Simple Statistics

To my son, David

SIMPLE STATISTICS

A course book for the social sciences

Frances Clegg
Honorary Research Associate, University of Hull

CAMBRIDGE
UNIVERSITY PRESS

PUBLISHED BY THE PRESS SYNDICATE OF THE UNIVERSITY OF CAMBRIDGE
The Pitt Building, Trumpington Street, Cambridge, United Kingdom

CAMBRIDGE UNIVERSITY PRESS
The Edinburgh Building, Cambridge CB2 2RU, UK
40 West 20th Street, New York, NY 10011–4211, USA
477 Williamstown Road, Port Melbourne, VIC 3207, Australia
Ruiz de Alarcón 13, 28014 Madrid, Spain
Dock House, The Waterfront, Cape Town 8001, South Africa

http://www.cambridge.org

First published 1982
Nineteenth printing 2003

Printed in the United Kingdom at the University Press, Cambridge

A catalogue record for this book is available from the British Library

ISBN 0 521 28802 9 paperback

CONTENTS

Contents

The drawings and cartoons on the cover and within this book were drawn by Elivia Savadier.

The report 'Some observations on the diseases of Brunus edwardii (species nova)' by D. K. Blackmore, D. G. Owen and C. M. Young first appeared in *The Veterinary Record*, 1 April 1972. The extracts from it on pages 148–52 are reproduced with permission from the journal's editor, Edward Boden.

Table S2 is based on table 2 of *Some rapid approximate statistical procedures* by F. Wilcoxon and R. A. Wilcox (1964, New York: Lederle Laboratories) and is reproduced with the permission of the American Cyanamid Company.

Tables S4 and S7 are from tables C.7 and C.6 of *The numbers game: statistics for psychology* by Joan Gay Snodgrass (1978, New York: Oxford University Press). Table S4 draws on table 11.4 of *Handbook of statistical tables* by D. B. Owen (1962, Reading, Mass.: Addison Wesley) and on D. Auble's article 'Extended tables for the Mann-Whitney statistic', *Bulletin of the Institute of Educational Research at Indiana University*, vol. 1, no. 2, 1953.

Acknowledgements

Like many other teachers of introductory statistics, I felt a need to supplement the available textbooks with my own handouts. When time permitted I compiled these into a single manual; at that point, thanks to illustrations drawn by Chris Hinds and Patrick Sammon, the project took on a life of its own. I still remember with gratitude the ideas, the time for discussion and the support which Chris and Patrick gave to me. It was quite a challenge to turn a statistics manual – potentially the dreariest and most off-putting kind of book – into something which students might positively enjoy using. However, the response to the manual was very encouraging and the book you are now looking at is, I hope, an improved version which retains the early spirit. If you can suggest further improvements, I will be pleased to receive your comments and ideas for further amendments.

The original illustrations have now been replaced by Elivia Savadier's skilfully drawn cartoons. The debt to Patrick and Chris remains – but Elivia has also succeeded in making another valued contribution to the finished product. I must also thank Dodie Masterman, a leading authority on Tennyson's poem 'Maud', for providing the lovely little illustration on page 180.

Several members of the Psychology and Mathematical Statistics Department at Hull University also gave me advice and help. Professor A. D. B. Clarke and Dr Ann Clarke, Dave and Jean Williams and Lorraine Hudson must be named in particular. More recently I have valued the enthusiasm and patient comments I have received from Graham Hart, Sue Glover and Marcus Askwith at Cambridge University Press. It will be largely due to their efforts that the book has improved over the two-year interval. Needless to say, any errors which remain are due to my own misjudgements and oversights, and should not be associated with anyone else who has been involved in the book's production.

I am constantly amazed by the great tolerance shown to me by the members of my family; without their understanding and assistance I doubt that I could have written the book. I must thank my husband, Brent Elliott, in particular, for he has helped me considerably with many aspects of the final manuscript preparation.

Finally I would like to acknowledge the role of all the A-level students I taught at Hull College of Further Education – and who were exposed to much of the written material in 'live' form! It was their needs and responses which inspired my first attempts to teach statistics, and from them I started not only to learn how to do it, but also to appreciate the value of humour in the classroom.

As a nonstatistician I feel some trepidation in producing a statistics textbook.

Acknowledgements

Ironically though, it seems that people who are less expert in statistics are better able to understand the problems that students (and particularly those who label themselves 'non-numerate') encounter when starting the subject, and are thus in a position to cover the ground more gently. If you are about to embark on statistics, then I hope that I manage to explain clearly what the subject is all about. When you have finished this book you will then be in a position to turn to standard textbooks for further information – and I will consider that I have truly succeeded in my aim if you are able to do this with interest and pleasure.

Frances Clegg

THOSE OF YOU WHO APPROACH STATISTICS WITH FEAR AND FOREBODING...

1 Why do we need statistics?

Perhaps when you began your course in one of the life sciences, you felt dismayed to discover that you would have to start doing statistics. You wouldn't be the first person to feel like this! Understandably, many students imagine that the new syllabus will concentrate entirely on aspects of behaviour or mental processes shown by living organisms, and that knowledge of maths will not be needed. So why is it your bad luck that you now have to start statistics – just when you thought that at last you would be able to devote all your attention to a really *interesting* subject? In the next sections I shall outline the main uses of statistics in the life sciences, and conclude the chapter by considering the matter of just why it is that so many students dislike the subject and find it difficult.

Statistics for description

In the social and biological sciences, although we are very happy to be able to understand precisely what makes one living organism 'tick', at the same time, our overall aim is to be able to comprehend the mechanics which underlie the behaviour of an entire species. Then we can use our knowledge to make predictions about individuals or groups of individuals which we have not previously encountered or studied. Thus in our studies of living beings and their activities, we will often be working with several individuals at any one time. In surveys, the numbers may run into thousands, but there will normally be smaller numbers in the more carefully controlled experimental type of investigation. Inevitably our efforts will reward us with sets of data which usually, although not always, take the form of numbers. It is in conveying information about, and trying to interpret, these large sets of numbers in an efficient and convenient manner that we really need *descriptive* statistics. An example will make this clear.

Suppose someone was studying road accidents, with a view to making road safety recommendations. The first thing to discover is when, where, and under what circumstances accidents occur. We will look at 'when' in more detail. The times of road accidents can easily be obtained from police records, and the researcher could find out how many accidents occur each year, month, week, day, and even hour. The data could be put into the form of daily tables. Well, here it is, looking very impressive, but taking up an awful lot of space! Constantly wading through sheets of daily accident tables is not going to be particularly useful, either, until some kind of overall picture or summary can be gleaned. A good starting point would be an indication of the 'normal', or 'usual', number of accidents per year, month, week,

1

Why do we need statistics?

etc., these figures being called *averages*. You all know, even if only vaguely, what an average is. Our researcher might say:

'On average, there are about 100 accidents per week in Dodge City,'

using as his basis the fact that 10 000 accident reports came in over a two-year period. Notice the word 'about'. It indicates that you would not expect precisely 100 accidents to occur each week, but that some variation around the figure of 100 is to be expected. The researcher might then go on to give more specific details . . .

'Usually, most of the accidents involving other cars occur between 10.30 pm and midnight on Fridays and Saturdays. Of the accidents involving children and pedestrians, which comprise about 40 each week, roughly an eighth happen between 8 and 9 am, Mondays to Fridays, a quarter on the same days, but between 3.30 and 6.30 pm, and the remainder during the weekend daylight hours.'

These sentences describe briefly, yet fairly accurately, the wealth of information contained in the 10 000 reported incidents. But no one is yawning, or feeling the minor panic induced in the researcher when confronted with the original data – in twenty cardboard boxes! The *average* is one kind of descriptive statistic. It is a number which indicates a 'typical' or 'central' figure for a group of numbers, and is officially called a *measure of central tendency*. From the example just given, averages could be quoted for any of the groups of numbers comprising yearly, weekly, daily or hourly accident rates.

Another type of descriptive statistic is used to qualify the word 'about', as in the sentence 'There are *about* 100 accidents per week.' Clearly, there is a difference between a town in which anything from 50 to 150 accidents is usual, and one where no less than 98 and no more than 103 accidents occur in any single week. Although both towns might have an average of 100 accidents each week, 'about' signifies that there may be a very large departure from the average in the first town, but only two or three more or less than the average in the second. Used on its own the word 'about' is far too vague, and we need some means of giving more details about the variation which occurs. The solution is to use the kind of descriptive statistic which is called a *measure of spread*, or sometimes, a *measure of dispersion*; it simply indicates just how much the word 'about' means for a particular set of figures.

As living creatures show the most tremendous variety in their attributes, behaviour, and just about every characteristic you care to name, variation is an inescapable fact of life. On the whole, the simpler the organism, the less variation it will display; but most readers of this book will be especially interested in studying the behaviour of mammals – the most complex animals – and man in particular – the most complex of the lot! If humans were fairly similar in their behaviour and characteristics, then we would not need to study so many of them to be able to make statements about mankind as a whole. As it is, humans vary tremendously, not only on a world-wide scale, and with regard to cultural differences and appearance but also within cultures, and, as we all know, within nations and families. Even identical twins, who have the same genetic make-up, are not entirely alike, due to the effect of the different experiences they have had from conception onwards. In other words, living organisms are unique entities, and the more complex the organism, the less likely it is to behave in the same way as its neighbour. So we often need statistics to describe adequately the large numbers of people, other animals, or events which we are studying, both in terms of *typical* patterns and the *variation* which we might expect.

Statistics for drawing conclusions

The other main use of statistics is in making decisions about situations where you are not entirely confident that the 'truth' has been revealed. In an experiment certain events take place (hopefully, ones which are more or less anticipated by the experimenter!), changes are recorded, and the findings, which will usually comprise numbers of some sort or another, are used as a basis for drawing conclusions about the underlying events. Statistics used in arriving at conclusions in this way are called *inferential* statistics. Think about the following example.

Suppose you gave two people of similar age and intelligence a long list of words to read, and asked them to recall the words later. Despite their similarity as humans, and in age and intelligence, their recall of the information would undoubtedly differ – or show variability. No doubt you can think of several reasons why this should be so. They may have concentrated to different extents whilst reading the words; some of the words might have conjured up strong association or visual images for either of the learners; one of them might have been very anxious about the purpose of the reading task, whilst the other took it more light-heartedly; one of the learners might have spent the immediate pre-learning period propping up a nearby bar . . . These, or a score of other factors, could have influenced the learners' recall.

WE MUST SOMETIMES BEAR IN MIND PRE-EXPERIMENTAL EVENTS...

Why do we need statistics?

Suppose that you have just invented a new memorising technique, and you wish to find out whether it works as well as you hope. Common-sense will tell you that you must try out your technique on more than one person, and also that you must compare the technique in actual use with memorisation which is carried out by another, similar, group of people who have not had the benefit of your wisdom. If you didn't have such a group (called a *control* or *control group*), then you would have no idea what sort of aid your technique is providing. For all you know, it might turn out to make recall harder, rather than easier! So you must have this other group of memorisers acting under identical conditions to those using the new method, except that they are not actually using the new technique.

If the group using the new method comprised people who had good memories, whilst the other group was made up of poor memorisers, then the comparison would hardly be a fair one. But although it is easy to see *why* the two groups should be similar to each other, in practice it is often difficult to achieve complete similarity, as you might have guessed. We shall return to this topic later in the book. Meanwhile, a set-up like the one just described is called an *experiment*. When it has been completed the investigator will be the proud owner of sets of scores (the *results*, which in this case represent success in memorising), obtained from the victims, who are usually referred to as *subjects*. Another piece of jargon used in experimental work is the verb used to describe the participation of subjects in an experiment. We say that they *ran* in an experiment, and also talk of experimenters *running* either subjects or experiments.

Let's return to the memory experiment, in which two groups have participated and provided us with recall scores. Suppose that *all* the people who used the new technique recalled the same words correctly, and that these were 80% of the total number of words on the list, whilst the unaided group, the control subjects, recalled the same kinds of words, but only 40% of the list. Doubtless you would hurry off to patent your new memory technique! This is not a plausible situation though, is it? It would be much more likely that the aided group got *about* 80% of the words right, and the unaided group *about* 40%. Probably the words recalled would also be different for each person. A different, but even more realistic, outcome would be the aided group getting *about* 60% of the words correct, and the unaided group *about* 50%. Would you be so certain now that your technique was an improvement? Let's consider again the word 'about'. It describes a scattering of result scores which will occur over and over again in experimental work. With the last set of results mentioned for the memory experiment, it could have been that the lowest score in the aided group was 45% and the highest 70%; in the unaided group, the lowest 30% and the highest 80%. In other words, some people in the unaided group did *better* than some in the aided group. The overlap of scores is presented visually in figure 1.

It is this problem of overlapping sets of scores which creates the need for statistical analysis – and inferential techniques in particular. The overlapping is largely due to the following factors. Notice that the first two are a direct result of the natural variation which occurs in complex organisms.

1 We can never match our comparison (control) group *exactly* with the experimental group on every single relevant attribute (e.g. age, intelligence, motivation, previous experiences, family background, personality, etc.).
2 There are dimensions of personality or experience which we *should* match on, but

we may not be able to, because our methods of assessment are not sophisticated enough. Some of the ways in which we measure personality and intelligence are still very crude. There may be other aspects of organisms which we should consider, but our lack of knowledge means that we have not yet learned the importance or relevance of these features, and so we ignore them.

3 Even when we have matched the groups soundly, our experimental efforts may still not result in their presenting scores which are clearly different, because our understanding of the phenomenon under consideration was too limited. Put another way, the experiment didn't 'work'!

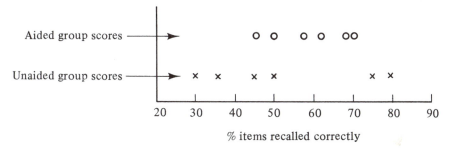

Figure 1. Overlap of scores in a memory experiment

These factors will become very real to you when you actually start to carry out experiments – situations in which we change something and then try to decide whether our change brought about other changes. *Surveys* provide another way of gathering information about organisms or events. Our role is less active than in experiments however, for here we draw data from groups already occurring naturally, and don't actually induce any changes. When it comes to analysing the results though, just as with experiments, we find that our data may not indicate clearly distinguishable groups, but ones with a certain degree of overlap. Once more, inferential statistics come to our aid in helping us decide the extent to which the groups really differ.

Exercise

1 The results of four memory experiments are shown in table 1. Study the numbers and decide for yourself which experiments suggest that the memory technique being tried out actually does help people to memorise better. Answers are given at the end of the book.

Table 1. Results from four separate memory experiments

Experiment 1		Experiment 2		Experiment 3		Experiment 4	
Aided	Unaided	Aided	Unaided	Aided	Unaided	Aided	Unaided
55	30	50	40	50	45	30	50
60	35	55	45	55	50	40	52
65	40	60	50	60	55	50	58
70	45	65	55	65	60	52	60
75	50	70	58	70	65	54	65
80	55	75					70

Why do we need statistics?

You probably found that it was most difficult to decide whether the memory technique worked in experiments 2 and 3. This is why we need inferential statistics – or the dreaded statistical tests! When we can merely glance at sets of scores, as in experiments 1 and 4, and see immediately that they are different, we call this, jokingly, the 'eye-ball' test. Unfortunately, we are not able to get away with this test very often. It is far more typical to obtain scores which need careful analysis in order to find out whether one of the groups is *really* different from the other; that is to say, when our experimental conditions have not created a sufficient difference for us to be able to easily distinguish the two sets of scores.

Another explanation for the failure to show a clear difference in the sets of scores lies in an element of luck. Our memory technique might be a perfectly good one, but just through bad luck, the items listed for recall might have given rise to particularly strong visual images or associations for members of the unaided group, thus making that set of scores as a whole higher. It might have been the other way round in experiments 1 and 2. Chance factors may have made it *seem* as though our memory aid groups were better, though we would find, if we used different subjects, that really the technique isn't as good as the two sets of results led us to believe initially. Unfortunately, this element of luck can never be completely ruled out; even after we have carried out a statistical analysis, we usually feel that we cannot state our conclusions with complete confidence, but must qualify them according to the role we think that chance may have had. The qualifications we make – our cautiousness in concluding whether an experiment 'worked' or not – are built into the statistical analysis techniques, and so at the end of our calculations we are able to estimate precisely the part we consider chance factors (or luck!) to have played. Note that although I have attributed results to luck, or been forced to consider that an element of luck is involved, what has happened is that we haven't really known enough about our subjects' memories, personalities, etc., to be able to control these variabilities precisely. If we knew all that there was to know, then of course we could choose our subjects with exact precision, and would not be left with quite such a hard task of deciding whether or not our new technique had altered events.

So, one of the main uses of statistics in biological and social sciences is to decide whether a particular treatment (e.g. using a new memory aid; seeing whether a certain mineral affects plant growth; trying out a new drug; looking for links between housing conditions and delinquency) causes one group under study to obtain scores which are *really* different from a comparable group or groups. The statistical techniques used for this are called inferential, because on the basis of the scores which we obtain and analyse, we make inferences (or inspired guesses!) about what has been happening to the groups of subjects or materials which we are studying.

Statistics in practice

Using statistics is rather like using a tool box. Certain jobs have to be done, and in order to do them, you must select from the tool box implements which are appropriate. If your dentist kept a handyman's drill amongst his or her instruments, no doubt you would hope that you never needed a filling! Equally, you would be a little surprised to see a joiner attempting to cut a plank with a scalpel, or a decorator putting plaster on with a ruler. Instead, decorators, joiners, dentists, and everyone else who needs to use tools for particular tasks, will select instruments appropriate for the job. Appropriateness will be decided on the basis of the particular materials involved and the degree of precision sought. Think of statistics in the same way. The 'job' we undertake is to describe events and attempt to draw conclusions from them; the 'tools' are the various statistical techniques which are available. In order to pass statistics exams you will need to know something about certain techniques (the tools), and, of course, how to use them.

If you asked a driver how the engine of his car worked, he would probably be able to describe the basic principles and name and locate the main parts. However, it is unlikely that he would be able to identify the causes of, or rectify, an engine failure other than a simple one. Most people who use engines and tools are similar in this respect. They know *how* to use the instrument, *when* to use it, and when *not* to use it, but have only a rough idea of how it actually works. The same is true of statistics. You are only required to have a rough idea of how the techniques work – more detailed knowledge and understanding is the province of the mathematical statistician. Like engineers, statisticians are constantly devising new techniques and modifying existing ones, and it is their expertise which filters down to the many people who use statistical techniques in their daily work. The workmen themselves are not expected to understand in great detail how the tools work, or to carry out modifications or improvements.

Learning about statistics is also like being a workman in another respect. Although you may learn about the theoretical aspects of statistical techniques – uses of tests, their strengths and weaknesses, etc. – your knowledge would not be entirely complete if it did not include a certain amount of practice at using the various procedures. So it is necessary to practise using the tools. There are several things to be gained: better learning and retention through the *active* use of information; a good understanding of the contexts in which certain techniques can be appropriately used; first-hand knowledge of the various problems arising with statistical techniques and data analysis; and through the computational steps carried out, an appreciation of the principles which underlie the techniques. As a final bonus, you begin to see that even *you* can do statistics! For these reasons, many exercises are included in this text.

But I'm hopeless at maths!

If you are a typical social science student, you probably dislike maths and feel that it is one of your weakest subjects. You may also feel anxious or inferior because of this very fact. Let's look at these sources of worry – and I hope that I can offer some reassurance to those of you who are approaching statistics with fear and foreboding!

AN EVERYDAY USE OF SYMBOLS

Why do we need statistics?

First, statistics is *not* maths. True, it is a branch of mathematics, but it only involves the simplest of arithmetical operations. I expect that you will have the use of a calculator, and so these days you can study statistics and escape doing even basic arithmetic. Both maths and statistics rely heavily upon the use of symbols, and this is possibly responsible for the confusion – and also, for the dislike and dread which the subjects seem to generate.

We all use symbols a great deal. You are now reading symbols – i.e. the letters of the alphabet which have been strung together to make the words written on this page. However, are you experiencing difficulty and distaste over the act of reading them? Of course not. You have been reading for long enough, and frequently enough, to do it 'automatically'. No doubt a seven year old child would find these pages a little heavy going. You could imagine the youngster struggling to read and pronounce the words 'arithmetic' or 'enough', and perhaps wondering what 'symbol' means. These difficulties are quite reasonable, for seven year old children do not normally have an adult vocabulary at their command, and there are many abstract concepts which are completely beyond their experience. Well, you are the equivalent of a seven year old child as far as mathematical symbols go!

You may be quite happy about the symbols

$$+ \text{ and } - \text{ and } =,$$

perhaps scratch your head over

$$< \text{ and } \pm \text{ and } \neq,$$

and definitely start to stammer when you see

$$\bar{X} \text{ and } \Sigma.$$

Yet you are already familiar with the *operations* which all these symbols refer to, and may in fact use the concepts involved quite frequently, if only you knew it!

Other concepts, such as those expressed by the symbols

$$\hat{\sigma} \text{ and } \chi^2,$$

are a little more specialist, and it is unlikely that you will have needed to use them in your everyday (non-statistical) life.

Remember though:

SYMBOLS ARE NOT IMPOSSIBLE TO UNDERSTAND!

What you must understand is that it takes thought and patience and time and practice . . . and yet more practice, to become familiar and at ease with symbols. It is quite possible to acquire a working knowledge of statistics without knowing much about the symbols which could be used to describe the various arithmetical operations involved. In the operational schedules included in this book I will tell you how to carry out the various statistical procedures in words, and through worked examples *show* you what to do. Ideally, you will get the background knowledge from the text. In the schedules I have also included the symbols for the various techniques or formulae, and for two reasons. First, so that you gain familiarity – even if only a vague familiarity – with them, and secondly because there may come a day when you actually find it easier to work from statistical steps as summarised in a single formula, rather than from a verbal description, which may involve many small steps. At the moment you may well feel that *you* will never achieve such dizzy heights of competence, but all I can say is that it has been known for so-called 'innumerate' people to come to prefer symbols to words!

The arithmetic you need for statistics is hardly mind-boggling. Basically you will need to add, subtract, multiply, use brackets, understand what squaring means, and know what a square root is. These operations are usually covered in the first few pages of introductory arithmetic books. Of course calculators can carry out all these operations for you, but there are two things which they can't cope with. Calculators can't think on your behalf, neither can they count. Statistics involves both thinking and counting now and again, I'm afraid!

The maths language

No doubt you have at some time picked up a book printed in a foreign language, noted fairly rapidly that it was not written in a language with which you were familiar, and replaced it on the shelf before looking for a book which you could understand. When you looked at the first book, did it make you entertain serious doubts about your intellectual ability?

What if you saw

ولم تكن مناهج العلوم والرياضيات ، في الأرد

These symbols don't make you feel inadequate, or worried about your intelligence either, do they? You recognise immediately that you don't understand what the heiroglyphics stand for (unless you have recently been doing Arabic at night classes!); you don't feel threatened by them.

Now let's take another language:

$$t = \bar{d} \div \sqrt{\left(\frac{\Sigma d^2 - (\Sigma d)^2/n}{n(n-1)}\right)}.$$

I expect that feelings of anxiety and inadequacy will promptly be aroused in most of you! Is this reasonable, do you think? Why are you somehow expecting that you should be able to make sense of these symbols – and maybe also thinking that you 'never will' manage them, when you face the Arabian squiggles quite unruffled? What has happened to make you feel like this? Possibly a sequence of events, not uncommon, which took place in the murky past of your school days. Let's look at the maths language in a little more detail.

Why do we need statistics?

Maths symbols are just like those used in any language. They stand for something else – in this case, operations with numbers – and unless you are familiar with what they stand for, of course you can't translate them. The snag is that fluency in another language takes time and effort and continuous practice – yet this is *all* that is needed to master mathematical notation. There are no mystical skills or insights available only to a few lucky geniuses – and denied to you. Maths is like any other language; given work and practice, anyone can become reasonably fluent. Unfortunately, many maths teachers fail to appreciate that they are using a foreign language. They rattle on at a fair to moderate speed, leaving the average pupil floundering, simply because the learner needs more time to interpret the symbols than the teacher (who has been speaking the language for years – if not decades) realises. The more time the pupil needs for translation, the further he or she gets behind; the further behind, the more *new* information is not coped with, and the more *extra* time is needed for translation and thought. This extra time is not forthcoming, usually. I am sure that you get the picture. The poor pupils slowly sink into a mire of incomprehension, frustration, fear, and finally, hatred of maths. The circle is complete when a person actively avoids contact with the subject, and we have another self-confessed failure at maths on our hands. It is very sad that such 'failures' tend to blame themselves, rather than perceive that they are reasonably competent intelligent people, who have simply been exposed to a disastrous teaching programme. What lessons can be learned from this analysis of an unfortunately common situation then?

The first one is: don't blame yourself for the nasty experiences you have had with maths in the past, but try to forget them and make this a fresh start. In other words, stop thinking and worrying over the fact that you are 'hopeless' at maths. With careful effort, you too can pass statistics exams!

Secondly, for success, you must regard maths as a language, and be prepared for continuous practice. Would you go to a French class once a week, fail to do the set homework, fail to speak in the language or listen to it between sessions, and expect to make progress? I doubt it. You know as well as I do that halfway through the week you would probably have forgotten nearly all the things you learned in the lesson, and during the first part of the next class you would be struggling to get back into the swing of things. The same is true of maths. If you don't practise pretty regularly, you'll rapidly forget what it's all about, and so will always need extra time for thought and translation. So do try to work at statistics, the branch of maths central to this book, frequently. Plenty of exercises are included to help you in this respect. Don't ignore them, or just glance at them without making any effort to work through them. They not only give you a chance to think about and apply new techniques, but they also make you more fluent in your new language.

You would also do well to follow the advice given over a century ago by the old school master Bartle Massey, in George Eliot's novel *Adam Bede*. He urges his pupils of accounts to make up and work through examples of their own devising whilst their hands are occupied but their minds are free.

'There's nothing you can't turn into a sum, for there's nothing but what's got number in it – even a fool. You may say to yourselves, "I'm one fool, and Jack's another; if my fool's head weighed four pound, and Jack's three pound three ounces and three-quarters, how many penny-weights heavier would my head be than Jack's?" A man that had got his heart in learning figures would make sums for himself, and work 'em in his head; when he sat at his shoemaking, he'd count his stitches by fives, and then put a price on his stitches, say half a farthing, and then see how much money he could get in an hour, . . .'

Nowadays, we are so accustomed to writing things down, unlike Bartle Massey's pupils, that we forget we can use our brains when our hands are occupied. Washing up, going to work on the bus, waiting in queues, are the modern equivalent of shoemaking. His pupils were learning accounts – a more appropriate example for statistics students might be . . .

A statistics class comprises 30 male and 24 female fools. Twenty males and 16 females pass the end of term exam; does this constitute evidence that male fools are better at statistics than female fools?

Another good way of learning something – and also of finding out that you do not understand quite as much as you imagined – is to explain the material to someone else. As you might imagine though, not all members of your family or acquaintances are simply longing to learn about statistics, but never had the courage to ask! It might need considerable diplomacy to persuade someone you know to make your studies a more worthwhile experience. Whilst it is more realistic to select a partner from your study group, and perhaps take it in turns to explain things to each other, even this course of action is not completely free of hazards. Neglect of other subjects, choice of partner, location of study sessions and the raising of rivalry feelings or anxiety all raise interesting possibilities. Consequently, much as I believe you should follow my advice, I disclaim all responsibility for the domestic and social consequences of your activities if you do follow it!

The logic of maths

But learning statistics is not *exactly* similar to learning a language. There is one important difference which needs attention right from the start. This is that statistics and maths must be learned in a logical sequence. If you were ill for a language lesson, and missed twenty new vocabulary words, no doubt you might experience a little difficulty if you subsequently encountered one of the missed words, or needed to use one. However, that small gap could easily be rectified. With mathematical subjects things are a little different though. Because they build up in a logical manner, it is the case that later learning is usually highly, or totally, dependent upon a good understanding of earlier work. You can't miss out little bits, and expect to go sailing on without them – or even expect to pop them in easily at some future date. This is another reason why many schoolchildren soon come unstuck at maths. After a period of absence from the classroom – and it may not necessarily be prolonged, as in illness, but perhaps only be the fleeting type, known as 'day-dreaming' – the pupil should receive tuition which will make good the missing knowledge. We all know that in the typical school class today such attention to an individual's needs is quite out of the question – and the penalty is the enormous number of people who end up failing, and hating, maths.

Do take care then, whilst you are working from this book or receiving instruction in statistics, to make sure that you grasp all relevant information at a particular level before you move on to more advanced material. If you don't understand something, don't just think that you might begin to, if you just listen more carefully than usual to

Why do we need statistics?

A FLEETING ABSENCE FROM CLASSROOM

the next bit. Invariably, the next bit will seem even worse, and so on. If you find that you have got problems of understanding, then try to discover at which particular point you have failed to grasp a point, return to that stage, and proceed from there, working in small steps, and being absolutely sure that you *do* understand everything. And remember the saying 'If in doubt, *ask*!'

Having said that maths and statistics are subjects which build up in an orderly sequence, I would now like to make a slight qualification, and add that in statistics certain basic principles underlie almost all techniques. Once these are established, the order in which individual topics are covered is not too important. At the start of each chapter I shall indicate whether any of the earlier material is necessary for a good understanding of the new topic, or whether the chapter can be read as an independent unit.

As far as symbols go, get used to looking at them, and try to use them whenever you can. This way you will gradually lose your fear of mathematical-looking notation. Indeed, I hope that you may even come to enjoy the mathematical aspects of material included in this book. Be careful to whom you admit this though, because enjoying statistics is rather like eating nettles – it gets you the reputation of being rather odd!

Exercise

2 Decide whether descriptive or inferential statistics are most appropriate for the following situations:

(a) A man decides to buy a car from a friend, but discovers that it is over-priced. In order to persuade his wife that the purchase isn't complete folly, he investigates the prices of similar models in expensive local garages. He obtains the prices of ten cars which he feels will help his case. How does he present this 'evidence' to his wife?

(b) Some children are undecided about which of two routes reaches the beach more quickly. Sometimes it seems quicker to go one way, at others by the second route. Statistics needed for a decision?

(c) On weekdays I diet, and at the weekends over-eat. My total weight change each week is zero, but this is due to five days' loss versus two days' gain. How can the weight changes be summarised so that this pattern can be discerned?

(d) I treat half my tomato plants with Wonder Whizzo and half with Gro-kwik. When they mature I count the number of tomatoes I obtain from each. What kind of statistics will be needed to see whether there is any difference between the two treatments?

(e) Roland Butter owns a rather large book collection, and he decides to insure it. For this he needs to know the total value of all the books. It would be far too tedious to find the cost of each one, and build up the total that way, so instead he works out the value of six 'sample' shelves, from which he hopes to calculate the worth of the remaining books. He is anxious not to under-insure though. Statistics used?

2 Measures of central tendency

AVERAGE SPEED 4 mph   AVERAGE SPEED 40 mph

I have already said that one of the main purposes of statistics is to describe sets of numbers briefly, yet accurately. The human brain is limited in its capacity to deal rapidly with incoming information, and when faced with large groups of numbers, most people cannot normally hold them all in mind at once. Also, it takes an appreciable length of time to read through big sets of numbers. So we find it convenient to describe such groups of numbers by means of other, but *fewer*, numbers. You will all be familiar with the idea of an 'average' – a number which is used to summarise information from a larger set of numbers – but you may not be aware that there are several types of average. We shall now look at three of them.

The first kind of average – the mean

It is quite likely that if I gave you some numbers and asked you to find the average, you would add together all the numbers in the set and then divide the total by the number of numbers you added up. This operation gives the kind of average which is called the *mean*. Although it is very easy to understand how we obtain a mean, the procedure has been broken down into the basic steps on the first operation schedule, page 153, so that you can see the way in which operation schedules work. Just to introduce an easy symbol here, the number of scores in a set is normally referred to as N. Now that wasn't hard, was it?

Exercises

1 Follow the steps given in operation schedule 1 to obtain the means of the following sets of numbers:
   (a) 25, 28, 31, 24, 30
   (b) 305, 269, 427, 499, 385, 377, 280, 316, 392, 454
   (c) 5.6, 4.5, 7.2, 0.6, 3.0, 2.1, 1.9, 3.8
   (d) 12, 15, 32, 21, 29, 19, 40, 0
   (e) 120, 5, 56, 131, 99, 62, 19, 107
   (f) 40, 40, 40, 80, 80, 80
2 Go through all the measures you have just obtained, and consider how *well* the means represent the numbers from which they were obtained.

Trouble looming up!

Often in life, something which at first sight looks straightforward and easy turns out to have some hidden complications. The mean is no exception. Consider again the

13

answer to exercise 1(f) for which you have just (I hope!) obtained a mean of 60. The particular numbers in the set were 40, 40, 40, 80, 80 and 80. Suppose that these numbers referred to the height in inches of a long-lost tribe of Scots mountain dwellers. An enquirer, perhaps a kilt manufacturer, might receive quite a nasty surprise when confronted with the tribe, having previously been given the information that their average height was 60 inches. He would have to sell his kilts elsewhere! The lesson to be learned is that when a mean is given for a set of figures, it does not follow that any of the figures in the set is of the same value – or even remotely resembles it.

Sometimes a mean may be worked out to several decimal places. Whilst this is fine in many cases, occasionally it is done on numbers which can't easily be divided up in 'real life'. When this happens, quoting a mean may result in some odd interpretations. For example, we are informed by sociologists that the mean number of children per family in Britain these days is 2.45. I have yet to see 0.45 of a child looking alive and well!

Another little tendency which often creeps in is for means to have a long string of decimal places. Whilst this is fine if the original numbers are very precisely measured, and the decimal places thus represent *real* accuracy, more often than not the original numbers were whole ones. Particularly in the social sciences even these whole numbers must often be regarded as, at best, approximations, and so a highly accurate-looking mean, with several decimal places, could be somewhat misleading. This kind of false accuracy is called *spurious accuracy* – and is best avoided. However, there are rare occasions when it is wrong to treat decimal places casually in statistical calculations, and I shall indicate them when they arise.

When can the mean be used safely?

On the whole, when numbers in a particular group cluster closely around a central value, the mean is a good way of indicating the 'typical' score, i.e. it is truly representative of the numbers. If, however, the numbers are very widely spread, are very unevenly distributed, or cluster round extreme values (as in the giant and pygmy example), then the mean can be positively misleading, and other measures of central tendency should be used instead. Two more of these – and they too are called 'averages' – are described next.

Exercises

3 Would the mean be a suitable descriptive statistic to use with the sets of numbers given in exercise 1(a)–(e)?

4 Would the mean be suitable for use with these sets of numbers?
(a) 10, 10, 10, 10, 10, 10, 20, 20
(b) 10, 10, 10, 10, 10, 10, 11
(c) A hundred values of 10 and one value of 50
(d) 10, 11, 12, 13, 13, 14, 15, 15, 16, 17, 18, 21

Another average – the median

If you have a set of values, and wish to obtain a figure which represents the central point, then a sensible way of doing this might be to arrange the numbers in order of size and pick the number which falls in the middle as being of typical value. This can be illustrated with an example using apples of different sizes, the weight of each apple being inscribed on its side in grams. The apples would look like those shown in figure 1, and when the set has been arranged in order of magnitude, like figure 2. The apple in the middle, i.e. the fourth from either end, weighs 130 g. This value then is the *median* for the set of apples illustrated.

That was a nice easy example, where it was simple to find the mid-point of a set comprising seven items. What would happen if there had been eight apples in the set? Keeping them in order, but adding an extra one, the row now looks like figure 3.

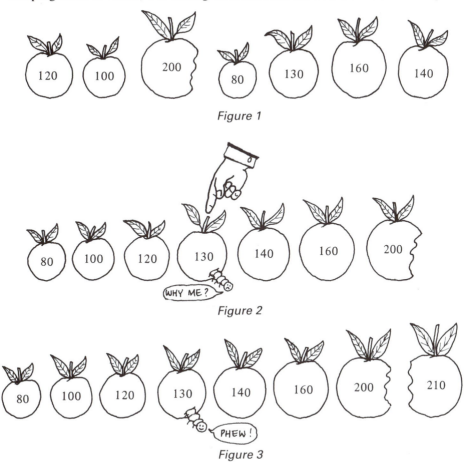

Figure 1

Figure 2

Figure 3

15

Measures of central tendency

Counting in from the ends, to find our centre, we find that as eight divides evenly into two sets of four, we don't have a *single* number at the centre, but two numbers – or apples of weights 130 g and 140 g. We don't abandon finding the median in this sort of case, but now take the *two* central numbers, and find the point which is halfway between them. In this example then, the median will be 135 g.

If the two central numbers had been 140 g and 180 g, the median would be 160 g, again the mid-point between the two figures. You may have noticed that you can find this mid-point by adding the two numbers in question and then dividing by two; that is, by finding their mean!

Exercises

5 Using the steps given in operation schedule 2, find the median for the following sets of numbers:
  (a) 25, 28, 31, 24, 30
  (b) 305, 269, 427, 499, 385, 377, 280, 316, 392, 454
  (c) 305, 269, 427, 499, 385, 377, 280, 316, 392, 454, 499
  (d) 5.6, 4.5, 7.2, 0.6, 3.0, 2.1, 1.9, 3.8
  (e) 12, 15, 32, 21, 29, 19, 40, 0
  (f) 40, 40, 40, 80, 80, 80
6 Compare the medians from groups (a), (b), (d), (e) and (f) above with the means which you obtained from the same sets in exercise 1. Which measure of central tendency do you consider to be the most representative of each?

The median – pros and cons

It's all very well working out what the median of a set of numbers is when there are fewer than a dozen or so numbers in the group. Imagine how time-consuming it would be, though, to place a hundred or more numbers in ascending order of magnitude. Another disadvantage of the median as a descriptive statistic is that if one of the numbers near the middle of the distribution moves even slightly, then the median would alter, unlike the mean, which is relatively unaffected by a change in one of the central numbers.

In the median's favour though, it must be said that if one of the *extreme* values changes (and often in experiments and measuring processes it is the extreme values which are least reliable), then the median remains unaltered. When extreme values alter, and particularly if they disappear, the mean can change tremendously. Sometimes (although one is reluctant to admit this) simple writing or typing errors can occur, such that a small value becomes very large, or vice versa. When the numbers are analysed later, it might be quite difficult to find out whether the extreme value is a genuine score or an error. Single scores which are quite clearly 'deviant', when compared with the others, are known as *outliers*. When they occur, and for whatever reasons, the median becomes an appropriate choice of descriptive statistic.

Sometimes, in collecting information or scores, it happens that the procedure was such that you end up with scores all having rather high *or* rather low values. For instance a task in a psychology study might have been too hard for most people, a simple test too easy, or a questionnaire may contain items which didn't give enough weighting to one end of the continuum. You know that if you readjusted the task or scale, many scores would subsequently go beyond the limits of the first scale at the over-represented end, but the values at the other end would remain unchanged. In cases like this, and working from the original scores, the median would be a suitable descriptive statistic to use as a measure of central tendency, for the details of the top and bottom figures themselves will not influence its value. It will only be affected by the actual *numbers* of relatively high or low scores.

When scores have been obtained from a number of individuals or specimens, then the median will relate to either one source, or two if the set is even-numbered. This means that, if you wish, you can examine the source of the median score further and look at other characteristics shown by this specimen or individual. As we have already seen, when the mean is obtained its value may bear little resemblance to the actual scores and so it cannot always be used to select a 'representative' of the group.

Finally, if a set of numbers has a lop-sided pattern – if, for example, most of the scores are small, several medium sized, but only one or two high – then the median may again be more appropriate than the mean, as its value will be close to the *majority* of numbers in the set.

A TASK TOO HARD FOR MOST PEOPLE...

The mode – a fashionable figure

A third type of average is called the *mode*. 'Mode' means, among other things, 'fashionable'; this word describes very well just what the statistical mode is. It is simply the value in any set of scores which occurs most often – or is the most 'popular'.

Take the following set of numbers:

5, 6, 7, 8, 8, 8, 9, 10, 10, 12

As the number 8 occurs most often (three times), 8 is the value of the mode. It is as simple as that – and certainly doesn't justify an operation schedule!

What would the mode have been if one of the 8s vanished? Then we would be left with two 8s and two 10s, and only one of each remaining score value. In this case there would be two modes, of values 8 and 10. Or on the other hand, take the list 5, 6, 7, 8, 9, 10, in which there is no single number which occurs more than once. What now? In this group there is no mode, as all the numbers appear with the same frequency. If a set of numbers has two modes, then it is called *bimodal* – the prefix *bi* meaning two, as in 'bicycle'. An example of a bimodal distribution was given in the heights of the pygmy and giant Scots, where the numbers involved were 40, 40, 40, 80, 80, 80. Remember that although the mean was 60, this figure was not a good indication of the height of any single member of the tribe. An enquirer would be much better off knowing that there are two modes, of values 40 and 80.

What's the matter with the mode?

As you might have anticipated, such a pleasant and simple measure as the mode must have some drawbacks. Perhaps the saddest thing about the mode is that it is hardly ever used! One of the reasons for this is that it is a very unstable figure, and can swing wildly through the whole breadth of a set of numbers at the drop of a hat. Take these numbers:

     1, 1, 6, 7, 8, 10.

The mode here is 1, which is not a very representative figure of the group as a whole. However, change the score of 1 into another value of 10, and the mode shifts right to the other end of the scale. Thus it can be seen that merely a single number change can alter the mode dramatically. This is in great contrast to the mean and median, where number changes can take place and leave them virtually unaffected.

    If a distribution of numbers has more than two modes – and with large sets of numbers it might be possible to have many modes – then the modal values themselves could need summarising, and so the usefulness of the mode as a descriptive statistic starts to dwindle.

What use is the mode?

Despite the criticisms just made, the mode can be a useful statistic. One of its main assets is that it can be used to indicate a 'normal' or 'usual' figure. It is exactly opposite to the mean in this respect, as the modal value *must* be a commonly occurring figure. Often the value of the mean is a number with decimal points (and in cases where *none* of the original scores had decimal points), and sometimes it may not even remotely resemble any of the values in the set – as with the giants and pygmies. Often it is the mode which is used as an average in expressions such as 'the *average* person', or 'the *average* holiday length'. The figure quoted is the *usual*, or *typical*, value – and quite often will not be the mean. We might also speak of the *normal* value of such-and-such, meaning the mode. It is important to realise that 'normal', in a statistical context, means 'usual', and not the opposite of 'abnormal', in its familiar sense of 'peculiar' or 'odd'.

    The mode is also a useful descriptive statistic when the numbers in a distribution are not spread evenly around a central value. Such a lop-sided pattern is called a *skewed* distribution, and you may recall that it was described in connection with the median, which is often also quoted in summaries of asymmetrically spread scores. The numbers

    6, 7, 7, 8, 8, 8, 10, 10, 13, 15, 18

make a skewed distribution, and they are shown diagrammatically in figure 4.

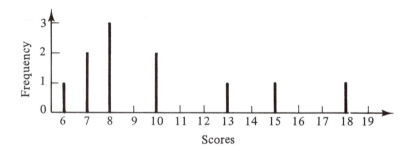

Figure 4. A skewed distribution

The vertical line (or axis) labelled 'frequency' refers to the number of instances of each individual number which occurs in the set. You can easily see that there are three number 8s, and that this is the most commonly occurring number, for with score 8, the vertical line is the highest. The mode for this set of numbers, then, is 8. If you obtained the mean of the group, you would find that it was 10, a figure which is rather on the high side to be regarded as typical. Remember that the mean is very sensitive to extreme scores; it is the three high scores of 13, 15 and 18 which are responsible for giving it a relatively high value. The median for these numbers is the same as the mode, 8 (the sixth number along the list from either end), and for these particular numbers, we would feel happier about summarising them by means of the median and mode, rather than the mean.

Averages as measures of central tendency

The three averages which have just been described are all *descriptive statistics*, and are used in an attempt to supply a quick 'picture' of a set of numbers by indicating roughly where the middle of the set lies. They differ in that each is obtained by using a slightly different definition of the word 'middle' – although with the mode, there is merely an assumption that the most typical value will be in the middle, which is not always the case. However, these three averages are all known as *measures of central tendency*.

The various advantages and disadvantages associated with each kind of average have been noted, and in deciding which figure is most appropriate, you must now use this information. Ask yourself: 'Does the figure selected give a fair indication of what the scores are like?', not forgetting that the descriptive statistic needn't be an extremely precise number (for instance a figure with five decimal places), but rather one which is not misleading in some respect. Finally, remember that other peoples' motives when describing sets of numbers may not be quite as pure as one would wish, and so occasionally an 'average' figure may be quoted which, whilst it undoubtedly *is* an average, is very misleading. Consideration of figure 5 (page 20) should make this clear. The firm for which the figures are shown could quite legitimately claim that its *average* length of holiday is 2 months. It is this kind of deliberate attempt to mislead, by using statistical terms in such a way that those unfamiliar with the subject are likely to come to the wrong conclusion, that gives statistics a bad reputation. We have all heard the saying 'lies, damned lies, and statistics'; quoting the mean when the mode would be a more appropriate 'average' is a perfect illustration of the type of thing which gives statistics a bad name!

Exercises

7 State the mean, median and mode for the following sets of scores:
  (a) 9, 10, 11, 12, 13, 13, 14, 15, 16, 18, 20
  (b) 8, 10, 11, 12, 13, 14, 15, 16, 18, 20
  (c) 7, 8, 10, 10, 11, 13, 17, 18, 19, 19, 21, 22
  (d) 10, 12, 15, 20, 22, 23, 23, 24, 25, 25, 25, 28, 30
8 Go through the measures of central tendency you have just obtained, and decide which average or averages convey the best picture of each. Give reasons.
9 Make a table summarising the relative merits and problems associated with the three averages described in this chapter.

A note on distributions

Up to now, groups of numbers used in examples have usually been referred to as 'groups' or 'sets' of numbers. Occasionally the word 'distribution' has been used for a set of numbers. It means virtually the same as 'group', except that the word carries the vague implication that the numbers fall into a particular kind of pattern.

Distributions, or groups of numbers, are often shown by means of diagrams, as these afford the clearest way of conveying information about large sets of numerical

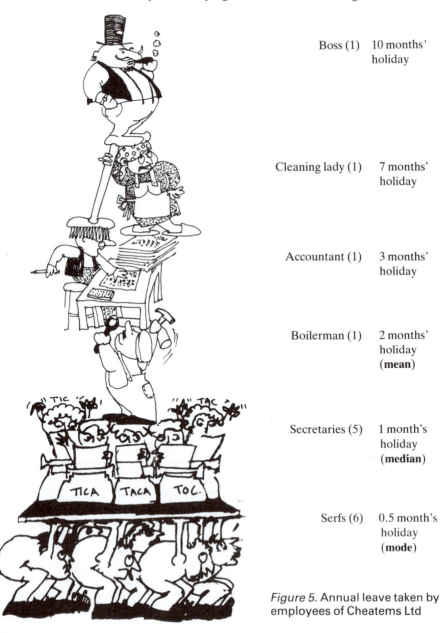

Boss (1)	10 months' holiday
Cleaning lady (1)	7 months' holiday
Accountant (1)	3 months' holiday
Boilerman (1)	2 months' holiday (**mean**)
Secretaries (5)	1 month's holiday (**median**)
Serfs (6)	0.5 month's holiday (**mode**)

Figure 5. Annual leave taken by employees of Cheatems Ltd

data. Diagrams like figure 4 in this chapter are called 'frequency diagrams' or 'frequency distributions', and you will see many more throughout this book. The vertical axis is the one which tells you how many numbers there are having a particular value, or how *frequently* particular scores occur; it is usually labelled 'frequency', or just *f*.

Distributions can comprise numbers covering a very wide range, or at the opposite extreme, can be made up of numbers which are closely huddled together. In a fairly symmetrical distribution, like the one shown in figure 6, the mean, median and mode

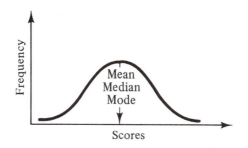

Figure 6. The normal distribution

all have the same value – or are extremely similar. Whilst the majority of scores are clustered around these measures, there are still quite a few which occur both below and above the central area. This type of distribution is called the *normal* distribution, and it will be examined in more detail in chapter 4.

In some distributions the numbers may be spread fairly evenly above and below the mid-point, but in others the spread may be uneven. Figure 4 showed this kind of distribution. There are two sorts; one in which the scores fall mainly below the mean (as in figure 5, showing the firm's holiday allowance), and those in which the scores fall mainly above the mean. These are called *positively* and *negatively skewed*, respectively, and they are shown, together with the relative positions of the averages, in figure 7. You can see from the diagram why the mean alone is not a good descriptive statistic to use; with skewed distributions it is usual to give the values of all three averages. Note that the actual value for each is obtained from the scores

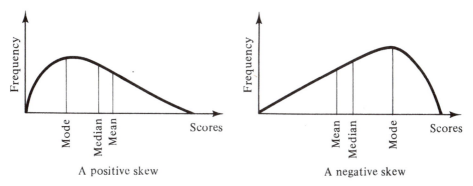

Figure 7. Skewed distributions

given along the horizontal axes. It is also interesting to note that in skewed distributions the mode is approximately twice as far from the median as the mean.

Hint
You can easily remember which kind of skew is positive and which negative by the following strategy. Looking at the distribution from left to right (the normal reading direction), you come first to *either* a line which goes up fairly sharply, *or* to a line travelling relatively horizontally. The distribution which swings upward sooner is the *positive* skew – and the (nearly) vertical line can be associated with the vertical stroke on the positive plus (+) sign. The earlier relatively horizontal line seen on the other skewed distribution, the *negative* skew, can be associated with the negative minus (−) sign.

You have already been given an example of a bimodal distribution, in the giant and pygmy heights. Shown diagrammatically, it is characterised by two 'humps', as in figure 8.

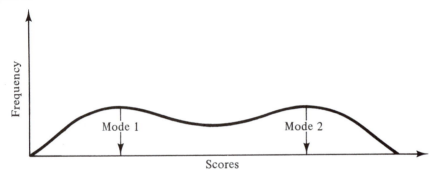

Figure 8. A bimodal distribution

There are many other kinds of distributions, i.e. scores falling into recognisable shapes – but most of them have rather long names! Fortunately you will not often encounter any of them, and the ones which I have just described will be the ones which you will come across most frequently.

Exercises

10 For each of the following sets of descriptive statistics, draw a rough shape of the distribution they have come from.

Table 1

Distribution	Mean	Median	Mode
A	50	50	50
B	10	20	—
C	30	20	10
D	60	60	20, 80

11 The table below shows the exam marks (in broad bands) obtained by 60 students. Put the data into the form of a diagram, and comment on the use of the mean, median and mode in connection with the figures.

Table 2

Marks	0–19	20–39	40–59	60–79	80–99
Number of students	1	8	22	28	1

3 Measures of dispersion

In the last chapter you learned about some of the ways of describing sets of numbers, or distributions, by giving a rough indication of the middle of the set. Make sure that you are quite happy about using the three measures of central tendency before you move on to the material presented in this chapter.

You will have probably already realised that simply indicating the central point of a distribution certainly does not give a complete picture of its shape, and on occasions may be quite misleading. In order to give a better impression of a distribution's shape, a second kind of summarising statistic is normally used, a measure of *dispersion*, or *spread*. As the names suggest, these measures indicate how widely scattered the numbers are. If one of these measures is used together with one of the averages then the two summary numbers together will give an extremely concise and useful description of the particular distribution. As was the case with the measures of central tendency, there are three commonly used measures of dispersion, and we shall consider them all in turn, starting with the simplest.

The range

The range tells you over how many numbers altogether a distribution is spread. It is easily obtained by subtracting the smallest score from the largest in the particular distribution of numbers under consideration. For example, if I found that various kinds of potatoes for sale in several greengrocers' shops were priced at

10p, 25p, 12p, 8p, 14p, 14p, 24p and 15p per lb

then the range for these prices would be 25p − 8p = 17p.

Consider next these two sets of numbers:

10, 11, 11, 12, 12, 13, 13, 13, 14

and

10, 11, 11, 12, 12, 13, 13, 13, 20.

Work out the values of the range for each set, and see whether you can spot the disadvantage which is associated with the use of the range.

The two ranges are 4 (=14 − 10) and 10 (=20 − 10) respectively. The problem with the range is the one previously encountered with the mean, namely that extreme values have a very big effect on the descriptive statistic. In the second distribution, only one number has changed; 14 has become 20. However, this single change has increased the range by 6 points. On the other hand, outliers (atypical extreme values) may cause distributions which overall look very different to have similar ranges.

Clearly then, the range can only be used sensibly as a descriptive statistic when *all* the scores are fairly well bunched together. Otherwise it gives the impression of an evenly widely spread group of members, when in fact the breadth of range may be due to only one or two extreme scores.

The mean deviation

The mean deviation is a number which indicates how much, *on average*, the scores in a distribution differ from a central point, the mean. I did hear you ask 'which average?', when I said 'on average', didn't I? You'll soon find out. Suppose you take the numbers:

8, 9, 10, 11, 12.

The *mean* is 10 and the *range* is 4. The number 8 is 2 points away from the mean, and so is the number 12. Numbers 9 and 11 are both 1 point away from the mean, and 10, the remaining number in the set *is* the mean, so does not differ at all. Listing these differences, you get

2 + 1 + 0 + 1 + 2 = **6**.

There are five numbers in the group, and so you can say that the average (mean) amount they all vary from the mean is 6 divided by 5, i.e. 1.2 points. The differences, 2, 1, 0, etc., which were obtained are called *deviations*; it might be better if the mean deviation of 1.2, just calculated, was called the 'mean of the deviations from the mean' as this is what it is.

Now let's look at another set of numbers, again with a mean of 10:

4, 8, 10, 12, 16.

First, find the range.

You should have obtained 16 − 4 = 12, and this, a much larger number than the 4 which was obtained with the previous set, is a fair indication of the wider spread of scores. Again, find out how far each number is away from the mean of the set, and then add up the five numbers. You should get a total of 16, which, when divided by 5 (the number of scores comprising the group, or N), gives 3.2. This figure is the mean deviation, and you can see that there has been an increase of only 2 from the first set (mean deviation 1.2) – not such a big increase as that shown by the range, which increased by 8 points. However, there was an increase, reflecting the wider spread of scores, but as the mean deviation is based on *all* the numbers in a distribution it is a much more stable statistic than the range, which is only based on two of them.

The method for working out the mean deviation is given in operation schedule 3. You will see that if all the numbers are subtracted from the mean, some of them will be negative. When you worked out the mean deviations from the examples just given, you did not have to deal with negative numbers, because we asked how many points *different* each score was from the mean. We didn't make any distinction between scores which were above and ones which were below it. When we calculate the mean deviation formally, we have to be a little more precise, and state how far each score is *above* or *below* the mean, by using plus (+) and minus (−) signs. Provided that you worked out the mean correctly, and did your additions and subtractions accurately, *and* remembered to put the signs in the right way round, you will find that the total of the deviations is zero. This *always* happens. If it doesn't, then there is something wrong with your arithmetic! It happens because the very nature of the mean makes it the central score arithmetically, unlike the mode and median which are obtained by counting. Because the mean is an arithmetic centre, so the deviations of all the scores on either side will always be equal, and will cancel each other out when the signs are taken into consideration. This isn't very helpful. The problem is overcome simply by ignoring the signs (or direction of the differences) in adding up, just as we did in the examples given above. The mathematical symbol which indicates that we find the *difference* between two scores, disregarding their signs, is two vertical lines. For example, the difference between 5 and 9 (4) would be written $|5 - 9|$.

Exercises

1 Work out the mean deviations for the following distributions:
  (a) 12, 10, 8, 4, 18, 8   (b) 0, 0, 4, 5, 20, 22, 19
  (c) 0, 19, 21, 18, 22   (d) 2, 3, 3, 3, 4, 4, 4, 4, 5, 5, 5, 6
2 State whether the range would be a good measure of dispersion to use in the distributions given in exercise 1.
3 In the next example the mean is 10. Find the mode, median, range and mean deviation; comment upon the aptness of these descriptive statistics for the particular distribution.
    0, 1, 2, 20, 1, 3, 51, 20, 1, 1

Final comments on the mean deviation

It is easy to remember what the mean deviation actually is, and how to work it out, if you privately call it 'the mean of the deviations from the mean'.

Sadly, the way in which we add the differences together, ignoring the signs so that the total does not equal zero, is not pleasing to mathematicians. Partly for this reason, but mainly because the mean deviation is a very simple figure without any powerful mathematical properties, it is rarely used as a measure of dispersion. The preferred measure, the *standard deviation*, is used far more often, usually in conjunction with the mean and range. You will learn why the standard deviation is a 'better' statistic when we come to examine the normal distribution and its properties.

Don't forget, for it's less obvious with the mean deviation than with the range, that the larger the mean deviation is, the more spread out the scores in the distribution are.

The standard deviation

In principle, the standard deviation (often shortened to SD) is very similar to the mean deviation. It summarises an average distance of all the scores from the mean of a particular set, but it is calculated in a slightly different manner.

You may recall that the problem of the signs of the deviations from the mean was dwelt on at some length. If they are taken into consideration, the mean deviation will always be zero, but this was overcome by ignoring them. There is another solution to the problem. You may remember from your basic arithmetic that if you multiply two *negative* numbers together you get a *positive* result. The same applies to squaring a negative number, for it is a negative number being multiplied by another negative number of the same value.

Now, suppose you have the set of deviations:

$-2, -1, 0, +1, +2.$

These equal 0 when added together 'correctly', or 6 when the signs are ignored. What happens if instead of adding the deviations you square each one? You will now get

$+4, +1, 0, +1, +4$

for the squared deviations – and all are *positive* numbers. Magic! Now add these numbers and find *their* mean, just as you did with the mean deviation calculations. You should get a total of 10, divided by 5, to obtain the value 2. The figure 10 is called the *sum of squares*, or sometimes, the *sum of squared differences*, for obvious reasons, and 2, the mean of the sum of squares, is called the *variance*. Notice that 2 is *not* the standard deviation; the operation for obtaining it is not quite complete yet, although we are nearly there. As we *squared* all the differences, the figure which we obtained must now be 'unsquared', so to speak, to bring it back into the right kind of perspective. No doubt you know how to 'unsquare' a number – you find its square root. In this case, the square root of 2 is 1.4142. This then is the standard deviation. You can see that it is slightly higher than the figure of 1.2 which was the value of the mean deviation for the same set of numbers.

The process of squaring and unsquaring numbers during this operation can be likened to looking at something under a microscope. The lens makes the object in view appear very much larger. An object seems just as real when enlarged, and it is easy to forget that something is being magnified – until the lens is removed, and it rapidly shrinks back to the right proportions. Squaring the differences makes the total much larger, and in taking the square root, we are putting the number back into its correct 'perspective'. So be careful to remember to do this, and don't make the simple mistake of giving the variance instead of the standard deviation. Another common error is to take the square root too early in the proceedings, obtaining it from the sum of squares, rather than the variance. This mistake gives you a very convincing-looking answer – unfortunately, not the correct one!

Exercises

4 Obtain the sums of squares, variances and standard deviations for the following sets of numbers:
  (a) 12, 10, 8, 4, 18, 8   (b) 0, 0, 4, 5, 20, 22, 19
  (c) 0, 19, 21, 18, 22   (d) 2, 3, 3, 3, 4, 4, 4, 4, 5, 5, 5, 6
5 How do the standard deviations compare with the mean deviations which you obtained from the same figures in exercise 1?

Slight – but not serious – complications with the standard deviation

The first complication concerns the use of N in obtaining the variance from the sum of squares. To refresh your memory, N refers to the number of scores in the particular set you are working with. If you look at a selection of statistics books, you will find that many of them tell you to divide the sum of squares by $N - 1$ (i.e. one item less than the number of scores making up the set), instead of N. Thus in the previous example you would divide 10 by 4, rather than 5. Before reading any further, work out for yourself what effect this change is going to have on the final figure.

The effect, which I am sure you did work out, is that dividing by a smaller number will give a larger variance (of 2.5 in the example), and hence a larger standard deviation. It will be 1.58 instead of 1.41. The procedure of using $N - 1$ is not always used, but it is very common in calculations involving data from experiments. This is because when we obtain a set of numbers which we wish to describe or analyse, we have not usually collected every single score possible, but only a *sample* of scores. If we are measuring the height of all adults aged 20 to 40 years in Britain, we could not hope to measure everyone who falls into the category, but instead, and after careful planning, we would take our measurements from a representative sample. A sample *is* only a sample though, and inevitably some error will occur. The sensible way to compensate for this is to make an allowance for it which is included in the calculation

of the standard deviation. If the standard deviation has been made a little larger, by subtracting 1 from N, then the figure obtained allows a margin of error. It could perhaps be called a 'guesstimate'! Thus a formula involving $N - 1$ is preferred whenever we are working with samples rather than a set of scores which is absolutely complete. Such a complete set of scores is called a *population*, and you will hear much more about samples and populations in later chapters.

Exercise

6 Check for yourself that the standard deviation increases when $N - 1$ is used, by using it instead of N with the numbers given in exercise 4.

The second complication I want to discuss concerns another alternative procedure for obtaining the standard deviation. The steps given in operation schedule 4 barely differ from those given for obtaining the mean deviation. Suppose though that in the figures given for exercise 4 (a) there had been an extra score of 8. This would have meant a total of 78, and a new mean of 9.7. If you bother to work through the figures again, with the extra number and new mean, you will be rewarded for your efforts by finding that the calculations are now much more fiddly. Subtracting 9.7 from every score takes longer than subtracting a mean which is a whole number. Suppose that your sample comprised a hundred scores, and their mean was the very inconvenient figure of 7.62. It would be extremely tedious and time-consuming to obtain all the deviations, even with a calculator, and it is not appropriate to round off decimal figures in the *middle* of calculations. So, a simpler method of obtaining the standard deviation has been devised, which produces exactly the same figure, but going by a different mathematical route. It is given on operation schedule 5. Briefly, you square the individual scores, sum the results, and then subtract from this (usually immense) total, the average of the squared sum of all the observations. This figure is called the *correction factor*, and when it has been subtracted, the remaining amount is referred to as the *corrected sum of squares*. If you have done your sums carefully, this figure will be identical to the sum of squares which you would have obtained using the first method. All this may sound technical and confusing. Don't worry! Just remember that there are two methods for obtaining the standard deviation, and that the second one is better with large sets of numbers and/or when the mean is not a convenient round figure – as is usually the case in 'real-life' work! Also, keep an eye on the symbols used in the second method:

ΣX^2 means the sum of all the individual squared scores
whilst $(\Sigma X)^2$ means the sum of the original scores, which is *then* squared.

It is ever so easy to get the totalling and squaring operations in the wrong order, so do take care over them.

Exercises

7 Summarise the following distributions as aptly as you can. They are all complete populations.
   (a) 4, 4, 4, 5, 5, 5, 5, 5, 5, 6, 6, 6
   (b) 1, 2, 3, 3, 4, 4, 4, 5, 5, 9
   (c) 0, 0, 0, 10, 10, 10
8 Recalculate the standard deviations for the figures just given, but on the basis that they are now only samples, not complete distributions.
9 To gain familiarity with the alternative method of obtaining the standard deviation, rework all the numbers provided above, but this time using the general method which you *didn't* use the first time round. You should obtain identical values.

Variance

The term *variance* was mentioned earlier in this chapter, when I said that it is the number obtained immediately prior to the standard deviation. Variance is the standard deviation squared, and as it changes exactly in step with the standard deviation, we can often use it as an alternative measure of spread. Later in this book we will encounter a statistical test called the *variance ratio* (or *F*) *test*, in which we compare the spreads of different distributions by looking at their variances. In fact a whole bunch of statistical tests, coming under the umbrella term 'Analysis of Variance', and shortened to ANOVA, exists, and as the name implies, they focus on variance. They are not particularly difficult to understand, but there are several kinds, and the beginner is not likely to encounter them early in a statistics course, as

Measures of dispersion

they are usually used for complex experimental designs and data analysis arising during fairly advanced practical work. However, the basic principles underlying analysis of variance do not differ from those behind the statistical tests covered in this book.

As with the mean deviation and standard deviation, the larger the variance, the greater the variation, or spread, seen in the numbers involved.

4 The normal distribution

Before you start this chapter, make sure that you are comfortable with the idea and details of describing sets of numbers by means of other, fewer, numbers, as covered in chapters 2 and 3.

The characteristics of the normal distribution

The normal distribution is a bell-shaped curve which is shown in figure 1 below. Its main feature is that the three measures of central tendency, the mean, median and mode, all lie at the same place on the curve. That is to say, they all have the same, or nearly the same, value. If the scores making up a distribution are either very squashed up, or very spread out, then we have the shapes shown in figures 2 and 3, overleaf. These are *not* normal distributions, despite the fact that their means, modes and medians all fall at the same point (and this is what gives them their symmetry); the normal distribution is always bell-shaped. As it was 'discovered' by the mathematician Gauss, it is sometimes called the *Gaussian* distribution.

It so happens that much of the data gathered during studies of living organisms fall into this pattern. From the shape of the curve we can see that there are very few extremely low and extremely high scores (the curve drops at the left- and right-hand ends, this drop being due to the very low frequencies found), whilst the majority of scores lie at the values around the mean. We shall look at the pattern of scores much more closely soon, but at this point another feature of the normal distribution must be mentioned. This is that *theoretically* the curve never actually descends to touch the horizontal axis, but continues to approach it over an infinite distance. This is a mathematical property of the distribution, and one which is not reflected in 'real-life'

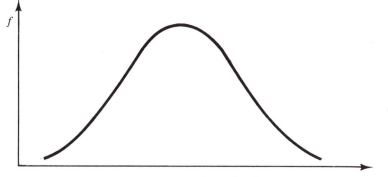

Figure 1. A normal distribution

The normal distribution

data gathering. We don't come across humans of absolutely gargantuan or micro-scopic dimensions – whatever creative yarn-spinners would like to have us believe!

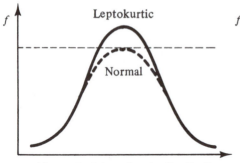

Figure 2. A leptokurtic distribution

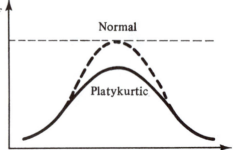

Figure 3. A platykurtic distribution

Properties of the normal distribution are then:

(i) It is symmetrical.
(ii) It is bell-shaped.
(iii) Its mean, median and mode fall in the same place on the curve.
(iv) The two tails never actually touch the horizontal axis.

You may wonder how strictly defined, in terms of scores, the normal distribution is. In other words, how much can a shape deviate from the ideal bell-shape, before it has to be regarded as 'non-normal'? There are two approaches commonly used in reaching a decision about this; the problem is a fairly important one for you to consider actually, for some of the statistical tests described later in this book can only be carried out on sets of data which are normally distributed.

One approach is to decide on the basis of simply looking at the scores – 'by inspection', to give it a more impressive-sounding label. If there is a large number of scores in a set, then drawing a frequency distribution will make the task of inspecting and deciding much easier. The other way is to follow one of the mathematical procedures available for determining whether a set of scores is normally distributed. A version of the *chi*-square test which is included in this book is one of these. In fact it is fairly unlikely that at this stage of your statistical career you would need to know with great precision whether or not a distribution can be regarded as normal, and you will usually be able to get away with the 'eye-ball' test! However, you will be expected to show some awareness that the problem exists fairly early in the proceedings.

Exercises

1 For revision, and without referring back to the previous figures, draw a skewed distribution and mark on it the positions of the mean, median and mode. You should be able to work out where they lie, even if you can't remember.

2 State, after looking at the following numbers, or drawing frequency distributions, whether each set is normally distributed:
   (a) 0, 5, 5, 5, 5, 5, 5, 5, 5, 5, 0
   (b) 0, 0, 1, 1, 1, 2, 2, 2, 2, 3, 3, 6, 6, 8, 10
   (c) 0, 2, 3, 3, 5, 5, 5, 6, 7, 9, 12
   (d) 0, 2, 3, 3, 3, 4, 5, 8, 9, 9, 10, 10, 11, 11, 11, 11, 12, 12, 13
   (e) 0, 3, 5, 8, 9, 9, 11, 11, 12, 12, 12, 13, 15, 18

The area under the curve

We now move on to a property of the normal distribution which is of tremendous importance to life scientists, geographers, economists, market researchers and statisticians. This is that when you have a normal distribution, you always have the *same relative proportions* of scores falling between particular values of the numbers involved. I said earlier that there will only be a few extreme scores occurring, and that the majority of scores will lie in the middle region; we will now look at this in somewhat more detail. It is usual for explanations of the distribution pattern of scores to mention 'areas under the curve'. By this is meant the proportions of scores lying in the various parts of the complete distribution.

To begin – and using an easy example which does not involve mental exertion! – we know from property (i) that the normal distribution is symmetrical. Thus if we draw a line down the middle, through the central point which is the value of the mean, mode and median, we know from our work on the median that we have 50% of all the scores above the line and 50% below. Did you have any problems with that? Think it over, and don't proceed if you can't see why, but return to the material on measures of central tendency, paying particular attention to the median. It follows that if there is a point on the normal distribution at which 50% of the scores can be obtained, that there must also be points along the curve where division into 25% and 75%; 30% and 70%; 80% and 20%; or indeed, any proportions totalling 100% can be made. The essential point is that division into parts – say 85% and 15% – will always lie at the same *relative* positions on any normal distributions. This is shown in figures 4 and 5, where you have curves for the height of leprechauns and the speed of reaction to a drug. The point below which 85% of the leprechaun population lies in terms of height is 5 feet, whilst 85% of the subjects who take the drug Dynow will show a response within 15 minutes. The shaded areas contain 85% of all scores.

Now the problem is, how can we describe exactly where any given portion of the population, as shown on the curve, is going to fall? In figures 4 and 5, it can be more or less guessed that the cut-off point for 85% of the scores is going to fall in the places shown. How can it be known precisely though, and how can it be described to others without the aid of a diagram? The answer to the first question is that the mathematical properties of the normal distribution enable us to specify the precise location of any proportional division of the curve; to the second, that we are able to specify locations by means of the standard deviation – the measure of dispersion described in the previous chapter.

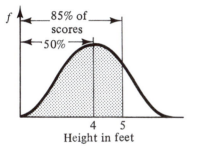

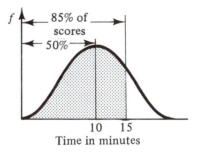

Figure 4. Height of leprechauns

Figure 5. Reaction time to Dynow

A VIGOROUS REACTION TO THE DRUG DYNOW

The normal curve and standard deviations

Suppose you take a set of numbers, the mean of which is 50, and you calculate that the standard deviation is 5. We call this value (inches, seconds, points on a rating scale or whatever) *one* standard deviation. Ten of the inches, seconds, etc., would comprise *two* standard deviations, and 15, *three* standard deviations – always with reference to the particular set of numbers from which we obtained the value of 5. It is as though we take the standard deviation and make its value in the original units into one unit of a new measurement scale; rather like saying that one inch is the same as 2.54 centimetres. You wouldn't ever mix inches and centimetres in calculations, but convert from one to the other. Likewise, you don't mix actual scores with standard deviations, but convert from one type of scale to the other.

Let's return to the proportions of numbers in different parts of the distribution. If I take one part of the curve between the mean, marked on the horizontal axis in figure 6 as 50, and one standard deviation, marked on the horizontal axis at a score of 55 units, then I know that I shall have roughly *one-third* of all the scores in the group lying between them. I know this because it is always the case with the normal distribution. Strictly speaking, the exact proportion of the total set of scores falling between the mean and one standard deviation above the mean (50 and 55 in this case) is 34.13%. Because the normal distribution is symmetrical, exactly the same thing must occur *below* the mean, i.e. we shall have another 34.13% of the scores falling

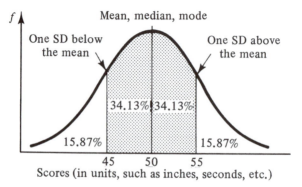

Figure 6. Proportions of the distribution cut off by one SD below and one SD above the mean

between the values of 50 and 45 – 45 being the mean score *minus* one standard deviation of 5 points.

Now look at the two proportions which are shaded. Elementary arithmetic tells you that 68.26% of the total number of scores is now accounted for, between the values of 45 and 55, leaving a remainder of 31.74% for the more extreme values on both sides. Again, the symmetry of the curve means that for this proportion, half of 31.74%, i.e. 15.87%, must lie in each tail part. In other words, about 16% of *all* the numbers in that particular set will be *less than* 45, and the same amount will be *greater than* the value of 55.

The normal distribution and scores from 'real-life'

It is now time to use this information in an example taken from the classroom. Let's suppose that a teacher obtains marks from a reading test given to 200 schoolchildren. The scores are normally distributed with a mean of 60 and a standard deviation (SD) of 8. From the properties of the normal distribution, we will find that roughly two-thirds of all the marks, i.e. those obtained from about 136 of the children tested, will be between 52 and 68. About 32 children (16%) will have marks below 52, and roughly another 32 will have marks above 68. Thus everyone is accounted for. Now – and here we come into one of the main uses of the standard deviation and the normal distribution in psychological measurement – suppose the parents of a child who had obtained a mark of 68 enquired about their little Johnnie's progress. Being told that their child's mark was 'above average' might at first please them, but soon they would probe again, and want to know just how much above average it was, compared with the other 50% of the children who also obtained 'above average' marks. In other words, they want to know the *relative standing* of their child's performance. If the marks had all been squashed up around the mean, with a top mark of 68, then the parents would have continued to feel delighted. Less pleasing to them would be the news that the top mark had been 90, with a very thick spread of marks going upwards, even above 70. However, the teacher knows that the SD of the marks was 8, and thus that a third of all the marks were between 60 and 68. Knowing that 50% of all the marks obtained were 'below average', it can be seen that this particular child's position is roughly 84% of the way up the complete set of marks. And so the parents can be pleased, after all!

If the child had obtained a mark of 76, then the parents would have had even more cause for pride, knowing that he was almost 98% of the way up (a mark of 76 is two SDs above the mean), and a mark of 84 would have put Johnnie in the enviable position of being 99.87% of the way up – in other words, from a group of 200 children, quite possibly top. Standard deviations cut off fixed proportions of the normal

ENQUIRIES ABOUT LITTLE JOHNNIE'S PROGRESS

The normal distribution

distribution from the mean to (theoretically) infinity, in both directions. The normal distribution, with all the standard deviation cut-off points, is shown in detail on page 197.

Make sure that you understand how the relative standing of a mark of 76 is obtained (i.e. 50% + 33% + 15%) and how it can be calculated that this group of children would produce about four others who obtained marks above 76. See whether you can calculate what mark would have been likely to put a child in the less enviable position of being only four places away from the bottom. The answer is 44. To obtain it we need to know what the mark represented by two SDs below the mean is, and which gives a cut-off point of 2%. Thus if we take 60, the mean, and subtract the value of two SDs – 16, twice the value of 8, which comprises a *single* SD – we arrive at 44. Always be careful to avoid mixing SD values with the actual original scores. In this example we didn't subtract the value of 2 from the mean of 60, although we wanted to find the score which was two SDs below it. We subtracted 16 marks, these being the number making up two SDs for this particular set of scores.

Exercises

3 On the Bloggs Personality Test, which is meant for a population of one-eyed dwarfs, the mean score for kindness was 16. The standard deviation was 4. Are the dwarfs pretty similar with respect to kindness, or rather variable? Justify your answer.

4 Fifty dwarfs of the variety just described live in a community. On the assumption that they are representative of the species as a whole, how many of them would you expect to have scores of (a) less than 8, (b) less than 12, (c) more than 20, (d) more than 28?

5 How big would the sample have to be before we might reasonably expect to come across a very very kind dwarf, with a score of 28 or more (i.e. three SDs above the mean)?

6 In fact Bloggs finds, when he examines the 50 scores, that there are at least 3 dwarfs with scores of 30 (the maximum), 10 with scores from 26 to 29, 15 with scores from 21 to 25, 10 with scores from 16 to 21, and the remainder with less than 16. Using a frequency diagram to illustrate your answer, tell us what Bloggs might conclude from these scores.

7 In a technical college, pork pies prove a popular snack. Sales records show that the SD for daily sales is 200 pies, and that up to 1200 pies are eaten on 84% of the days included in the records. What is the mean daily pie consumption, and might the staff expect to sell 1600 pies in a single day?

8 Work out the scores marking three SDs above and below the mean for the following distributions:
   (a) mean 15 inches, SD 2.5 inches   (b) mean £500, SD £50
   (c) mean 8.4 seconds, SD 1.2 seconds   (d) mean 80 elephants, SD 5 elephants
9 Ms Scrooge has two secretaries, Ms Sweetie and Ms Wink. Hard times hit the firm, and one of the girls has to be made redundant. In an effort to assess their worth as typists, Ms Scrooge counts the number of typing errors each makes. She discovers that Ms Sweetie has a daily mean of 10 errors, SD 2, and Ms Wink a mean of 8 errors, SD 6. How will this information help her to reach a decision?

z scores

In the examples we have looked at so far, we have considered scores which have been on the mean, or exactly one, two or three SDs above or below it. The time has come to examine scores which are not quite as readily converted into standard deviations.

Suppose for instance that the child with anxious parents had obtained a reading mark of 64. The child's position on the curve would have been in the middle of the distance along the horizontal axis between the mean score of 60 and one SD above, of 68. Look at this in figure 7.

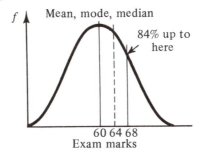

Figure 7. Position of a mark of 64 in relation to a mean of 60

The child's position is *exactly* halfway between the two points of 60 and 68. Does this mean that his relative standing in the group as a whole is halfway between the mean position of 50% and the 84% position of a mark of 68? That is to say, his position is about 67% of the way up the complete set of scores? Look carefully at the two portions of the curve divided by the line drawn at the 64 mark. Are they even? No – and here we have a problem which makes the computation of relative standing into a much more tiresome affair than we would like. As we get further and further away from the mean, the number of scores falling into the various proportions specified diminishes rapidly. So, if you take two portions, say between 60 and 64, and between 64 and 68, there will be fewer scores in the latter. There are even less in the next half SD, between the marks of 68 and 72, and so on. The same holds true of scores which are below the average, except that in this case it is the higher rather than the lower scores which are closer to the mean. There will be far fewer scores falling between 44 and 48 than between 48 and 52, although in both cases the range of marks covers 4 points, or half an SD. When you look at the shape of a normal distribution the changing size of the proportions enclosed by the various SD cut-off points seems obvious. However, the problem of deciding on the relative position of a mark of 64, compared with the remaining scores, hasn't disappeared. How do we determine it? The answer is by means of *z scores*.

The normal distribution

z scores correspond very closely to standard deviations, and in fact are virtually the same thing, except that a z score always refers to a point's position with regard to the mean. This will become clearer shortly. For the moment think that a z score of 1 is the same thing as an SD of 1, a z score of 2 like an SD of 2, and so on. Because there is virtually nothing left in the normal distribution after the third SD or z score away from the mean has been passed – in either direction – it is rare for SDs or z scores which exceed 4 to be mentioned. It is usual to refer to z scores as *plus* or *minus*; but in using SDs we tend to describe them as being either above or below the mean, rather than plus or minus.

An SD will have an unvarying actual value, whilst a z score refers to a relative position on the curve, and always in relation to the mean. In so far as a z score of 1 means 1 SD above the mean, then a z score and SD are identical. However, an SD of 1 might refer to a group of scores making up that SD at *any* place on the curve, i.e. throughout the whole set of numbers, whilst z scores have fixed positions on the curve. A z score of +1 means the point exactly 1 SD above the mean, and not any group of scores making up an SD.

We shall now return to our problem score of 64 and its relative standing. We know that its position is half a standard deviation above the mean, and so we give it a z score of +0.5. Very conveniently for us, tables have been devised which enable us to ascertain quickly whereabouts on the normal curve all the z scores between −3.99 and +3.99 lie. We shall use one version of the several types of table available to find out where a z score of 0.5 lies on the curve; it appears as table S1 in this book (page 159). The figures in the body of the table tell us the percentage of scores falling into the area between the mean and any particular z score. The small diagram at the top of the page indicates by the shaded portion that we are considering the area to the immediate right of the mean. Of course, as the curve is symmetrical. all the values will apply equally to the corresponding area to the left-hand side – or to z scores which have negative values. When we are considering positive z scores though, and wish to know how far up a total set of scores a particular z score (and its corresponding original score) is, we have to add 50% to the value we obtain from the table, as the left-hand half is not included in the shaded area. Let's see what happens with our score of 64 then, which has a z score of +0.5. We can read that value off by moving down the first column on the left, headed z, until we arrive at 0.5. Then we move one step to the right, and see the number 19.15. We have to add 50%, and so obtain the figure 69.15. Now we know that there were 69.15% of the scores lying below 64, and 30.85% above. It would be appropriate to round the percentages off, to 69% and 31% respectively.

Let's take another example, this time the mark of 65. This is 5 points above the mean, and the SD for the group was 8. A mark 5 points above the mean is thus 5/8 of an SD above the mean. Turned into a decimal, we can calculate that its z score will be +0.63. As it is above the mean its value is positive. Again turn to table S1. As the z score is now expressed to two decimal places the procedure is slightly different. Move down the first column once more, but this time proceed until you reach 0.6. The value to the immediate right (22.57) would be the correct percentage for a z score of 0.6. However, our z score is 0.63, and so we need to move along the body of the table three more columns, until we reach the one headed 0.03. That value, added to our 0.6, gives us a z score of 0.63 – and so we read from the body of the table the value 23.57.

As our z score was positive, we must add 50% for our final pronouncement, which will be 73.57. Hence the mark of 65 is almost 74% of the way up the scale. You can see from the table that 49% of all the marks on each side of the curve are included by the time the z score is as high as 2.33 (or just very slightly below, to be completely accurate). Note also though, that the complete 50% is never given – don't forget that mathematically, the tails of the curve never do actually touch the horizontal axis, nor enclose *all* possible scores.

Now let's look at the relative standing of a person who obtains a score which is *below* the mean, say a mark of 41 from the original example. This mark is 19 points below the mean, and so just a little more than 2 SDs away. To be precise, it is ¹⁹⁄₈, or 2.375 SDs below. Its z score will be −2.375. From table S1, we see that a z score of +2.3 encloses 48.93% of all the scores, but our z score was a slightly higher figure of 2.375. As the table is for use with two decimal places only, we will round the score off to 2.38. Moving along the rows, we now stop at the column headed 0.08, and read off the value of 49.13. So a z score of +2.38 would include 50% plus 49.13% = 99.13% of all the scores. So far so good, but our value was negative. We simply turn our curve round, as it were, and work from the mirror image. Thus with our value of −2.38, we know that 99.13% of all the marks in the distribution will be above it, and so only 0.87% below. If we call this tiny proportion 1%, then from our original sample of 200, we might expect 1%, or two of the marks to be as low or lower than 41. At the other end of the range of marks, we would only expect to find two pupils with marks 19 or more points above the mean, i.e. with marks exceeding 79.

The way we obtain the value of a z score is given formally in the expression:

$$z \text{ score} = \frac{\text{the mark's deviation from the mean}}{\text{the standard deviation}}$$

If you express your deviation from the mean with a plus or minus sign, according to whether it is above or below respectively, then your z score will emerge with the correct sign.

A word of warning

The relative proportion of numbers in a set of scores falling between standard deviations is unchanging. You *always* get about 68% of all the scores falling between one SD below and one SD above the mean (i.e., between z scores of −1 and +1), regardless of the actual values of the scores from which the SD was derived. It is similar in principle to the way in which an area of a circle is always expressed by the formula πr^2. It doesn't matter how big or small the circle is, or what it represents – the

The normal distribution

formula is the same. However, you would not say that the area of an *oval* shape is πr^2, although there is nothing to prevent you from taking a rough average radius of the oval, and then putting that number into the formula. You would obtain a figure which looked valid enough as an area, but it would be incorrect, as the formula holds good for circles only. Take care not to do a similar thing when you are working with standard deviations, z scores, or areas under the curve, by working out values using numbers obtained from distributions which are *not* normal. **These standardised scores apply only to numbers obtained from normal distributions.** You may obtain a figure which looks authentic, but which in fact is nonsense! For instance, take a skewed distribution . . . We will work with one which has a mean of 30 points. This in itself is a dubious descriptive statistic to use in communicating information about this set of numbers, but it can be obtained quite legitimately. The standard deviation of our numbers might also be calculated, and we could emerge with the value 4. Fine – or is it? Take a look at figure 8. To use SDs and z scores meaningfully, we *must* have a symmetrical distribution, at the very least. A z score of -1 must include the same proportion of the total number of scores in the distribution away from the mean as a z score of $+1$. In figure 8 you can see quite clearly that this is not the case. There are far more scores to the left of the mean than to the right. So any statements in which z scores and similar measures are used are not only incorrect, but may be very misleading.

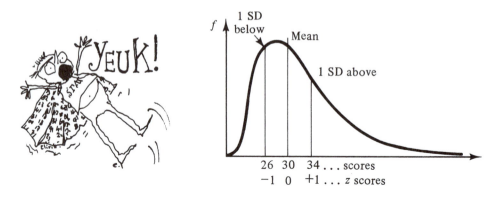

Figure 8. SDs and z scores marked on a skewed distribution

The message is then: Take care when working with z scores and SDs to use them only when the data from which they were derived are normally, or approximately normally distributed. Otherwise you will end up in trouble!

Exercises

10 Locate z score values of +1, +2, +3, −1, −2 and −3 for these sets of numbers, assuming that they are samples, not complete populations:
(a) 48, 55, 58, 59, 60, 60, 61, 61, 62, 63, 65, 68
(b) 2, 4, 5, 5, 6, 6, 6, 7, 7, 7, 7, 8, 8, 8, 8, 9, 10, 10, 11

11 A distribution has a mean of 48 and an SD of 6. What are the scores which correspond to:
(a) $z = -2.5$ (b) $z = +2.33$ (c) $z = +1.66$ (d) $z = 0$ (e) $z = -0.33$?

12 From a normally distributed sample with 100 scores, mean 30 and SD 2, how many would you expect to find:
(a) over 20 (b) under 29 (c) over 32 (d) over 33?
And what scores would the following z scores represent?
(e) −2 (f) −0.5 (g) +1.5 (h) +4

13 Using table S1, translate the following z scores into percentage areas under the curve:
(a) −2.43 (b) −1.88 (c) −0.36 (d) 0 (e) +0.9 (f) +1.47 (g) +2.61

14 Now turn these percentages into z scores:
(a) 50% (b) 67% (c) 99.2% (d) 75.8% (e) 33% (f) 1%

15 You will now need to *think*, as I haven't specifically told you how to do this. Although you can get the information needed for the first few problems from the diagram on page 34, make sure that you can also get it from table S1. For the remainder, you will need table S1, and also have to do some addition and subtraction here and there.
In a normally distributed sample of 100 marks, the mean was 60 and the SD 10. How many of the marks would be expected to fall:
(a) between 50 and 70 (b) between 40 and 80 (c) between 60 and 100 (d) over 90
(e) between 70 and 90 (f) between 58 and 62 (g) between 49 and 72
(h) between 0 and 40?

16 An intelligence test developed in Never-Never Land has a mean of 109 and SD of 12. What proportion of the population will be expected to have IQs of:
(a) less than 91 (b) between 94 and 124 (c) above 137?
Brillia, the society for highly intelligent people, requires a minimum IQ of 115 for membership. If the adult population in this country is 30 million people, how many members might Brillia expect to get if everyone suddenly applied for membership?

17 The weights of 10 000 onions are normally distributed. Their mean is 11.5 g, and SD 0.3 g. How many would weigh:
(a) between 11.5 and 11.8 g (b) 11.2 and 11.5 g (c) 10.9 and 12.1 g (d) 10.6 and 12.4 g?

Standard scores and standardisation

z scores are also called *standard scores*. This is because their values, ranging from −3 or −4 through 0 to +3 or +4, are unchanging, and actual scores, marks, etc. can be converted into z scores, and given relative positions on the normal curve.

In some widely used personality and intelligence tests, such as Cattell's 16 Personality Factor (16 PF) test and the Wechsler Adult Intelligence Scale, actual scores (called 'raw' scores) can be converted into z scores and expressed this way. Thus the standing of a person can very rapidly be compared with others from the same population. z scores are consistent, and are thus used to make comparisons between scores obtained on different tests, in a way which is not possible with the raw scores. For instance an IQ of 150 points might be extremely high, but a score of 150 on another test – perhaps a personality test – might be close to the mean. Expressing the same scores by using the z scores of $+3$ or $+0.01$ would give a rapid and clear comparison however.

We speak of some psychological tests as being 'standardised'. This means that they have been tried out on very many people comprising a representative sample of a particular society or population. The scores obtained may often show a normal distribution, but often tests are constructed so that they give rise to scores which are normally distributed, and in the case of many intelligence tests, around a mean of 100.

Finally, we talk of tests being administered under 'standard' conditions. This means that the tester goes through exactly the same routine in giving the test to all his or her customers, and that other testers have also been trained to follow an identical procedure. The result is that test scores obtained from different sources can be meaningfully compared. It would not be very helpful for any scientific investigation if, for instance, one research laboratory became known for 'helping' subjects to get good scores on tests – and even worse if this was happening, but undiscovered. Unfortunately though, a test can never be administered under *completely* identical conditions from one occasion to the next, or when more than one tester is involved; standardisation of procedure is an attempt to make the best of a difficult job.

THE TESTER'S APPEARANCE CAN MATTER

5 Probability

This chapter is about the way we use the concept of chance, or probability, in our statistical work, and why we need to do so. You should be able to understand all the ideas and information presented without having to refer to any of the previous chapters.

The main reason we use statements of probability in conjunction with statistical tests in our work is that over and over again we are having to answer the question: Could that event, situation or pattern of numbers have arisen by chance?

We all know that if something can go wrong it will! In scientific measurement, surveys and experiments, we are not immune from this law of nature and so must consider the likelihood of freak occurrences and accidental events when we consider and communicate our data. However, when referring to a particular set of data, rather than vaguely speculate by means of *words* how lucky or unlucky we think we have been, in true mathematical tradition we specify *numerically* the element of luck which we consider might be involved.

Everyone has heard the phrases 'two-to-one', 'fifty-fifty', 'a million-to-one' and 'one-in-twenty'; they will all have been heard in connection with events involving a certain amount of uncertainty, and are numerical estimates of the likelihood of something occurring or not occurring. Each expression can be translated: 'two-to-one' means that there are twice as many chances that one specified thing will happen rather than the other; with 'fifty-fifty', there is an equal chance of either of two events occurring; 'a million-to-one' states that it is a million times more likely that one thing rather than another will occur – i.e., one of the events in question is *extremely* unlikely. Consider this problem. An airline company, Fly by Night, is known to have accidents at a rate of about one in twenty flights. Its main rival, the High Flier company advertises quite truthfully that its accident rate is one in a million. You win the pools, and decide to take your dream trip to the Bahamas. Which airline company would you prefer to travel with? Unless you get your kicks from fear of death, no doubt you would opt for the second firm, the High Flier! This decision shows that you already have a good understanding of the way we express probability in numbers rather than words. We shall now proceed to build a little more knowledge on this foundation.

The chances are . . .

The expressions of probability you read earlier are based on two ways of describing chance events numerically. One is to use a *ratio* description – 'one-in-ten', 'one-in-twenty', 'a thousand-to-one', 'three-in-four', etc. – whilst the other uses *percentages*, as in 'fifty-fifty'. This means exactly the same as 'one-in-two', but has been converted to 50% and 50%. It could have been expressed as 'There is a 50% probability that . . .' In fact all probabilities can be expressed in percentages, although this is not very common in everyday speech. The 99 whole numbers lying between the two extremes of 0% and 100% describe the gradually altering likelihood of something happening or not happening, as the case may be. However, we wouldn't speak of a probability of 1000%. Although numerically there could be such a thing, the system of expressing likelihoods in percentages dictates that 100% is the highest percentage which can be used. This figure indicates *absolute inevitability*, and increasing it cannot be meaningful, as an event cannot become more inevitable than that! Table 1 below shows a scale which gives the probability, or likelihood of particular events, using both ratio and percentage methods. The very top of the scale represents absolute certainty that some event will occur, whilst at the bottom, there is equal certainty that something will not take place. Most speculations can be expressed either as an event or a non-event. For instance 'I am 95% sure that I won't score a bull's-eye' can become 'I have a 5% chance of scoring a bull's-eye'. Also, if it is possible to specify the probability of one outcome out of several possible events, then the remaining probability will apply to the other events. For instance if I throw a dice, I know that I have a one-in-six (or 18%) chance of obtaining any specified number – a 'one' for instance – and that I can then say that there is an 82% chance of *any one* of the remaining five faces coming up. Can you work out the probability of obtaining any *even* number on a single throw? The answer is 50%. Half the six faces are even-numbered and half odd. Therefore there is an equal chance of obtaining either sort of number.

Table 1. A probability scale in ratios and percentages

Ratio description	Event	Percentage description
Certain	That you were born	100%
Two-to-one	Racing fans can supply their own examples!	$66\frac{2}{3}$% (rare)
Fifty-fifty	A tossed coin coming up heads	50%
One-in-three	That Eve is displaying one of her faces	$33\frac{1}{3}$% (rare)
One-in-six	That a dice will come up with a 'six'	$16\frac{2}{3}$% (rare)
One-in-twenty	Both used in connection with experimental work	5%
One-in-a-hundred		1%
Impossible	That you will fly to the moon without mechanical assistance	0%

Just to complicate matters

There is one more way of expressing probability, and it is a simple extension of the percentage method. It is to express the likelihood as a decimal fraction. To do this, the decimal place on the percentage which has been stated needs to be moved two places to the left, so that 100% becomes 1, 50% becomes 0.5, 10% becomes 0.1 and 1% becomes 0.01. This method is in fact the most commonly used way of expressing probability in connection with statistical tests. Basically, it is very simple – the biggest danger being that it is easy to get the decimal place in the wrong position. The 0.5 (50%) value is often written by students when they mean 0.05 (5%). This value is used frequently in statistical work, as you will soon find out. The abbreviation for probability is p.

Exercises

1 It is important that you gain fluency in expressing probabilities in terms of ratios, percentages and decimals. By drawing three columns and giving them the headings shown in table 2, construct your own conversion chart and fill in the following values:
   100%, 99%, 95%, 75%, 67%, 50%, 33%, 25%, 10%, 5%, 2.5%, 1%, 0.1%.

Table 2. An incomplete probability conversion table

Percentage	Decimal probability (p)	Ratio or verbal description
100%	1.0	Completely certain
		Dead cert!

2 Convert the following figures to percentage statements of probability:
   (a) one-in-thirty   (b) one-in-a-hundred   (c) 40:60
   (d) 1:20   (e) one-in-a-thousand   (f) one-in-five-hundred
   (g) 1:1   (h) one-in-ten
3 Convert the same figures to decimal statements of probability.

Know your onions

To illustrate our need for expressions of probability in statistical work, I am going to describe a situation which at first glance seems far removed from the world of the statistician. It concerns the proprietor of a transport café, and the problems he experiences when buying onions. Strange though it might seem, his problems, and the decisions he has to make, are rather similar to the ones we encounter in science laboratories, or when we conduct surveys which provide data for analysis.

Joe Bloggs and his wife need to buy about 100 onions every week for the cheese and onion sandwiches which they sell in the café. Normally they obtain their onions from the nearest greengrocer, Johnnie Appleseed, and find that in a typical weekly purchase, about 10 onions will be bad. One week, Ms Bloggs takes command, and decides to patronise a different greengrocer, Bill Bashem. Anxious to demonstrate to her husband how much better her choice is, she systematically checks through the weekly purchase, counting the bad onions. To her annoyance, she finds that the sack contains 20 bad onions, i.e. the proportion of rejects has doubled, and is one-in-five. Now the question is: Does that doubling of proportion *really* indicate that Bill Bashem's goods are inferior to Johnnie Appleseed's, or is it just that she has bought them during a 'bad' week, or when some accident has made them worse than usual?

Let's assume for the moment that both the greengrocers buy onions of similar quality from one wholesaler. Any differences in the onions are due to different treatments during the transport, storage and selling processes. When we buy vegetables, whatever the quantity, greengrocers do not normally supply us with details of what they paid for them, or how they have handled and stored them, etc.

ARE BILL BASHEM'S ONIONS REALLY INFERIOR?

What happens is that on the basis of what we see when we unpack the purchases at home we decide for ourselves whether goods from a particular source are better than from another – always providing that we are comparing goods of roughly similar quality of course. We would not usually base our decision about the relative merits of greengrocers' goods on the strength of only one purchase, but prefer to make several. Over a period of time we would get a good idea of the average quality of the goods, and how much variability we might anticipate from week to week. Our weekly purchases are called *samples* and the knowledge we gain from them, of what comprises 'typical' proportions of sound and unsound vegetables, is called a *baseline*. Our baseline with Johnnie Appleseed was established as being one-in-ten for unsound onions. There is nothing to prevent some accident occurring which could on one week turn half the onions into a mushy pulp – although that week's sample would be in sharp contrast to what we know the baseline to be. If another supplier normally sold onions which were of very poor quality, then in this case, half the onions being bad would not be much different from the baseline performance.

To return to the Bloggs couple. You can just imagine that while Joe uses the doubling of bad onions to prove how right *he* was in patronising Johnnie Appleseed, Ms Bloggs could equally well assert that it isn't fair to judge Bill Bashem on the basis of one week's purchase (sample) only. Which one of them is correct? In a sense, both of them. A rise from 10 to 20 bad onions is a large enough difference to make one suspect that it signifies a real difference in quality – but on the other hand, it *could* have been due to the fact that some unlikely event has taken place. It might have been that one of Bill Bashem's assistants had been asked to leave, and on his last day in the shop was getting his own back by deliberately including in the deliveries onions which Bill Bashem would never dream of selling. Obviously, the ideal way to solve the dispute is to continue to buy 'samples' from both sources, and compare them over a period of time. Often though, this solution is not practicable.

Now I want to show you how this problem reflects the problems we encounter in scientific work. When we conduct an experiment we usually obtain two sets of scores for comparison, and these comprise our samples. One set measures some kind of event which occurred under the experimental conditions, and the other, the same kind of event, but without the experimental treatment. The two sets of scores are said to come from experimental and control groups respectively. Just as in the memory experiment results described in chapter 1, it often happens that our two sets of scores are not radically different, but only differ by a small amount. Like Joe Bloggs, we are left wondering whether the difference is due to a real effect, or just to some chance variation. The ideal solution is the same. We would repeat our experiment several times, and thus quickly discover exactly what 'typical' results comprise. Just a small difference in the scores, but repeated over and over again, would indicate a real, even if small, difference in treatments. However, if we established that the baselines were indistinguishable, then we would conclude that our treatment did not have any effect. Fine – except that considerations of time and cost usually mean that we do not repeat experiments in order to reach a decision about what the results signify.

In other words, we make a preliminary judgement on the basis of one sample only. Of course, the experiment will probably be repeated, sooner or later, and particularly if it concerns some effect which is deemed to be of importance. However, each single experiment is still judged initially on its own merits – and this is where we need statistical techniques. The tests we carry out on sets of scores will indicate to us just how safe it is to attribute any difference we obtain to a real difference in baseline, as opposed to being due to an unusual accidental occurrence. In fact had Joe Bloggs taken a statistics course, he would have been able to use a statistical test to decide on a rational basis where the next purchase of onions should be made! As it is, we might note in passing that although statistical techniques can easily tell us what the probability of some event is, or whether a sample can be regarded as typical, it can never tell us directly what to do. There are many factors which have to be taken into consideration. If an experiment or survey is very costly, in terms of time or skill, then we would not wish to have to repeat it unnecessarily. However, if the experiment concerns a matter which will prove to be of immense benefit to humanity – or if there is some chance that a certain treatment carries with it some danger (as in drug development, or brain surgery) – then most of us would prefer that *replications* (repeat experiments) are carried out. This repeated 'sampling' gives us a baseline to work from, and is safer than 'one-off' judgements. Even when we have established that some treatment works, statistical tests cannot tell us whether the benefits outweigh the costs. So Joe and his wife could still argue about whether the superiority of one batch of onions justifies travelling to a more distant greengrocer, or whether

Probability

the pleasantness of Johnnie Appleseed compensated for the fact that his produce is slightly below the standard of his less friendly rivals!

In chapter 6 there will be much more information about the relationship between statistical tests and statements of probability, and another example will show the connection between them and experimental work. Meanwhile, make sure that you are quite happy about the several ways in which we express probability numerically.

6 What are statistical tests all about?

TYPICAL FIELDWORK WEATHER

All the statistical procedures described so far have been concerned with summarising information as briefly and accurately as possible – hence the name *descriptive statistics*. Now we move on to the second main type of statistical techniques, *inferential statistics* – or, the dreaded tests! We use them to draw inferences (informed guesses) about situations from which we have only been able to gather a part of the total information which exists. As the aim of experimental work is to make predictions on the basis of limited information, we have frequent occasion to use statistical tests in analysing the results of experiments. The information contained in the next few chapters will be directly applicable to most kinds of scientific work, although the examples I give will mainly be drawn from the social sciences. The only material needed for a good understanding of this chapter is that given on probability, in chapter 5.

The dreaded statistical tests

I would like to begin by considering briefly why statistics tests are dreaded and disliked by many students. First, few people understand the rationale behind inferential tests and techniques – in other words, they don't have much of a clue about what is going on! Then, having ploughed through a number of tests, most of which are somewhat different from each other, yet all of which are used in fairly similar situations, students find it hard to fathom out which test is appropriate for a given set of data. Finally, statistical formulae and tests *look* really difficult, and are very off-putting – especially for people who were nervous of maths in the first place!

I hope to describe and explain the use of statistical tests in such a way that you understand quite clearly just why you are using them, and what is going on when you carry one out. Page 198 (just before the index) tells you how to decide on which test to use for the various experimental designs, and with different types of data. As for the fact that tests look difficult, I couldn't agree more! The *t* test formula in particular looks quite horrific. Bold readers look at it now – on page 172 – nervous readers, perhaps not just yet! Who knows what that pile of square root signs, brackets, bars and lines is trying to convey?

Take heart. First of all, those of you who have read the chapter on measures of dispersion will already be in a better position to cope with nasty-looking formulae. Look at the one for obtaining the standard deviation, given on page 156. That too looks off-putting, although admittedly not quite as bad as the *t* test formula. However, if you do have some insight into what it means, and have actually worked through it to obtain a measure of spread, it doesn't seem quite as bad, does it? You now know that it is possible to use the formula by going through the series of steps which the symbols stand for, in small stages. The *t* test formula is just the same. It can be tackled in a series of steps, each of which is quite simple, and instead of looking like a pile of mysterious mumbo-jumbo, it can be seen to represent a longish sequence of arithmetical operations. If you doubt this, take your courage in one hand, and with the other, turn to the formula on page 172. Even nervous readers should now do this. Examine every symbol in turn, and decide what each one signifies. You will already know that $\sqrt{}$ means 'take the square root of', a line —— means 'divide by', and that + means 'add together'. Σ was encountered in obtaining the standard deviation, and just means everything given in a particular list added together. The only really new symbol is *t* itself – but you obtain *that* by ploughing steadily through the instructions contained in the formula.

Perhaps it is worth mentioning here a common misconception. When you did maths, and algebra in particular, you learnt that formulae and equations have to be regarded as puzzles, in which the various symbols must be taken apart, shuffled and reassembled in such a way that the correct 'answer' emerges. Formulae in statistics aren't like this. All the puzzling and shuffling have already been done by statisticians, and a formula represents a series of operations which must be carried out in the order laid down by the rules of arithmetic – rather like the operations conveyed in a recipe, or a knitting pattern. The *t* test formula does not have to be *solved* in any way, but just worked through, and you only need very elementary skills in arithmetic to be able to cope. Perhaps the crucial thing is to know in which order the various operations should be undertaken (given in the detailed operation schedule steps) – and also, to prevent yourself from dying of boredom whilst slowly ploughing through the longer sequences of calculations!

Populations and samples

I shall now spend some time talking about the rationale which underlies statistical testing. In gathering scores for analysis, we are normally working with only a fraction of the information which is theoretically available. This partial availability of data, coupled with the variability commonly found in complex organisms, is basically what gives rise to our need for statistics tests. We call the large pool of information from which we draw a portion for study a *population*, whilst the smaller portion itself is known as a *sample*.

The first thing to realise about the term *population* is that it does not necessarily refer to people. In everyday language it means people, but its official definition in statistics is: **any group of numbers, finite or infinite, which refer to real or hypothetical objects or events**. This definition has quite a broad scope! It doesn't only cover people (or rather, some numerical aspect derived from those people), but any numbers taken from a group which shares some common characteristic. Examples of populations are the number of: fishes in the sea, fishes in fresh water, left-handed people living in Scotland, people living in England, giraffes in the world, giraffes kept in captivity, sufferers from schizophrenia, plankton in a pond, measured heights of a group of people, road accidents occurring in Great Britain, stars in the universe, cows in Yorkshire, memory test scores from adults. So a population can refer not only to humans, but also to other animals, events, scores, or simply anything which can give rise to numbers.

Populations can also vary in size. They may be quite small, as in the case of left-handed blind people; very large, as in the number of inhabitants of a country or continent; large and virtually infinite, as with stars in the universe or fishes in the sea. Some numbers are derived from populations of flexible and unknown size. Examples are the scores obtained from people participating in a personality test, or the number of bull's-eyes scored by a rifle marksman. In theory he could spend his entire life shooting at a target – just as theoretically, people could spend their lives completing personality questionnaires – but of course this doesn't happen in reality, and so the scores obtained from people participating in experiments or trials of some sort are regarded as samples from populations of virtually infinite size.

In fact it is very unusual to conduct experimental work on a complete population. The examples which spring most readily to mind are those of sufferers from a rare disease, or a species of animal which is approaching extinction. Even then, any scores or measurements taken from these populations would still only be a sample of a larger set of numbers available if the researcher spent longer measuring his or her subjects' behaviour or attributes. It is extremely unlikely that you will ever work with a complete population, although your aim, if you do experimental work, will be to make statements about them, and not restrict your conclusions to the sample which you have actually studied.

The skill with which you select your sample, and its size, will determine just how accurately you can make statements about the populations from which it was drawn. This population is called the *parent population*, and inferences you make about it, on the basis of samples, are known as *generalisations*. In statistical formulae it is traditional to distinguish populations from samples by using the letters of the Greek alphabet to denote an estimate based on a sample, as opposed to the more precise figure obtained from an entire population. Apart from the difference this creates when calculating standard deviations – and we virtually always use sample estimates – this need be of no further concern to you.

Exercise

1 Identify the parent population of the following things:
   (a) your pet cat   (b) your best friend's IQ score   (c) a raindrop   (d) a sardine from a tin   (e) yourself   (f) the third person you saw on your way to work this morning   (g) the people you pass on your way home in the late afternoon   (h) slowing of responses after alcohol consumption   (i) the Victorian cemetery at Highgate   (j) Queen Victoria

Populations, samples and statistical tests

So far then, you should have grasped the idea that a population is a large, often infinitely large, set of numbers derived from virtually anything at all. Also, that we usually only deal with samples, which are smaller portions of the populations currently under study. How do populations and samples fit in with statistical tests? In evaluating the results of an experiment, or some sets of observations, we are normally asking the question: Is one set of results *really* different from the other?

What happens next is that if we decide, after using the appropriate statistical tests, that the two sets of results really *are* different, then we conclude that they have been drawn from *two different populations*. If the numbers are not 'really' different, as decided by the tests, then what we state is that they appear to have come from just *one* population. This is where populations come into statistical testing, and I shall soon give more details. Samples are involved in so far as we normally work with them, rather than populations, and as a sample is not usually a perfect representative of its parent population, we can never be quite certain that the conclusions based upon them are absolutely correct.

Before I go on to describe how statistics tests might be used to evaluate the results of a particular experiment, I would like to present an analogy to testing which involves strong visual associations, and which should help you to achieve insight into the rationale of statistical testing.

Fieldwork in biology

Imagine a country scene, and two ponds which are fairly close together. One of the ponds is in a wood, and the other in an open field. A biologist wishes to study the micro-organisms which inhabit the ponds, and so sets out with test-tubes, nets, wellies and all the other essential paraphernalia. At great personal risk, he manages to obtain two test-tubes full of pond water. I shall pause here, to point out how the ponds relate to statistics. All micro-organisms in the pond in the woods comprise *population A*. Similarly, the micro-organisms in the field pond make up *population B*. What has the biologist done in taking test-tubes full of water from each pond? You've got it! He has drawn two *samples*.

As is usual in fieldwork, a downpour sets in, and the rain makes the labels which the biologist had stuck onto the test-tubes, fall off. On his arrival at the lab., then, the

YES I THINK WE MIGHT SAFELY SAY······THAT THESE SAMPLES *differ*.

biologist does not know which test-tube contains water from which pond. However, just by looking at the two samples he can see that one is much greener than the other – due to the different kinds of micro-organisms which inhabit wood and field ponds.

Let's pause again to take stock. The test-tubes contain samples of micro-organisms. Our statistical samples comprise sets of numbers. The biologist's two samples might *look* different. So can numbers. A 'test-tube' containing the digits:

  1, 4, 5, 2, 7, 9, 4, 3, 0, 5

looks very different from one containing:

  22, 31, 6, 44, 25, 18, 39, 27

This is the old eye-ball test again!

Just as the biologist could *see* that the test-tubes contained different micro-organisms, so we can sometimes *see* that samples of numbers differ radically from each other. No need for any stats tests at all! Unfortunately, experiments rarely oblige by giving rise to sets of scores which are as obviously different as the ones above, but more often to ones like those I list in the next comparison. If the samples of pond water hadn't looked very different, then the equivalent in numbers might be:

  Test-tube 1: 1 4 5 3 0 2 3
  Test-tube 2: 3 6 4 8 9 2 7

Now it has become quite hard to distinguish the two sets simply by looking at the numbers. This is another version of the problem concerning the results of the new memory technique experiment, which was described in chapter 1. We want to know, by some means, whether the two sets of numbers really do differ from each other, or not.

Returning to the field, we must make some rather odd events overtake our biologist in order to illustrate the rationale behind statistical testing. The biologist sets off, obtains his two samples of pond water, loses the labels from the test-tubes, and on his arrival at the lab. leaves them on a table while he goes to change his wet clothes. His colleague arrives on the scene. She knew that the samples of pond water were to have been collected, but can't remember whether the samples were to have been taken from two ponds that day, or just one of them. Can you translate these events into the statistical equivalent? You have two sets of numbers which *look* different. You wonder whether these samples have come from one source (population), or whether they were drawn from two different sources (populations). If the numbers look completely different, then with no more ado you can conclude that they have probably come from two different underlying populations.

But how would the biologist solve the problem if the samples looked fairly similar? She would put the pond water under a microscope, and with the aid of this tool, and the details it revealed, make a decision. How do we solve problems with similar-looking sets of numbers? We take our samples and subject them to statistical analysis – the appropriate tool – to reach a conclusion about their source or sources. Because we have worked with a sample (water taken from a pond, or scores obtained from a subject), and not a complete population, we cannot be 100% certain that the portion we have inspected was truly representative of the parent population, and so we have to allow for this potential source of error in our final decision. This will be covered in more detail later. Meanwhile, that's it. *That's* what all the fuss is about! We use statistical tests to tell us (when we can't just see) whether samples of numbers appear to have been drawn from one or two populations. The statistical test will also inform us what our likely margin of error is.

A summary of experimental work

In an experiment, we set up some alteration of conditions, and then compare the scores derived from the altered situation with those obtained from the control, i.e. from the one in which there was no alteration. We thus obtain two sets of scores. Our question is: Did the altered condition make any difference? The difference will be reflected in the scores, and so the question can be turned into one relating to a statistical evaluation: Are the scores from the two groups different in any way? This in turn is converted to: Do the scores seem to have come from one or two populations? We then carry out a statistical test – if the question cannot be determined simply by the eye-ball test. If the scores *do* appear to have been drawn from one population only, then we have to conclude that our experimental manipulations failed to bring about any change in the scores, and the experimental group scores will closely resemble the control group scores.

A note about the use of the word 'population' with respect to statistical tests. It is traditional to state the statistical aspects of experimental work in the terms I have just given. There is a potential source of confusion over the word 'population' though, and I will try to explain it, so that you can avoid the confusion. You may remember from exercise 1 that some groups of things can form an entire population in their own right, or form a part of another population – and both at the same time. In experimental work, whenever we take, say, a sample of subjects, then these subjects are drawn from a particular parent population. We then (usually) proceed to divide our sample into two, and apply one treatment to one of the groups whilst the other serves as a control. We get our two sets of results, and apply statistical techniques to them. Now it was said above, that we look to see (statistically) whether they have come from one or two populations. But we have been working with what was originally one sample, which was obtained from one population, before it was divided into two. For statistical purposes, the *sample* we took becomes the population, and in fact if our experimental treatment did have an effect, the sample becomes two populations. The point is that here we are talking about populations of scores, and these must not be confused with populations of subjects. If it helps, try to separate entirely the idea of the scores which we obtain from subjects, or the scores we are going to analyse, from the subjects, or populations of living things which actually give the scores. In statistical work, it is just as if we take the sets of scores (maybe you can imagine them contained in test-tubes) and look at the numbers themselves, when asking the question about their source. It does not matter to statisticians whether the source itself was a population, sub-population, or sub-sub-population. They treat the numbers as if they have been directly derived from one or two populations – and so the word in this case means just a 'pool' of numbers.

A psychology experiment

I shall now describe a psychology experiment on learning, and examine the role of samples, populations and statistical tests in this set-up. Twelve sets of identical twins aged 18 were selected. These subjects represent a very small sample from the fairly large population of adult identical twins aged 18 – or the larger population of all adult identical twins – or the even larger population of humans. The twins were asked to learn some poetry. From each pair of twins, one was chosen to join the group which was to do the learning under quiet conditions, while the other was put into the group which was to learn poetry under noisy conditions. By dividing our sample into two groups, and by giving them different treatments, we will (we hope) create two populations of scores. These scores are obtained after 10 minutes of learning, and they reflect the degree of material mastered. The stages of the experiment are shown in Figure 1.

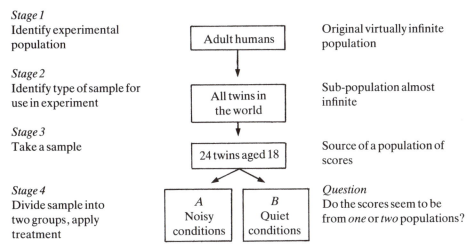

Stage 1
Identify experimental population

Adult humans

Original virtually infinite population

Stage 2
Identify type of sample for use in experiment

All twins in the world

Sub-population almost infinite

Stage 3
Take a sample

24 twins aged 18

Source of a population of scores

Stage 4
Divide sample into two groups, apply treatment

A Noisy conditions

B Quiet conditions

Question
Do the scores seem to be from *one* or *two* populations?

Figure 1. The stages of an experiment on learning

From an *experimental* point of view, the scores obtained in A and B can now be regarded as two populations. From a statistical point of view, we can't tell whether the numbers from A and B have come from two populations until we have carried out tests. If they seem to have come from one population, then we have to conclude that in applying our experimental treatment we did not create enough effect for the scores to be distinguishable. Our experiment did not 'work'. If, on the other hand, our scores are distinguishable, we can conclude that the experimental manipulations did have an effect.

Although we know what we did when we conducted the experiment, in terms of applying this or that treatment, we can't tell whether what we did had any effect until after we have looked at the results, and perhaps subjected them to statistical analysis. It is as if, when we conduct our analysis, we have to pretend that we don't really know what happened before – like the biologist's colleague, mentioned earlier in the chapter. If the learning ability scores appear to have come from two populations, *A* with noise and *B* without noise, then it can be concluded that noise does have a particular effect. However, taking the experiment as part of the broader context of psychological understanding, we would hope to generalise our findings from the twins actually used in the study to all humans. If we talk of 'learning' generally, as opposed to poetry learning, then we are making another generalisation, but this time in terms of the material being learnt. You might wonder why the experiment was carried out on twins, if the aim was to make statements about 'untwinned' humans. Twins are particularly favoured in experimental psychology. This is because they have the same genetic make-up, thus reducing somewhat the amount of variability in their behaviour, and so helping to make the effect of experimental manipulations more discernible.

Summary

In experimental work we go through the following sequence of activities:

1 We try to create two separate populations by giving different treatments to a sample drawn from the parent population.

2 We obtain scores from the two groups we have created.

3 We examine the sets of scores, using statistical techniques if necessary, to see whether they really do differ from each other.

4 If they differ, then our statistical test will enable us to put a figure on the element of chance likely to have been involved. If it is low, we conclude that the sets of scores seemed to have come from two sources (populations), and that our experiment was a success. If it is high, we conclude that the scores are not distinguishable, and that our treatment did not bring about the effect which we had originally anticipated.

7 Hypotheses

STATISTICIANS TAKE A NEGATIVE APPROACH

In the previous chapter you were given, in somewhat laborious detail, the sequence of operations we follow in carrying out an experiment. Make sure that you have thoroughly grasped that material, for this chapter is simply an extension: some more steps will be added, and then the whole routine re-expressed, using the formal terms in common usage. By the end of the chapter you will know about all the steps undertaken in experimental work, and most of the remainder of this book will be spent on giving further details of some of the steps themselves – for instance statistical tests, aspects of experimental design, and sampling.

Hypotheses and variables

In putting together an experiment, we start off by naming the phenomenon which is at the centre of our investigation, stating which conditions we intend to manipulate – and how – and considering what kind of data we hope to collect from experimental and control groups for comparison purposes. The major step to be added to this sequence of events occurs right at the start of an experiment, and it concerns our belief about the effect which the experimental manipulation of conditions will have. Any idea or theory which makes certain provisional predictions is called a *hypothesis*, and the preliminary idea we have in our experimental work is termed – not surprisingly – the *experimental hypothesis*. Examples of experimental hypotheses are:

> That a particular drug changes specified organic tissue
> That diet influences intelligence
> That facial appearance matters in inter-personal perception
> That advertising policy affects beer sales
> That environmental pollution is responsible for altering plant life
> That study habits influence exam marks

We have named particular things (organic tissue, intelligence, inter-personal perception, etc.) and stated our belief that each is influenced in some way by something else – the 'something elses' being a drug, diet and facial appearance, etc. All these 'things' and 'something elses' are called *variables*. The term 'variable', used in an experimental context, means anything which is free to vary, and in order to describe them in a quantitative way, they have to be expressed in appropriate units. Sometimes the units will be quite obvious, like inches, IQ scores, success rate on a task, pints of beer sold, etc., but at other times ingenuity will be called for. For instance how do we measure and express taste, attitudes, beliefs and motivation? Often we have to devise a rating scale specially for expressing a particular variable in an appropriate kind of unit. Such 'home-made' scales are often regarded as being less trustworthy than well-established units in common usage. As you will discover in chapter 10, the kinds of units we use to quantify variables have an important bearing on the statistical test we will choose for data analysis.

The pairs of variables which occur in each experiment have separate names. The variable we manipulate is called the *independent variable*, and abbreviated to IV. The variable which we hypothesise will alter as a consequence of our manipulations is called the *dependent variable*, or DV. It is easy to remember which way round the IV and DV are. The dependent variable alters as a consequence of the value of the independent variable – its value is *dependent* upon this. The value of the independent variable is free to vary according to the whims of the experimenters. The IV's and DV's named in the hypotheses listed above are given in table 1.

Table 1

Independent variable	Dependent variable
A particular drug	Specific organic tissue
Diet	Intelligence
Facial appearance	Inter-personal perception
Advertising policy	Beer sales
Environmental pollution	Plant life
Study habits	Exam marks

Most variables can be either dependent or independent, within the context of a particular experiment. For instance, in the final example given above, it was hypothesised that students' study habits will affect their exam performance. However, it is also reasonable to wonder whether students' exam marks might actually lead them to seek to improve their study habits! Beer sales, given as a DV above, would become an IV in the context of studies concerning alcoholism, road accidents or sales of soft drinks.

Directional hypotheses

You might feel that the hypotheses listed earlier were all rather vague, for the words 'influence', 'affect', 'change', etc., are not precise. It often happens that we feel we can make more specific predictions about the effect our manipulations of the IV will have. For example we might predict that a specific diet will improve intelligence; certain experiences might cause a deterioration in a skill, perceptual or mental process; environmental pollution may reduce plant growth or altered study habits might improve exam marks. When a hypothesis states a predicted direction of outcome – as seen by the use of such words as 'reduce', 'increase', 'lower' or 'raise' – then it is called a *directional*, or *one-tailed hypothesis*. The vaguer types of hypothesis, like the ones given earlier, are known as *nondirectional*, or *two-tailed hypotheses*.

The terms one- and two-tailed are more commonly used than directional or nondirectional. It is extremely important to know whether an experimental hypothesis is one- or two-tailed, for this information will be used in conjunction with the statistical analysis to state the level of chance expectancy associated with a particular experimental outcome.

Exercises

1 Identify the IV and DV in each of the following proverbs:
   (a) Spare the rod and spoil the child
   (b) Two heads are better than one
   (c) Absence makes the heart grow fonder
   (d) Out of sight, out of mind
   (e) A rolling stone gathers no moss
   (f) He laughs best who laughs last
   Are the statements likely to be framed as one- or two-tailed hypotheses?
2 Decide whether each of the following research hypotheses is one- or two-tailed:
   (a) Older people make slower learners
   (b) Alcohol affects reaction time
   (c) Anxiety influences performance
   (d) Sunlight makes plants grow faster
   (e) Quality of bar staff influences the sale of drinks
   (f) Vandalism rises with over-crowding
3 Compose three one-tailed and three two-tailed hypotheses. Check your creations with a fellow student or your teacher.

The null hypothesis

Regardless of whether a hypothesis is one- or two-tailed, it is known as an *experimental* or *research hypothesis*. Experimental hypotheses can go by yet another name, just to confuse matters, this being the *alternative hypothesis*. Alternative to what, I hear you asking? We'll discover in a few moments, when I have reviewed the state of the game so far.

The stages undertaken in experimental work are:

1 From an idea, formulate a one- or two-tailed hypothesis.
2 Decide what the units of measurement for the IV and DV are.
3 Decide what values the IV will have in your experimental manipulations.
4 Identify the parent population and select a sample of subjects from it. Divide this sample into two.
5 Apply the experimental treatment to one group of subjects, and treat the other in an identical manner, but with different values of the IV. The latter forms the control group. In some experiments it is possible for subjects to take part twice, under comparable conditions, and in this case we speak of subjects acting as their own controls.
6 Collect the results, i.e. two sets of scores reflecting different values of the IV. The scores will be values of the DV.
7 Analyse the results. In doing so, you will be able to decide how likely it is that any difference found between the sets of scores is a real one, as opposed to one which may have been due to chance factors.
8 Draw a conclusion about whether the original experimental hypothesis has been confirmed or not.

Hypotheses

This all seems reasonably straightforward. You might guess that it can't possibly remain as simple as this, and that something will become more complicated. Right again! The 'something' which becomes more complex concerns the way we express our prediction of whether or not the experiment worked, when we start to carry out the statistical analysis. For reasons best known to mathematicians and philosophers, when we start to grind our scores through the statistical treatment mill, we begin by making the statement that **we will assume the experiment has not worked** – this being reflected in the expectation that the two sets of scores which we obtain will not differ. The mathematical rationale behind this strange turn of events is beyond the scope of this book. However, what you *do* need to know is that when you start the mathematical treatment of the data, you make the tentative statement: **The independent variable does *not* affect the dependent variable in the way we anticipated.** This is known as the *null hypothesis*. It is because of this gloomy creature that the experimental hypothesis – its exact opposite – is sometimes called the alternative hypothesis.

I think that it is helpful, when trying to fit experimental work and statistical analysis together, to think along the following lines . . .

The scientist has an idea which is put into the form of an experimental hypothesis. An experiment, designed to test the hypothesis, is subsequently undertaken. The results are collected, and a statistical technique or test is needed in order to decide whether the experimental hypothesis was correct or not, i.e., whether the IV *did* influence the DV in the manner predicted. At this stage, envisage the scientist handing the results over to a statistician, saying 'I collected these results in such and such a way; can you tell me whether they really differ from each other or not?' The statistician then takes the numbers, and in fact need know nothing about the purpose of the experiment or the scientist's prediction, to be able to analyse the data. All that must be known is what *kinds* of scores the numbers represent, for instance IQ, minutes, item recall, people, inches, attitude ratings, acidity, etc., and how well the experimental and control groups were matched. On receipt of the data, the statistician makes the initial statement which comprises the null hypothesis: **The sets of numbers do not differ.** Whatever the IV was, it is assumed not to have had the predicted effect on the DV.

The statistician then carries out the appropriate analysis on the data. If it is found that the numbers *do* appear to differ, and it is very unlikely that this is due to chance, then the null hypothesis can be *rejected*. When this happens, the conclusion is that the experimental hypothesis can be taken as correct. If the numbers do not differ, then the statistician's gloomy statement is confirmed, and the null hypothesis stands. When this information is conveyed back to the scientist, then it is concluded that the experimental hypothesis was either wrong (and so must be discarded), or incorrect because of some other variable whose influence was overlooked. In this case, the experimental hypothesis may be rejected as it stands, but modified at some future date, in the light of the experimental findings.

This may seem unnecessarily complicated, because of the statistician's negative approach to the experimental hypothesis. Also, an understanding of the processes involved is not helped by the fact that many of the concepts have more than one name. Anyhow, it seems easier to think of the statistical operations, which occur in the middle of the experimental procedure, as purely mathematical events which are rather separate from the practical activities. When the statistical fun starts, it is as though you have to forget everything you already knew about the treatments you have given the samples, and start afresh, with the pessimistic prediction that the sets of numbers you are now inspecting do not differ from each other.

The null hypothesis can be defined as: **The statistical hypothesis of no difference**. The word 'statistical' should serve as a reminder that it is the concoction of statisticians, and not an integral part of experimental procedure.

Exercise

4 Decide what kind of hypothesis each of the following is:
   (a) That drinking blood makes the teeth grow
   (b) That there is no difference between two sets of scores obtained during an experiment on perseverance
   (c) That sunshine affects mood
   (d) That the drug Gromor makes you shrink
   (e) That there is no difference in social status between the residents of a council house estate and the owners of stately homes
   (f) That the provision of maternity hospitals changes the perinatal mortality rate
   (g) That children who eat breakfast show better concentration at school
   (h) That the perceived redness of sunsets is altered by the quantity of volcanic dust circling the Earth
   (i) That vegetarians have a lower incidence of athlete's foot
   (j) That traffic vibrations accelerate the decay of old buildings

Like a dog with two tails!

Returning to the fact that experimental hypotheses are of two kinds, one- and two-tailed, I would like to say a little more about why the choice of hypothesis has consequences for the evaluation of results.

Suppose you say that you expect a certain drug to *aid* recovery. This is a one-tailed or directional hypothesis, and you are claiming that you expect recovery rates to improve when subjects take the drug. So far so good. The statistical null hypothesis applied to the data will be an expectation of no difference. If the sets of results do appear to differ, as shown by a statistical test, and the recovery rate is better with the drug than without it, then all is well. No difference between the sets of scores, and you would conclude that the experimental hypothesis was incorrect, and reject it in favour of the null hypothesis. But what happens if your sets of results are quite clearly different, but that the drug has made recovery *slower*? From the statistical point of view, the sets differ. However, as you set up a directional hypothesis, and the results are in the wrong direction, then you have no option but to reject your experimental hypothesis. If you had established a nondirectional (two-tailed) hypothesis, then it would not have mattered in which direction the experimental group scores had altered. In either case you would be able to reject the null hypothesis and accept the experimental hypothesis, which would have been that the drug would have *altered* the rate of recovery.

Why should experimenters ever make directional hypotheses then? In brief, because it is easier, from a statistical point of view, to show a difference between sets of scores if a direction is predicted at the outset. As most researchers prefer to report experiments which have worked – and indeed, it is harder to get the results of unsuccessful experiments published – there is some motivation here. This is quite a pity though, for it is often the case that an experiment which hasn't 'worked' is just as valuable in leading the way to further research.

Space-saving abbreviations

Rather than writing out the word 'hypothesis', together with its type, it is usual to refer to a hypothesis simply as H, and to add another letter or digit to signify the kind of hypothesis being referred to. For reference, the various hypotheses and their abbreviations are given in table 2. Notice that there is no distinction between one- and two-tailed hypotheses in terms of the abbreviations used. It is also usual to make the following abbreviations:

E for experimenter – to be used in writing reports instead of the first person singular, which is avoided.

S in work involving animals; the long-suffering subjects, ranging from insects and worms, through goldfish and rats, to humans.

Table 2. Hypotheses commonly encountered in scientific work

Hypothesis	Abbreviation	Description of hypothesis
Alternative	H_1 or H_A	The experimental hypothesis; a statement of the
Experimental	H_1 or H_A	predicted influence of the IV on the DV
Research	H_1 or H_A	
Null	H_0	The statistical hypothesis of no difference
Directional	None	An experimental hypothesis in which the specific
One-tailed	None	direction of score differences is predicted
Nondirectional	None	An experimental hypothesis in which the specific
Two-tailed	None	direction of score differences is *not* predicted

A summary of experimental procedure

To end this chapter, I shall now give a summary of the steps undertaken in a scientific investigation, from start to finish. The fourth and fifth steps have not yet been covered, but are included at this stage so that you now have a complete list of the procedure.

1 Have an idea about the effect of one variable upon another.
2 Define the IV and DV, and decide how they will be quantified.
3 Express the idea formally, and by means of a one- or two-tailed experimental hypothesis.
4 Decide what kind of statistical analysis will be appropriate.
5 Specify a significance level and sample size.
6 Select the sample to be used from the parent population which is under scrutiny.
7 Apply the experimental treatment to one part of the sample, and treat the other as a control group.
8 Collect the data.
9 Analyse the data.
  (i) Establish the null hypothesis.
  (ii) Apply appropriate statistical test or technique.
  (iii) Accept or reject the null hypothesis in the light of Step 9 (ii).
10 According to the outcome of Step 9 (iii), decide whether the experimental hypothesis can be accepted (if the null hypothesis is rejected) or rejected (if the null hypothesis has been accepted).

THUMP   DOUBLE THUMP.

A TWO-TAILED BEAST?

8 Significance

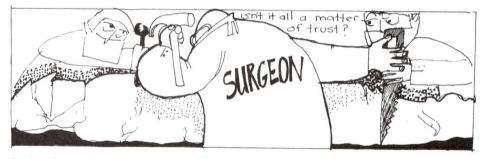

In this chapter I am going to enlarge upon what happens when we analyse our scores, and are forced to consider the element that chance factors might have contributed. Material introduced here builds upon that presented in the three previous chapters.

A very significant experiment

When we evaluate the results of an experiment, we normally describe the findings in terms of their *significance*. The term has a rather special meaning in this context. It doesn't just refer to the importance of the experiment, and whether it represents a significant advance in the field of scientific endeavour, but rather the outcome of the statistical analysis of the data. The significance, expressed as a precise numerical probability value, tells us how sure we can be that our scores really are different, and our experimental treatment did work, as opposed to being the result of some fluke – like an atypical sample, or the effects of some unconsidered variable. In other words, even if you have decided that your scores appear to come from two populations rather than one – i.e. your manipulation of the IV *did* alter the DV – you must state how certain you are of this.

You may recall from the chapter on probability that we can indicate our degree of confidence in something by putting a numerical value on it. We could say, for instance, that we are not very convinced of our success in an experiment, and state 20% as our level of confidence. We would mean that on one out of every five occasions we carried out the study (20% of the time) we would get these particular results accidentally – regardless of our manipulations of the IV. If we wanted, we could say the same thing a different way and give the figure of 80%, meaning that on only 80% of the occasions would the difference in scores represent a real difference due to the action of the IV on the DV. The lowest level of confidence which is acceptable to scientists is the 5%, or one-in-twenty level. In the 'Results' section of a report it would normally be expressed as the 0.05 level of probability – or significance – following a brief note saying which particular statistical treatment has been employed. If our treatment of the data had come up with a certainty of 0.01 (1%), then we would feel much more confidence in accepting our experimental hypothesis, as the chance of fluke occurrences would now only be one-in-a-hundred. Finally, and most pleasing, is when our results can only be attributed to chance factors at an estimated one-in-a-thousand rate, which is expressed as the 0.001 or 0.1% level. The three levels of 0.05, 0.01 and 0.001 (5%, 1% and 0.1%) are the ones traditionally used in reporting the results of statistical treatment. A probability level of more than

5% is not acceptable, and if this outcome occurs, then the null hypothesis cannot be rejected. Yet another tradition is followed in the way we word our final statement. We say that the null hypothesis 'cannot be rejected' – not that it has been accepted.

We refer to the level of probability, or significance, by using the abbreviation p. Also, in stating the value formally, another symbol, $\leq$, is used. This means 'less than or equal to'. So if our results turned out to have a significance level of 0.05, we would write either $p = 0.05$, or $p \leq 0.05$. If the significance level fell between the values of 0.05 and the next one of 0.01, we would state the most conservative value, and give $p \leq 0.05$ in our results. Similarly, between 0.01 and 0.001 would be stated as $p \leq 0.01$. Note that as the probability levels fall, from a numerical point of view, so our confidence in the results rises, and we speak of *higher* significance levels – the highest which is normally quoted being the much-desired 0.001 level.

In principle, as many writers on statistics point out, we should state the level of significance we are prepared to accept *before* we carry out our experimental or observational work. The level we choose rather depends upon the importance of being correct in our final conclusion. One writer, Siegel, illustrates this with the example of an experiment in brain surgery. If we were to investigate some new treatment for a brain disease, then we would not be too happy about deciding that it worked if our level of significance for trial experiments had only been 0.05. The cost of 5% of the brain surgery operations failing, both in terms of human suffering and expense, would be too great for us to wish to recommend that particular treatment. We would probably adopt the most stringent level before we felt that we could recommend it for general use. Notice though that our choice of a significance level doesn't in itself tell us what to *do* about our findings. It merely tells us what kind of confidence we can have in them. Naturally, we demand a high level of confidence for matters involving life or death outcomes (literally), or any other work in which the consequences of accepting the research hypothesis are not trivial.

Interpreting the outcome of statistical tests

Many statistical tests finish off with a particular 'statistic', for instance:

> t from the t test
> U from the Mann-Whitney U test
> T from the Wilcoxon test
> and F from the variance-ratio test

The statistic is then evaluated to see how significant it is, using the special tables drawn up for each. It is then possible to state whether a particular difference in sets of scores was likely to be due to a real effect rather than chance factors.

A common mistake made by students is to think of the final statistic – e.g. $U = 31$, or $t = 2.58$ – as some sort of answer, which may be correct or incorrect, like the answer to a sum in arithmetic. The statistics you obtain aren't really answers, although it is true that they do represent the final stages of working through an analysis, and so can be seen as the finish of it all. The particular value obtained won't be subsequently evaluated as right or wrong, but according to how likely it is that it might be the product of scores reflecting chance factors.

But what if I was wrong?

As you will have gathered, in stating a certain degree of confidence in your results, you are also admitting to the possibility of being wrong. (We will discount the possibility of being wrong because you made arithmetical errors during the calculations!) From a logical point of view, you can be wrong in two ways:

1 You decide that your sets of results differed, and accepted the experimental hypothesis, when in fact the IV hadn't really affected the DV in the manner predicted, but the one-in-twenty, or one-in-a-hundred event had occurred.
2 You decide that your sets of results didn't really differ, and so didn't reject (i.e. you accepted) the null hypothesis, and concluded that the experiment hadn't worked – when really, it had. It might be that great variability in the scores prevented the statistical technique from showing a significant difference, for instance. Or it might have been that your method for quantifying the DV was not precise and fine enough to show up rather subtle changes which took place.

These mistakes are called, respectively, *Type I* and *Type II errors*. Again, in 'real life' (whatever that is!), your willingness to make either of these mistakes will be dependent upon the kind of research you are doing, and the consequences of drawing incorrect conclusions.

9 Simple statistical tests

It is now time to tackle the much-dreaded statistical tests! Actually, I am sure that you will be surprised by just how easy they are to carry out. The difficulties associated with statistical tests lie in the rationale behind testing and interpretation, rather than in arithmetical aspects. Before we embark on the first test, make sure that you understand the topics covered in the last four chapters.

A fictitious experiment

First I will outline an investigation, and then I will use the results in a statistical analysis.

A keen market research student wished to discover whether his nine fellow residents in a student hostel consider the washing up liquid Gresego to be better than its cheaper rival, Kwikclene. Privately, he thought that Gresego was better, but he was careful not to let any of the others know this. He asked them to participate in a small study, and requested that each person wash up an identical pile of dirty dishes on two occasions on consecutive days. Half the students were to use Gresego first, and the other half Kwikclene first. As soon as they had finished the washing up, the students were required to give a score out of ten to the liquid they had just used. The higher the score, the better they judged the washing up liquid to have done its job. The investigator was careful to regulate such variables as the temperature of the water, the amount of washing up liquid used, and the amount of time and effort put into washing up. In addition, he did not let the students know which liquid was being used on each occasion, just in case that knowledge and certain prior expectations caused the student to give a biased judgement.

Exercise

1 In the experiment just outlined, identify the IV and DV. State the experimental hypothesis and decide whether it is one- or two-tailed. State the null hypothesis.

So, the market researcher obtained eighteen observations in all, collected in pairs from the nine participants in the study. He is now in a position to evaluate their judgements, which are given in table 1. If you hadn't worked it out (and shame on you!), the experimental hypothesis established here was a one-tailed one, as the prediction had been that Gresego would give *better* results (i.e. higher scores) than Kwikclene.

Simple statistical tests

Table 1. Ratings obtained for the efficiency of the washing up liquids Gresego and Kwikclene

Subject	Judgements of performance Gresego	Kwikclene
1	8	5
2	7	5
3	9	2
4	7	6
5	8	9
6	7	6
7	9	5
8	6	5
9	5	6

The eye-ball test indicates that Gresego has indeed produced better results – it obtained a median score of 7, as compared with Kwikclene's median of 5. Also, there are only two students who gave the higher rating to Kwikclene in their paired comparisons. Not content with the eye-ball test however, and maybe in an effort to convince the others that this was a 'proper' scientific investigation, not just a scheme devised to get the washing up done by others, the investigator decided to carry out a statistical test on the sets of scores. A test which is appropriate for this type of data is the *Wilcoxon* test. It can be used whenever sets of scores are 'paired off' in some way. In this experiment, each subject has contributed scores towards both sets of ratings, and in presenting and analysing the data, the pairs are kept in line with each other. The workings for the Wilcoxon test are given in operation schedule 7. Study the steps involved, and note that they finish with the final triumphant statement:

$$T = 6$$

Now that's not the answer, but a value for the T statistic which we must proceed to interpret, using the appropriate table. Our evaluation is the final step of the analysis, for it is this which gives us a probability level, which in turn indicates whether our results might have arisen by chance or not. If the final value of T could have arisen on more than one in twenty occasions, then we cannot reject the null hypothesis, and we must conclude that the original experimental hypothesis was wrong, i.e., that Gresego is *not* judged to be better than Kwikclene. If, however, the table indicates that on only one in twenty, or even fewer occasions, might the results have arisen 'by accident', then we are in business! The experimental hypothesis can be accepted, and the investigator would conclude with some confidence that Gresego is the superior brand of washing up liquid.

Let's see what happened then. The results of the analysis, $T = 6$, are evaluated using table S2. The steps involved in evaluation are given in operation schedule 7a. The outcome is a significant value of 0.025 for our particular T – in other words, we might have expected to get this value due to chance factors on only two and a half out of a hundred occasions. Perhaps five out of two hundred is an easier way of thinking about this particular value. Our confidence in the results is stronger than it would have been if the probability level of 0.05 (five out of one hundred) had been the outcome. Thus we can reject the null hypothesis quite happily, and accept the experimental hypothesis. The two sets of numbers which our samples comprise appear to have been drawn from two different parent populations, not one, and so the market research student can conclude that Gresego does in fact appear to produce better results than Kwikclene. Of course, whether it is better to the extent that its higher price can be justified is quite another question, and not one which is answered by the investigation just described. In a formal report, at the end of the 'Results' section, it would be said of this analysis:

> The results of the statistical analysis were significant at the $p \leqslant 0.025$ level (one-tailed Wilcoxon test; $T = 6$; $N = 9$), and so the experimental hypothesis was accepted. It was concluded that the performance of Gresego was judged to be superior to that of Kwikclene.

Exercises

2 Carry out the Wilcoxon test on the following pairs of scores, and interpret the test results with a one-tailed hypothesis established.

(a)	(b)
210, 200	250, 244
240, 220	235, 238
190, 260	202, 221
170, 220	196, 215
270, 440	227, 234
230, 260	218, 232
220, 580	232, 237
220, 920	224, 245
	215, 224
	203, 192

3 Interpret the following values of T, assuming that they were derived from experiments or investigations involving one-tailed hypotheses.
(a) $N = 10$, $T = 7$ (b) $N = 12$, $T = 57$ (c) $N = 20$, $T = 7$ (d) $N = 10$, $T = 4$
(e) $N = 16$, $T = 29$ (f) $N = 18$, $T = 49$ (g) $N = 13$, $T = 17$ (h) $N = 15$, $T = 29$

Interpretation with a two-tailed hypothesis

Suppose that in the original investigation the student had not had an opinion about the relative merits of Gresego and Kwikclene, but merely wondered whether *either* of them might turn out to be a better brand. Here we have a two-tailed hypothesis rather than a one-tailed, or directional, hypothesis. In the results we would look for a consistent difference between the two sets of scores which would reflect differences in washing up power (the DV), but we are not anticipating that one particular brand will produce either higher *or* lower scores than the other. The difference could be in either direction. Of course, if there isn't any difference, then the null hypothesis will stand, and we would conclude that the washing up liquids cannot be distinguished in terms of their performance.

We will use the data obtained earlier to see what would happen at the analysis stage if the student had established a two-tailed, rather than a one-tailed hypothesis. The calculations carried out in the Wilcoxon test are unchanged, and once more we have a value of T which is 6. The procedure for interpretation of T then alters as follows.

Simple statistical tests

Instead of taking the table's value for $T = 6$ when $N = 9$, using the *top* line of table S2, we refer to the line immediately below, which is headed 'Level of significance for two-tailed test'. A value of $T = 6$ will still be in the same position in the body of the table, but instead of reading off the significance level of 0.025, we now give it a probability value of 0.05. This is precisely twice the first value, and equivalent to the one in twenty accidental occurrence rate, rather than the one in forty (or two and a half out of a hundred), which was obtained previously. Thus the result has diminished in terms of level of significance. A swift glance at the top of table S2 will tell you that whatever significance level you decided upon for the interpretation of a one-tailed test, it will be doubled for a two-tailed one. Thus it is easier to obtain significant results with a one-tailed hypothesis. You can check this out for yourself by considering a T value of 7, obtained from nine pairs of scores which have been subjected to the Wilcoxon test. This value is just a little too large to be significant at the 0.05 level for a two-tailed test, but you can see that it would be significant for a one-tailed test, as it does not exceed the figure of 8, given in the far left column. In presenting the significance level in a formal report, we would say that the value of $T = 7$, for a one-tailed test, would be significant at the 0.05 level. This would be written something along these lines:

> The results of the Wilcoxon test were significant ($p \leq 0.05$, when $N = 9$, $T = 7$), and so the null hypothesis can be rejected.

You may suspect that temptation can arise over this business of relative significance levels of one- and two-tailed hypotheses. You would be correct! Suppose that it had been predicted that the two types of washing up liquid might differ, and a relatively vague, two-tailed hypothesis had been established. The investigator finds out that there is no significant difference between the two sets of scores when they are interpreted as two-tailed results, but that there *is* a significant difference if they are treated as one-tailed test data. The temptation is to say at that stage 'Well, I really suspected all along that such a set of results (naming the list with the higher set of scores) would be better.' If the investigation formed the basis for an experimental report, the experimental hypothesis could then be written up as a one-tailed hypothesis, and no-one would know that things had ever been imagined to be otherwise. As I mentioned earlier, publication traditions make life much easier for researchers who obtain significant results, and so rather strong will-power is needed to avoid succumbing to this temptation if it arises.

The same temptation to go back on a statement made at the outset of an experiment can occur in another situation. This is the one which was described in chapter 7, in which you start off with a one-tailed hypothesis, but find that although your results are statistically significant, the *direction* of difference is the wrong one. Actually, it is harder than it sounds to alter the original hypothesis in this case, because it is more than likely that the experimental work (and hypothesis) fits into a general background of known phenomena or some theoretical model. It is this background or model (or maybe only a simple observation), which governs the direction of the prediction, and so it is not usually possible to change the experimental hypothesis without altering the underlying assumptions or model quite radically. In the event of an unexpected direction cropping up in the results, most scientists would decide to carry out the experiment again – a process known as *replication*. They may or may not predict a new direction of results in the second attempt, depending upon whether they viewed the outcome of the first experiment as being due to the effect of some variable they had overlooked, or due to chance events. In carrying out the experiment once more, they have a second chance to look carefully at what is going on, and perhaps rule out the freak event explanation.

Exercise

4 Interpret the values of *T* which were given in exercise 3, but this time assume that the results have been obtained from investigations in which two-tailed predictions had been made.

An even simpler test – the sign test

If you have carried out the exercises and had a go at the Wilcoxon test, you were probably surprised by just how simple the arithmetic was, and found the evaluation of *T* to be the trickiest part of the procedure. The next test we will look at, the sign test, is even easier, and could probably be successfully carried out by a clever chimpanzee! I have chosen to describe it after the Wilcoxon test though, because I want to use its results to illustrate how tests can vary in their ability to detect significant differences in sets of scores. We call this ability *power-efficiency*, and it can be likened to degree of precision in tools. The finer an instrument, the more suitable it is for tasks requiring attention to detail; the more sophisticated a test is, the better it can detect subtle and perhaps small differences between sets of scores. You will soon be able to decide for yourself whether the sign test can be regarded as more sophisticated than the Wilcoxon.

The step-by-step procedure for the sign test is given in operation schedule 8, but I shall outline here what goes on. As with the Wilcoxon test, you obtain differences between the paired scores, and give each difference a plus (+) or minus (−) sign. In the sign test though, instead of ranking the differences between scores and then summing all the ranks which have the same sign, you merely *count* the number of differences with each sign. This is equivalent to saying 'There are so many (number stated) scores in one set which are *smaller* than their counterparts in the second set, and so many (state number) which are *larger*.' Having found out how many scores are in one particular direction (maybe having been moved there by your experimental manipulations), you then evaluate this number, using table S3. It tells you the probability of your particular directional change.

If I predict that one condition will give rise to *higher* scores than another, I am predicting that all (or most) of one group will be greater than their paired counterparts. If they *are* all higher, that is fine. The sign test will give a significant result. If a few of the scores are not higher though, then this is not quite so good, and the likelihood of obtaining a significant difference is diminished. It is common-sense really, but by using the mathematical wizardry incorporated into the sign test, we can give probabilities associated with all the different proportions of changes which might occur. Note that if we had predicted *lower* scores rather than *higher* ones, the procedure would be just the same, but with the signs reversed. Whether higher or lower scores are predicted from one group of scores, the hypothesis would be a directional, or one-tailed one. It is quite possible to use the sign test with two-tailed predictions, just as with the Wilcoxon test, and the chosen significance level is selected from the two indicated at the top of the columns of the evaluation table.

Let's suppose that in an experiment using twelve subjects, we obtained paired sets of scores. Without going into great detail, the data have been collected from an experiment on dieting. Each lady who participated contributed two scores; unaided weight loss over a certain time interval, and weight loss over an identical period, but during which they were also scoffing Waist-Away – the Wonder Weight Loss Powder. As we aren't cynical about the worth of commercial diet products, we predict a greater weight loss when the powder is being used than when it isn't – and so we have established a one-tailed hypothesis. The results of the experiment were that ten out of the twelve dieters did have greater losses with the treatment than without, whilst two subjects didn't. If we carry out the sign test on these data, then we shall end up with the value of S, the number of less frequent signs, being 2, and a value of N, the number of paired scores which are being analysed, being 12. If you inspect table S3, then you will see that the values in the body of the table, when $N = 12$, for the 0.05 and 0.025 levels, is 2. If our obtained value of S is equal to or smaller than the tabulated value, which it is, then we conclude our results are significant, and the scores really do come from two populations. So we would decide that the Wonder Weight Loss Powder does what it claims to do. Although our obtained value of 2 did not exceed the values given in the columns for *both* the 0.05 and 0.025 levels of probability, we would quote in our report whichever level we had decided upon before we undertook the data analysis, i.e. if we had said that we would accept the 0.05 level, we would claim significance at that level, but if we had said beforehand that we would not take anything higher than 0.025 as being significant, then we would give that level in our formal statement. In practice, what tends to happen is that we don't specify in advance that we will accept results of a particular significance level, and then quote that, but wait to see how things work out, and then report the best level of significance which was obtained. So, for instance, if *all* our dieters had done better with the treatment than without it, then the number of less frequent signs (S) would be 0, and we could claim significance at the 0.0005 level. If we had not predicted a direction of difference, but established a two-tailed hypothesis, then our obtained value of $S = 0$ would be significant at the 0.001 level.

Now cast your eye down table S3 to the line below the one we have just been referring to, for $N = 13$. Imagine that we found three out of thirteen ladies didn't lose weight with the treatment. What would you conclude? If you had set up a one-tailed prediction, then you would be safe, and could claim significance at the 0.05 level. Too bad if your prediction had been nondirectional though, for a probability of 0.1 is not judged significant; the maximum number of 'failures' you can have for significance, when $N = 13$, is two. What you can't do, is change your mind after the analysis!

Here's another example. A batch of 60 young tortoises is given the tortoise IQ test. On the basis of the score they obtain, and also their leg length, they are then paired off. Next, they are put individually into a nice maze on the lawn, and told that if they hurry along through it, then they will be able to give a hare a good punch on the snout. One group of tortoises is given a drug (cleverly disguised in a lettuce leaf) which is supposed to increase running speed; the other group is given a dummy pill, called a *placebo*, and which is also wrapped in a lettuce leaf. Placebos are always given in studies involving drugs, to ensure that all subjects appear to be receiving identical treatments. One by one, the tortoises all have their turn in the maze. Sure enough, the tortoises who have taken the drug race along like greased lightning – all except one that is, who lets the side down. Apart from his running time, all the others have shorter times than those in the group which had the placebo. Analysis: $N = 30$, and we have an S of 1. This is way below the value of 5 given for the 0.0005 probability (one-tailed test), and so the conclusion was that the results were highly significant. The experimenter is so pleased that she lets all the tortoises punch the hare!

What would be the conclusion if six of the tortoises had been members of the Hare Protection League, and only ambled along, despite having received the drug? An S value of 6 falls between the two tabulated values of 7 and 5, for the 0.005 and 0.0005 one-tailed significance levels. So these results would be stated as being significant at the 0.005 probability level, for they didn't quite make the 0.0005 mark. We always extrapolate to the most conservative value when a test statistic falls between tabulated values. To fail to get significance with a one-tailed prediction, we would need to have at least eleven tortoises whose speeds are slower than their matched counterparts, but it would be ten if we had set up a two-tailed hypothesis, for the maximum permitted number of 'deviants' at the 0.05 level is given as nine.

Earlier I said that scores might have been 'moved' in a particular direction by experimental manipulations. Don't take this to mean that in the sign test you must always use the results from the experimental group as if they were the ones which have 'moved'. In working through the calculations it is quite arbitrary which column of scores is subtracted from the other, and it is always the number of scores with the less frequent sign which gives us the value of S. The sign tests tells us the probability of obtaining a low number of scores which are in a different direction to the remainder – and like all statistical tests, it has nothing to say about cause and effect, predictions and interpretations. What it does say, is that if we get a certain number of scores which are out of step (in either direction), we can conclude with a specified degree of confidence that the two samples have been derived from different populations. The sign test can also be used on data which are not derived from experiments, e.g. observations of many types, opinions or information derived from surveys and questionnaires, etc. The chief requirement is that the scores are paired off for comparison purposes.

Exercises

5 Carry out the sign test on the data given in exercise 2. Evaluate for both one- and two-tailed tests.
6 Find the significance of the following values of S for both one- and two-tailed tests:
   (a) $S = 1$, $N = 8$ (b) $S = 5$, $N = 12$ (c) $S = 4$, $N = 18$ (d) $S = 3$, $N = 20$
   (e) $S = 0$, $N = 6$ (f) $S = 0$, $N = 25$ (g) $S = 4$, $N = 16$ (h) $S = 0$, $N = 5$

Comparison of the sign test and the Wilcoxon test

So far, I have described how the sign test works, and made some comparisons between it and the Wilcoxon test. I would now like to look at the two together a little more closely, so that you get better insight into what the power-efficiency of a test means, and also, so that you can see why it is that the Wilcoxon test is the better of the two, under most circumstances. We will work with the data obtained in the washing up experiment, and which are analysed in the steps comprising operation schedule 8. The values of 2 and 9 were obtained for S and N respectively, and after referring to table S3, it was concluded that the null hypothesis could not be rejected. However, when the Wilcoxon test was carried out on the same data (operation schedule 7) the conclusion had been reached that the null hypothesis *could* be rejected, as the sets of scores were significantly different at the 0.025 level. The conclusion differed despite the fact that both the Wilcoxon and sign tests were evaluated for one-tailed predictions. How is it that we get this difference between the two tests?

The Wilcoxon is the more powerful test of the two, because given the same sample size, it correctly rejects the null hypothesis, when the sign test doesn't. It can do this because it uses more information from the sets of scores than the sign test. It works on the actual *size* of the ranked 'wrong' direction differences, not just the *number* of scores which are in the wrong direction. In using more information it is thus a more precise instrument for detecting differences. You may be able to see, from the workings of the Wilcoxon test, that it is sometimes possible to get a significant difference between sets of data when there are many scores in the wrong direction, but only slightly so, and also, that a single score in the opposite direction could count heavily in the test by giving rise to a large value of T, and so forcing the researcher to conclude that the data were drawn from one population. This is the old problem of the outlier again, by the way. Does the extremely large, unique score mean that it is atypical in some way, and if so, can it be dropped from the analysis? If you are entirely confident that something very distinctive brought about the odd score, and so can justify dropping it, then do so. If you can't justify the decision, then don't, or you will be accused of fiddling your data!

It is best for you to gain insight into the relative merits of the Wilcoxon and sign tests by working through them, using the same scores. Even more illuminating is to create fictitious data for your calculations, and to attempt at the outset to obtain specific significance levels. Exercise like this is really good for you!

I hear a few voices asking how we know which test to do, when we are faced with the analysis of sets of scores which have been matched off for comparison purposes. Whenever we collect data which comprise definite scores, then the Wilcoxon would be preferable to the sign test. Sometimes however, the data can only really be expressed verbally. For example subjects' ratings of some food item as 'better', 'the same', or 'worse', after it has been subject to some change; whether people 'agree', 'don't know' or 'disagree' about something or other; whether animals seem to be 'more' or 'less' active under two conditions, etc. Whenever we can state that there is a difference in a particular direction, but are not able to quantify the amount precisely, then the sign test is the one to use. Items falling into one category are labelled as if they were pluses and into the other as if they were minuses. Items which don't change – or in the example above, the 'don't know' category – are counted as tied, and that particular pair of scores extracted from the analysis, with a consequent reduction of N. The sign test is thus a very useful instrument for many types of investigation in the social sciences when non-numerical data have been collected. I shall say more about the way we quantify variables, and the relevance this has for choice of statistical test, in the next chapter.

Another easy test – the Mann–Whitney U test

The investigation into washing up liquids described earlier involved nine subjects who kindly contributed pairs of scores for the advancement of human knowledge. It was the pairing which was the major factor in deciding that the Wilcoxon test was appropriate for the analysis of the results. In the experiment, pairing occurred because subjects acted as their own controls, but it would also have been possible to use it on *any* data which are paired off in some way – maybe scores collected from identical twins, or from unrelated subjects who had been matched up on the basis of some attributes considered relevant. The racing tortoises are an example; towns and cities in different countries which are 'twinned' provide another. Pairing can also be seen in 'before' and 'after' situations, although things get tricky here, for there is always the danger that exposure to the first condition is going to alter the reaction to the second in addition to change brought about by the deliberate experimental manipulations. Whenever possible scores are paired, because the matching reduces the amount of random variation which can occur, and which often acts to mask real differences. Stated more formally, this variation is more likely to increase the likelihood of Type II error.

Suppose that the experiment had *not* produced pairs of scores though. If we had just obtained data from eighteen subjects, with nine in each group, and the ordering of scores within each set was quite arbitrary, then it would not be correct to carry out either the Wilcoxon or sign test. If there were no matching, then you could not sensibly decide which score in one set would provide a 'partner' for a particular score in the other. Indeed, a test which worked on unmatched, or *independent*, sets of scores must be used. The equivalent test to the Wilcoxon, except for the matching requirement, is the Mann–Whitney U test. Because it does not involve working with pairs of scores, it is quite possible to set up an experiment and analyse data from groups of scores which are of unequal size. Obviously, this can't be the case when scores are matched!

Just as the Wilcoxon test gave us the statistic T, and the sign test S, so the Mann–Whitney test specifies certain operations which will enable us to find the value of a statistic termed U. In fact two statistics are derived, U and U' (read 'U prime'). In a sense the two are interchangeable: at the end of our calculations, the smaller becomes U, and the larger U'. It is the value of U which we then go on to look up in the tables to determine whether there is a significant difference between the two sets of scores.

The Mann–Whitney test in action

During investigations into the different eating habits of fat and thin people, volunteers (either overweight or underweight) were invited to a psychology lab. to take part in an experiment on visual perception. They were required to spend a few hours isolated in individual cubicles. Unknown to the subjects, the clocks in some cubicles had been tampered with, so that they ran a little fast, and gained one hour in every four. Towards the end of the session, subjects were told to help themselves to sandwiches which were provided. The experimenter, cleverly disguised as a lab. rat, carefully recorded what everyone ate. Lo and behold! The overweight people who believed it to be later in the day than it was, ate more than their underweight counterparts. The number of sandwiches consumed by both groups of subjects is shown in table 2. For reasons unrelated to the availability of fat and thin subjects, more fat subjects participated in the experiment than thin ones. The individual steps for working out the value of U are given in operation schedule 9.

You will notice that in Step 4, and after that, we take the smallest set of scores, and carry out our calculations with that group only. The choice of scores for working with is quite arbitrary, but the smaller is normally taken, for ease of calculation. Working with the larger set gives the same values for U and U', and in fact it is quite a useful check for arithmetical errors to rework the test, using the numbers from the larger set on the second occasion. When you have scores from groups of equal size, then it doesn't matter which ones you take to use in the calculations. Again, reworking the data, but using the other group's results, provides a useful check. When you have completed the calculations, the value of U obtained is looked up in table S4. This

Table 2. Sandwiches consumed by overweight and underweight subjects in the time-tampering experiment

Overweight subjects	Underweight subjects
14	10
12	4
9	6
11	3
15	8
18	
16	

table differs somewhat from the tables for the Wilcoxon and sign tests, as it has to cater for samples which may differ in size, and so which can't be given a single value of N. Instead, the numbers across the top indicate the size of sample B (which will be the smaller, if they aren't of equal size), and those down the left-hand side the size of sample A. At the points where particular values of N_A and N_B intersect, two values can be seen. The top number gives the maximum permitted value of U which can be permitted for significance at the 0.05 level (two-tailed test), and the lower number the maximum value of U for the 0.01 level (two-tailed test). The same tabled values can be used with one-tailed tests, but now the significance levels would be 0.025 and 0.005 respectively.

On the whole, the worst aspect of the Mann–Whitney U test is trying to remember its name!

THE EXPERIMENTER, CLEVERLY DISGUISED AS A LAB RAT...

Exercises

7 Carry out the Mann–Whitney test on the data provided in table 2. Give significance levels for both one- and two-tailed predictions.

Simple statistical tests

8 Carry out the Mann–Whitney test on the following sets of data:

(a) Set A	Set B	(b) Set A	Set B	(c) Set A	Set B
10	10	25	11	150	100
9	12	30	15	100	250
15	4	45	22	125	225
18	3	33	9	225	100
16	0	42	13	250	125
	1	29	8		
	7	32	7		
		22	16		
		27	15		
		37	18		
		55	15		

9 From the information given below, find the significance of the U statistics obtained for both one- and two-tailed hypotheses.
(a) $N_A = 4$, $N_B = 6$, $U = 3$ (b) $N_A = 3$, $N_B = 5$, $U = 6$
(c) $N_A = 6$, $N_B = 8$, $U = 8$ (d) $N_A = 10$, $N_B = 10$, $U = 19$
(e) $N_A = 12$, $N_B = 18$, $U = 46$ (f) $N_A = 20$, $N_B = 9$, $U = 50$

10 Decide which test is appropriate for data derived from the following experiments and investigations:
(a) Thirty people are given a questionnaire in which their attitudes towards corporal punishment are measured before and after they have been shown a film on the subject.
(b) Two groups of subjects participate in an experiment on sleep deprivation. They are not twins, and are not matched in any way.
(c) Identical twins take part in an experiment on alcohol consumption. One twin from each pair is in the experimental group, and the other in the control group. Each twin contributed one score to the results.
(d) Ten villages are selected from British rural districts, and on the basis of their scores in the Best Kept Village competition, they are paired off. One village from each pair is asked to display prominent anti-litter notices. At weekly intervals, an inspector goes around the villages and gives a rating out of 10 for each, dependent upon how much litter is visible.
(e) In a practical experiment in visual perception, subjects are asked to read letters of the alphabet which are placed to the right or to the left of their visual field. The aim is to discover the distance at which the letters can first be correctly identified. Each subject's right and left visual ability is measured. The data from several people are collected for the statistical analysis.

10 What's in a number?

Well! The probability of crashing with a 44 BUS must be one in a thousand!

The material included in this chapter is independent of earlier topics. It has probably not occurred to you before, but (and get ready for the great initiation!) **we use numbers in different ways**. Numbers are symbols, and sometimes they are used in a very rough and ready way. On the other hand though, when they meet with certain requirements, they can also be used in an extremely precise manner. It is important to know what kind of number a score is, for this partly determines the kind of statistical analysis or treatment which can be carried out on the data.

Levels of measurement

First, let's take a look at the different kinds of numbers which exist. As all numbers describe or measure something or other (a variable), we talk of the various kinds of numbers as achieving a certain *level of measurement*. Our measurements might be at a very crude and inaccurate level, they might be a little more precise, or extremely fine in the kind of discrimination which they make. There are four levels of measurement, and they are listed below in ascending order of precision.

1 Nominal
2 Ordinal
3 Interval
4 Ratio

The different levels have their own characteristics, and for each one, certain arithmetical operations are either permissible or not – this being determined by the characteristics themselves. If you violate the rules, then you may well emerge from your calculations with a number which might sound as if it means something, but which on closer examination will be seen to be nonsense. You will soon discover what I mean.

The nominal scale

At this level, numbers are simply used to classify things. They say something about the underlying phenomena – but not very much! In fact other symbols, such as letters of the alphabet, geometric forms or colours, would be equally appropriate. Sometimes a verbal label could easily be used instead of a number, but numbers are often preferred because a verbal description uses up more space and takes longer to say or write out. The 'classic' example of the nominal type of number is the digits seen on the backs of football players' jerseys. These numbers give us some information about the individual players – namely their position on the field – at a glance. Clearly, it would be impracticable to replace such numbers with a verbal description. Imagine the words 'halfway down the field on the right-hand side', replacing a single digit. It would be quite possible and meaningful to replace jersey numbers by letters of the alphabet though, or geometric symbols, or even different coloured jerseys. (Although how would the *teams* recognise each other then? Another system would be required.) As it is, each digit stands for a place, and to protect the sanity of football players and spectators, the symbols comply with an internationally accepted system.

Other examples of nominal measurement, and which don't necessarily involve numbers, are: blood groups, types of cheese, psychiatric classification schemes, car registration, bus route and convict numbers. Letters of the alphabet; A, AO, O; Stilton, Cheshire, Lancashire; schizophrenia, depression, etc., could easily be replaced by digits without any loss of meaning or information. For instance in psychiatric classification, doctors would agree on the symptoms which defined a category, and from then on merely refer to that category by its number. Notice that the use of a single symbol to indicate a category does not necessarily mean that it is a simple variable, or that it can easily be categorised. That is quite a different matter.

Properties of the nominal scale

The only thing which the nominal scale represents is equivalence. If several objects or phenomena are given a particular number, then they must, as just described, be similar to each other. That is why I stated that if footballers adopted a new system of coding their positions on the field, the system would have to be taken over by everyone – otherwise the information would only be of use to an individual team, and there would be no way of generalising it to other teams. It would be possible, if everyone used the same categories, but different symbols, for translation to take place. For example, the position a star represented in one team would be known to be a circle in another, or a yellow jersey in a third, etc. Thus the only arithmetical term which is relevant for nominal data is 'equals' ($=$). The nominal scale illustrates well why arithmetical operations (and statistical tests) are dependent upon what the numbers actually represent. Although it would be possible to add up all the numbers on a team of footballers' jerseys, to get 66, what would the total signify? We might go

even further, and take an average for the total, obtaining a mean of 6. What on earth does *that* figure represent? Certainly not the 'average' position of all the players on the field! The results of adding, subtracting, multiplying or dividing nominal numbers are quite meaningless – although it is easy to fall into the trap of believing that because they *are* numbers, they *do* represent something. The position is rather similar to that of spurious accuracy which I mentioned in connection with decimal places. If you are wondering why numbers are ever used in a nominal capacity, apart from considerations of time and space, there is another reason. It is that if categories are labelled from 1 upwards, consecutively, then the highest number used will tell you how many categories there are in the scheme. This can sometimes be a useful piece of information.

The ordinal scale

Slightly more sophisticated than the nominal, the ordinal scale, as its name would suggest, involves an ordering or ranking of the variable under consideration. Thus the numbers of an ordinal scale show a relationship between numbered items, and do not merely represent a class or category. When we speak of 'higher', 'lower', 'easier', 'faster', 'most often', etc., we are using verbal labels to imply the type of order found in an ordinal scale. The numbers in this kind of scale are used systematically so that on any one scale, 0 or 1 will represent either the lowest or the highest of all possible values. Examples of schemes are: social class gradings I, II, III, etc.; house numbers; fruit and vegetable grades I, II, III; examination grades A–F; army ranks and race positions first, second, third; Moh's scale of rock hardness, 1–10.

Properties of ordinal numbers

Like the nominal scale, the ordinary scale involves equivalence ($=$), but also relative size, indicated by the symbols $>$ (greater than) and $<$ (less than). Numbers on an ordinal scale represent a fairly rough and ready rank ordering, and there is no expectation that the difference between any two grades at different points along the scale is the same. For instance there is no guarantee that the difference between apples Grade I and II is the same as the difference between Grades II and III. What's more, the relative gradings of vegetables don't even remain constant, but alter according to season. What could be passed as a Grade II tomato in winter may be put into the inferior Grade III category in summer. For these reasons, when ordinal data are expressed as numbers, adding and subtracting, multiplying and dividing, and all calculations involving these operations are not permissible. As with nominal data, a number would emerge at the end of such calculations, but it could not be interpreted very well, and particularly if cross-scale comparisons were involved. If one were trying to describe a set of ordinal numbers using a measure of central tendency, then the median and the mode, which only involve counting, would be appropriate. There is no measure of spread which could be used, as they all involve addition or subtraction.

There is one kind of scale which is particularly controversial. It is the well-known IQ scale – the numbers being derived from the outcome of an IQ test. While many psychologists maintain that it achieves a higher degree of precision than that of ordinal data, others consider it to be ordinal and treat data which comprise IQ scores with great care.

The interval scale

We now arrive at the first level of measurement in which arithmetical operations are allowed. This is because at the interval level, the numbers are not only ordered, but the intervals between each step, *at all points along the scale*, are of equal size. Thus two numbers which are adjacent at a low point on the scale (e.g. 3 and 4) are separated by exactly the same distance as two which occur at a higher point (e.g. 343 and 344). This is where the problem arises over IQ scores, for it is difficult to believe that a difference of 5 points on the scale occurring between the values of 30 and 70 is the same as the difference of 5 points occurring between 90 and 110; the middle range of the IQ scale is much more precisely measured than the extremes at either end. As social scientists frequently wish to undertake analysis of their data using arithmetically precise methods, they will often aim to use methods of measuring the variable under consideration which achieve at least the precision of the interval scale.

A main feature of interval scales which distinguishes them from the most-sophisticated ratio scales, is that they have no absolute zero point, but only arbitrary zero points. This can be seen through consideration of two examples of the scale, temperature (Centigrade) and calendar years. On the Centigrade temperature scale the zero was fixed as the point at which water freezes, and much lower temperatures which occur are indicated by a negative sign. Calendar years were given the 'starting point' of 1 at the time of Christ's birth, and the many years which occurred before this date are denoted by the label BC.

Properties of the interval scale

Because the size of intervals is equal within any one scale, it is admissible to carry out all arithmetical operations meaningfully. However, cross-scale comparisons (e.g. Centigrade to Fahrenheit) must be handled with some care. The comparisons are difficult because the zero point is not the same for both scales, and because the size of the interval used in each scale differs. Conversion from one scale to another is quite possible, but usually involves a certain amount of arithmetical juggling.

The ratio scale

This is exactly like the interval scale, in having ranked numbers with equal intervals between the numbers throughout the scale, but it differs in that it has, in addition, an *absolute* zero. This means that 0 means, literally, 'nothing there', not, as in the case of temperature Centigrade and Fahrenheit, just 'very low'. You can remember what 'absolute' zero means by memorising the phrase '*absolutely* nothing there'. It is impossible to have minus numbers in a true ratio scale. If negatives are to be seen, they signify that the operation of subtraction should be carried out, not that the number is less than zero. Length (metric and imperial), weight, elapsed time, speed, temperature on the Kelvin scale and frequencies are all examples of ratio scale measurement. On the Kelvin scale the reading 0 signifies the lowest possible temperature attainable; the point at which even the movement of molecules ceases. It is way below zero on the other scales, its equivalent on the Centigrade scale being $-273\,°C$. It is easy to spot when a scale is ratio, as a minus sign makes the items nonsensical. You can't have -2 humans, -3 oz sugar, or -10 seconds!

Properties of ratio scales

All arithmetical operations are permissible on numbers in a ratio scale, and also, because of the fact that they all have absolute zeros, it is possible to convert fairly easily from one to another. This is because the *ratios* of stated intervals, even across different scales, are equal.

What about cardinals; and are they discrete?

The interval and ratio levels of measurement are sometimes classified together and called the *cardinal* scale. Cardinal numbers give *amounts* of something, whilst ordinals give order only, and nominal numbers are simply names for categories.

Another division – this time of cardinal numbers only – is into *discrete* or *continuous*. Discrete units are ones in which each value is clearly separated from its neighbours. For instance in counting the number of people attending an event, our money, or the number of shops in a street, a unit is a complete entity which can't be meaningfully divided. Half a person can't go very far (at least, not in a vertical position!), an establishment either is or isn't a shop, and we don't divide money into units smaller than 1p, in British currency. All kinds of currency have their smallest unit, and no further subdivision takes place. On the other hand, continuous units are ones which can be divided up over and over again. There is no theoretical limit to the number of times an inch, second or ounce can be subdivided; the constraints are purely practical, and with our advanced technology we are capable of obtaining some extremely fine units of measurement. You will be pleased to hear that for the majority of tests you will encounter, it doesn't matter whether the variables involved are of a discrete or continuous nature.

Exercise

State the level of measurement achieved in the following types of numbers:
(a) steam engine numbers (b) a child's age (c) hospital staff, grades 1–9 (d) football goals (e) the Beaufort scale of wind strengths, from 0 (calm) to 12 (hurricane) (f) opinion ratings, from 1 (agree) to 5 (disagree) (g) TIQ – Tortoise IQ scores (h) National Insurance numbers (i) centimetres (j) Types I and II errors.

Why do levels of measurement matter?

Scientists of every shape and form are always manipulating variables, and expressing different values of the variables by means of various numerical units. The units will then be used in the subsequent data analysis. Chemists, physicists and biologists do not often run into difficulties here, for the units they deal with most frequently are of the cardinal type, and quite suitable for sophisticated arithmetical treatment. In fact, ask a 'real' scientist (as they like to think of themselves) about levels of measurement, and the chances are that he or she won't know the first thing about the topic, for it does not create problems in their world. Unfortunately, level of measurement is a constant headache for social scientists, as many of the variables they must consider are measured in units which do not attain interval or ratio sophistication, and so are unsuitable for precise methods of analysis. The three simple tests which I have covered in chapter 9 are appropriate for any kind of numbers, but as mathematical tools they lack precision. They belong to the group of tests called *nonparametric*, and are relatively free of restrictions concerning their use. In contrast to them, we have the more-sophisticated, more-powerful, *parametric* tests. These tests work on the basis that the scores fed into them come from a normal distribution, and they are able to pull on the mathematical properties of this distribution in distinguishing sets of data. Just as the Wilcoxon test correctly rejects the null hypothesis when the sign test doesn't (and this failure constituted a Type II error), so the sophisticated parametric tests are also better able to reject correctly the null hypothesis than the nonparametric ones, and hence have greater *power*. Because social scientists are concerned with variables that sometimes achieve interval status, but more frequently don't, it is important for them to know which type of statistical treatment is the appropriate one. Using any kind of instrument on unsuitable raw material is likely to have unfortunate consequences; in statistical analysis, if you use the wrong technique, you either miss finding a subtle difference which is there (a Type II error), or on the other hand, produce a statistic which looks good, but in fact may be quite meaningless. Data evaluation – or 'crunching', as they say – must be very finely tuned to the *nature* of the data.

The assumptions underlying parametric techniques

Now we take a closer look at the assumptions which underlie the parametric techniques. There are three main restrictions, and they concern the following features of sets of scores:

1 The type of measure which the scores represent (i.e. the level of measurement).
2 The distribution of scores – usually, our main concern being over whether or not they come from a normal distribution.
3 The spread of the scores.

1 Level of measurement

As parametric tests involve several sophisticated (but not necessarily difficult) arithmetical operations, they are only suitable for use with data which are of interval or ratio level. It is always possible to use the simpler nonparametric tests on high level data, but this is rather like using an untrained person to make fine distinctions in wine-tasting. He would arrive at judgements of differences between wines fairly successfully, but they would only be crude, and would not compare very favourably with the precise descriptions and statements made by trained wine-tasters. If a trained taster is always available at no extra cost, and the wine to be tasted will not insult the taster, why use a novice?

2 The distribution of the scores

As I mentioned earlier, parametric tests can only be used on data which are derived from normal (or nearly normal) distributions. It may surprise you to learn that there is a certain amount of controversy among statisticians over how far you can break this 'rule' and get away with it. Personally, I think it's better for the uninitiated, such as ourselves, to err on the conservative side, and observe this rule.

Assuming that you decide to play safe in this respect, how would you decide whether your data do fall into a normal distribution? When the number of scores you are dealing with lies between five and fifty, the answer is that you use the old eye-ball test again – i.e. you decide by looking at them! Putting the scores into the form of a diagram in which the vertical axis indicates frequency, and the horizontal axis various groups of units (in ascending order), is an operation which makes the decision easier. But what if they show a shape which is not *quite* normal? After all, it would be fairly surprising if any smallish sample drawn from a population with a normal distribution mirrored the parent population *exactly*. There is always a certain amount of error in sampling. So to discover whether the extent of deviance from the normal shape is sufficient to suggest that the scores are derived from a non-normal distribution, you could apply one of the statistical tests designed to answer this question, such as a test of goodness-of-fit (chapter 12). At this stage in your statistical career it is usually quite sufficient to know that the normality of a distribution must be considered, without having to go into all the details.

Note that in deciding whether or not samples are normally distributed, you must consider the shapes of *both* samples. They must both meet the requirement of normality before a parametric test can be used. However, they needn't have come from the same normal distribution – that is, have identical means. Indeed, this is precisely what you have hoped to avoid in undertaking the experiment; you anticipated that the manipulation of the IV would create two groups of scores coming from distributions with very different means.

3 The spread of the scores

Similarity of spread between samples is called officially *homogeneity of variance*, and it means that the two sets of scores have similar variances. *Variance* is a measure of how spread out, or scattered, a set of scores is, and was covered in detail in chapter 5, where I explained that it is directly related to the *standard deviation*, another measure of spread. What we are saying here is that two sets of scores must be scattered by a roughly equal amount if a parametric technique is to be used on them. If the scores comprising one sample are widely spread out around the mean (i.e. have a large variance), while the other set is squashed up in close proximity to it (with a small variance), then one of the nonparametric techniques must be used in analysing these data. Think of 'homogenised' milk to remember what the official term for this rule means. Homogenised milk is milk which has been treated so that it becomes and stays the same throughout the whole bottle.

As with the question of normality, you may wonder just how similar the variances have to be before a parametric test can safely be used – or, how dissimilar they can be before parametric techniques have to be abandoned. And, as before, for cases which are not readily determined by means of the eye-ball test, so it is possible to use a particular statistical technique to answer the question. The appropriate technique is known as the *variance-ratio*, or *F* test. Basically, it involves obtaining the variance of each set of scores, placing the larger value over the smaller, and looking up the resulting ratio in a table. Actually, the *F* test can be regarded as a statistical test in its own right, for it can answer the old question of whether samples appear to have been drawn from one or two populations. Suppose you have two sets of scores representing reaction times after the administration of a drug in one case, or a placebo in another. (A *placebo* is a substance which appears to be identical to the drug externally, and which is believed by the 'victim' to be the drug, but which does not in fact contain any active substance at all.) If you obtained widely scattered scores from the experimental group, but results which showed hardly any variation at all from the controls, who received the placebo, then you would be able to conclude, with statistical justification, that the two samples differed, and that the experimental treatment had brought about the large variation of response which was evident.

If any of the three requirements listed above are not met by your data, then you should really use a nonparametric technique in your analysis, rather than one of the more powerful parametric tests.

11 Two parametric tests

t TESTS ARE LIKE RICH FRUIT CAKES

You will need to have read and understood the five previous chapters to be able to deal with the contents of this one. In it I will cover the two parametric tests which replace the Wilcoxon and Mann–Whitney tests when the data for analysis conform to the following requirements:

1 Both samples are normally distributed.
2 The variances of the samples are similar to each other.
3 The samples comprise scores of at least interval measurement.

You may recall that the main difference between the Wilcoxon and the Mann–Whitney tests is that in the Wilcoxon test the scores for each condition are paired off, while in the Mann–Whitney test, there is no matching of individual numbers *between* the samples at all. The sign test is meant for paired scores, and it is less powerful than the Wilcoxon test, which it can replace. The importance of whether scores are paired off, or matched, as the pairing is called, is paramount in the choice of a statistical test. How we plan our experiments to obtain paired scores, and the advantages and limitations of such experimental designs is fully covered in chapter 13.

The two *t* tests

So far then, you know about the Wilcoxon and sign tests which can be used on *matched* scores, and the Mann–Whitney test which is used on *unmatched*, or *independent*, samples. The more powerful tests which replace the Wilcoxon and Mann–Whitney tests are the two *t* tests. One of them is for matched samples, and the other for independent samples. There are no prizes for working out that the matched *t* test replaces the Wilcoxon, and the independent *t* test the Mann–Whitney. Sometimes, just to complicate things, the *t* tests appear with different names.

Originally, the *t* distribution was worked out by a certain William Gosset, who was employed as a research chemist at the Guinness brewery in Ireland at the start of this century. At that time, Guinness employees were never allowed to publish any discoveries they made. However, because of the exceptional importance of his statistical discovery (and perhaps also because it concerned a mathematical, rather than a beer recipe!), the strict rule was relaxed for Gosset, providing that he published under a pen name and remained anonymous. He chose the name 'student', and so the *t* distribution and its application in statistical tests became known as *student's t test*. This name has died out a little in recent years, although the distinction between the version of the *t* formula used for matched and unmatched samples remains, and is reflected in the variety of names commonly used. Those for the *t* test formula for use with unmatched data include: 'unmatched *t* test', '*t* test for two independent means', 'independent *t* test' and '*t* test for unrelated samples'. The other version goes by the names: 'paired *t* test', '*t* test for related measures', 'related *t* test' and 'correlated *t* test'. As the last name implies, this version of the *t* formula hinges on computing a *correlation* (chapter 15). However, thanks to the efforts of statisticians, a different formula has been derived, and it is now possible to use this replacement (which doesn't involve correlation computations) to arrive at exactly the same value of *t*. Thus the *correlated t* test now only refers to the pairing aspect of the data under consideration, and not to the method of computing a value for *t*. Anyhow, basically there are only two *t* tests, despite the abundance of names flying around, and I shall provide two (again of several possible) methods for calculating the statistic *t*. Step by step details are given in the usual way, in operation schedules 10 and 11.

The *t* tests indicate sample differences by using means and the distribution of sample scores around the mean. Because computation of *t* involves measures of dispersion around the mean, together with a few other things, its formula – and particularly the one for unmatched samples – looks quite horrific! Don't forget that the formula isn't some sort of practical problem in number rearrangement though. It is like a cake recipe (a rather rich fruit cake!), in which the steps you must take in order to obtain the finished article are summarised. There are many steps, and of course, just as in baking a cake, you must carry them out in the correct order. You wouldn't put a cake in the oven *before* you had mixed all the ingredients together, would you? (You would? Afternoon '*t*' at your house must be quite something!) All the steps involved in working out the *t* tests are given, and you just need to plod patiently through them before success, in the form of a *t* value, is yours. Don't imagine, when you come to do your first *t* test, that the existence of many steps means that it will be 'difficult'. The actual arithmetic is only a little more advanced than that needed for the nonparametric tests, but because the formula is so complex, there are many small steps involved in working through it all. It is better to have lots of small easy steps rather than half a dozen more complicated ones. As usual, having obtained a value for a test statistic, in this case *t*, you must then evaluate it using a table (table S5). It is a very easy one to use, and is appropriate regardless of whether your *t* was derived from matched or independent samples.

Degrees of freedom

Just before you evaluate your *t* statistic, you have to determine the value of something which goes by the name of *degrees of freedom*, or *df*. This value enables you to know whereabouts on table S5 you compare your obtained value of *t* – and it is obviously something to do with sample size, rather equivalent to using *N* for the evaluation of the Wilcoxon *T* statistic. Degrees of freedom means the total number of items from any given sample or samples which have to be known, when the overall total is known, before any missing ones can be filled in.

For instance, if I told you that the sum of five numbers was 16, and then that four of the numbers were 1, 5, 4 and 3, you would soon be able to work out that the missing number was 3. If there had been two missing numbers though, you would not have been able to say what each one was, only that *together* they must total such-and-such a value. If you do not know the total of a particular sample, then you cannot work out the value of one, or more than one, missing number. In the case of five numbers which total 16, because we need to know four of the numbers in order to fill in a missing one, we say that this particular sample has 'four degrees of freedom', or '*df* = 4'. If there were eight numbers in a set, then the *df* would be 7, because we would need to know what seven of the numbers were, in order to calculate the final missing number.

In working out the *df* for the evaluation of the *t* statistic, we have, in the case of matched scores, a figure which is the total number of pairs of scores minus one. This is because the *pairs* are units, for computational purposes. With the independent measures *t* test, each list has its own degrees of freedom, equal to the number of items it comprises minus one, and so the final *df* is the total number of items making up both samples, minus two. The only other tests in this book in which degrees of freedom figure are the tests of goodness-of-fit which are described in the next chapter.

Tea for two?

Here is a nice visual example which should help you to remember what *df* means. Suppose that in your place of work, the dining room sports two large urns for hot drinks. One contains a warm wet substance which is supposed to be tea, and the other a brown liquid which is trying hard to be coffee. One day, due to circumstances beyond someone's control, the label gets missed off the coffee urn. The tea urn is labelled as usual. Now, the big question! Would you have any trouble obtaining coffee, if you knew that the basic set-up (although not necessarily the *position* of the urns) was unaltered? The answer, of course, is 'no' – and it is because the urns have only one degree of freedom. If one item is known, tea, and the total (that one urn contains tea, and the other coffee – not the two mixed together!), then the unknown contents of the second urn are not free to vary. The unlabelled urn *must* contain coffee. Suppose that both labels were missing. Now you wouldn't know which urn contains which beverage, although you would only need to take *one* sample in order

Two parametric tests

to find out. If there were three urns, containing tea, coffee and hot chocolate, what would be the *df*? How many samples would you need to take before you knew what each contained? If two are known, then the content of the final urn is fixed – always provided that you know what the overall separate items in the containers are – and you would be able to name it. So because *two* items have to be known before the third can be named, the *df* = 2. Got it?

Exercises

1 Decide whether a related *t* test or an independent *t* test would be appropriate for the following:

(a) A comparison of heights in a twin study, where one twin is in the experimental group, and the other in the control group.

(b) An analysis of differences in exam marks obtained (assume interval data) by boys and girls in a particular year, with a view to showing that one of the sexes obtained better marks.

(c) Medical social workers in a hospital start to notice that people who live in the vicinity of the steel foundry have large ears. They measure ear length precisely in these people, and compare the lengths with measurements obtained from others who live in the vicinity of the colliery.

(d) 'Before' and 'after' reaction scores obtained from one person who took part in an experiment on several occasions.

(e) 'Before' and 'after' scores obtained from a group of people who only participated in an experiment once.

2 Carry out *t* tests on the following sets of data:

(a) The independent samples:

Set *A*: 3, 5, 2, 4, 6, 2, 7

Set *B*: 9, 25, 4, 16, 36, 4, 49

(b) The independent samples:

Set *A*: 7, 6, 8, 3, 9, 4, 9, 5

Set *B*: 11, 14, 17, 16, 15, 21

(c) The related samples:

Set *A*: 3, 8, 4, 6, 9, 2, 12

Set *B*: 6, 14, 8, 4, 16, 7, 19

ENRICHED DIET ANIMALS

(d) Use the data in 2(c), but treat as if unrelated. Compare the two values of *t* you obtain.

3 Evaluate the *t* statistics you obtained in exercise 2 for significance, (i) assuming a one-tailed and (ii) a two-tailed hypothesis.

4 Decide whether the following data would be best suited to parametric or nonparametric analysis:

(a) IQ scores from two samples with means of 95 and 110, and identical variances.

(b) The two sets of scores:

Set *A*: 1, 1, 1, 1, 1, 4, 5, 10, 10, 10, 10

Set *B*: 1, 3, 5, 6, 6, 7, 7, 7, 9, 10

(c) 'Before' and 'after' attitude assessments, carried out on a group of students exposed to an exhibition of modern art.

(d) Weight in grams of baby rats born to females who have been kept on an enriched or standard diet.

(e) The reactions to certain stimuli, measured in seconds, after a drug treatment, compared with scores from controls. Samples are normally distributed, have variances of 10 seconds and 100 seconds, with means of 50 and 55 seconds.

5 For samples with *df* equal to 10, and for a one-tailed test, interpret the following values of *t*:

(a) 0.500   (b) 1.812   (c) 2.200   (d) 3.0

12 Tests of goodness of fit

A vague idea of the contents of chapters 9–11 will be helpful for an understanding of why tests of goodness of fit differ from other statistical tests. The *t* tests, sign, Wilcoxon and Mann–Whitney tests are all designed to tell you whether two samples appear to have been derived from one or two sources – the underlying population or populations. This is true, regardless of whether the test is parametric or non-parametric, matched or unmatched. If the two samples differ in any important way from each other, then our test statistic will result in our decision to reject the null hypothesis.

Tests of goodness of fit; quite a different cup of tea!

The tests of goodness of fit work on slightly different principles to the ones already described; their name gives a clue as to how they work. Suppose you have a set of scores which clearly showed a normal distribution (figure 1(a)), and they had been derived from a control group in an experiment. Now take the experimental group scores. They show the strongly skewed distribution illustrated in figure 1(b). Imagine cutting out the pattern shown in figure 1(b), and placing the shape over that of figure 1(a). The result would resemble figure 1(c).

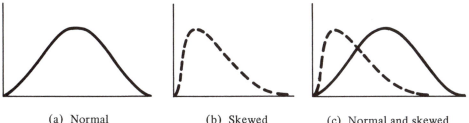

| (a) Normal distribution | (b) Skewed distribution | (c) Normal and skewed distributions together |

Figure 1. Tests of goodness of fit work on the extent to which distribution shapes overlap

The eye-ball test tells you immediately that the two distributions are very different – because they don't fit neatly on top of each other. So, with no more ado, we might conclude that scores showing such markedly different shapes must have come from two different underlying populations, one with a normal distribution and the other with a skewed distribution. Tests of goodness of fit work on the principle of distribution *shape*, rather than on actual scores. They compare overall patterns of results which are obtained by putting the actual scores into a frequency form.

Although our conclusion, about whether samples have been derived from the same or different underlying populations, will be the same with tests of goodness of fit as with the tests covered earlier, in these, we normally compare one sample with another of a particular distribution. An analogy might help.

Our samples are represented by two vanilla slices. The question we ask is: 'Were they bought in the same shop?' – the shop being equivalent to population. If they *are* similar, then we can conclude that they did come from a single source, and so not reject the null hypothesis. If they *differ*, then we would conclude that they have come from two shops, and so be able to reject the null hypothesis. In using any of the statistical tests described up to now, we wouldn't point to one of the slices and ask whether the other differs from *it*, but would ask whether they differ from each other. In using tests of goodness of fit, the question becomes 'If *this* slice (pointing to one of them) came from Ye Olde Tea Shoppe, did the other come from the same place?' There is a very subtle difference, and it is in specifying the characteristics of one of the samples, and asking whether the other resembles it. Apart from this, and the fact that we use *frequencies* of scores, rather than *actual* scores, tests of goodness of fit are similar to the other tests. Although the eye-ball test may be sufficient to decide that some distributions differ, as in figure 1(c), on occasions the difference may not be big enough to decide just by looking, and the usual question of whether a small difference might be the result of chance factors has to be answered by means of a formal statistical procedure. If you read about the requirements for parametric tests, in chapter 11, you will have already encountered a situation where a test of goodness of fit could be used. This is in the requirement that both samples for parametric tests are drawn from normal distributions. If either of the samples is skewed, then we know we cannot use a parametric test (and we might conclude immediately that they have been drawn from different sources). However, in many cases it is not too easy to decide whether the sample in question is sufficiently close to a normal distribution to justify the use of a parametric test, and in this case, we might well use a test of goodness of fit to help us to decide.

There is a whole group of tests based on the distribution of a statistic called χ^2, pronounced 'ky', rhyming with 'fly', and sometimes written out as '*chi-square*'. They all come under the heading of the *chi-square measure of association*. Although there are several varieties of the *chi*-square tests which, as usual, go by many names, and can also be calculated in various fashions, don't despair. You only really need to know that the *chi*-square test works on a slightly different principle from the other tests you have encountered, and to cope with the workings of just one of the variations, which is called, encouragingly, *simple chi-square* (see operation schedule 12). For the sake of completeness I include a little on the rationale of the *complex chi-square*, and include the steps involved in its computation in operation schedule 13.

Frequencies and rules in *chi*-square tests

In all tests of goodness of fit, the categories into which frequencies of scores fall are called *cells*. The cells contain counted items, such as the *number* of people who fall ill, have accidents, obtain various IQ scores, say 'No' to a question, give an opinion on a questionnaire, fall into particular social classes, show certain specified

behaviours; the *number* of times a coin came up heads, or a thrown die showed a 'six' (no statistics book would be complete without at least a mention of coins or dice!); the *number* of rats making false moves in mazes, of crimes committed by various kinds of people, of red blood cells found in a specified volume of blood, etc. In a beer sampling 'study', described in chapter 15, beer is rated according to five categories. Each category would form a cell, and a table could be drawn up indicating the number of times a sample pint was judged 'undrinkable', 'fair', or whatever. When you are using, or contemplating using, the *chi*-square test, the level of measurement involved in the categorisation scheme makes no difference to the kind of test of goodness of fit to be used. They all operate on frequency counts derived from any kind of data. However, there are some rules for *chi*-square tests, and they are listed below.

1 Items in cells must be independent. They cannot appear more than once, and they cannot be included if they are 'somehow' influenced by other items. Each item must be an isolated event.
2 The number of items appearing in the 'expected' category, obtained during the stages of computation, must be at least five.
3 The tests must be carried out on the actual numbers of items which appear in the cells, not on derived proportions or percentages. Even though the proportions of numbers are unaltered, the test is invalidated if the original numbers are not used.

As usual, there are some squabbles. The one concerning *chi*-square is over rule 2; that there must be at least five items in the 'expected' category. Some statisticians say that it doesn't matter all that much – but it is probably better to play safe and observe the rule. It is possible to overcome the problem of small expected frequencies by one of two methods. One way is to pool the data, which means putting some of the categories together. An example will make this clearer. Suppose I have carried out some observations on the age at which wisdom teeth appear in an obscure African tribe, and wish to compare the information with that already available for Europeans. I might have grouped my subjects according to the following broad divisions:

1 Children from birth to 9 years
2 Adolescents from 10–14 years
3 Adolescents from 15–18 years
4 Young people from 19–21 years
5 Adults from 22–25 years

It might turn out, during calculations, that fewer than five scores would be *expected* in the first category. Consequently, I could pool the cells of categories 1 and 2, giving one cell, labelled 'Children and adolescents from birth to 14 years'. Now the *expected* frequencies would be of sufficient size for me to proceed, but as a result of the pooling process, the new category would have become much broader, and so less useful. For this reason, pooling is avoided if possible.

The second way round the problem is to increase the size of the samples under consideration. Unfortunately, this is often impracticable, and almost always costly in terms of money and effort.

Sometimes, *chi*-square tests are called tests of association, for in survey studies, when we have counted the number of items falling into the categories, we conclude that the values of one variable are associated with particular values of another. However, because a survey is not an experiment, and we have not actually demonstrated a causal link, we cannot go on to say that '*X causes Y*' – only that '*X* is associated with *Y*, in such-and-such conditions'. We will encounter this kind of guarded statement again, when we come to consider another measure of association, *correlation*.

Simple *chi*-square

The simplest *chi*-square test involves only four cells, and their arrangement into what is known as a 2 × 2 *contingency table* (read 'two by two'). Such a table contains two samples, and both are divided into two values of a second variable. An example is given in table 1.

Table 1. A 2 × 2 contingency table, showing the relationship between weight and susceptibility to heart attack

Men	Have experienced heart attack(s)	Have not had a heart attack	Totals
Overweight	400	100	500
Underweight	100	400	500
Totals	500	500	1000

This example illustrates the relationship between weight and coronary heart disease – using fictitious data! The population comprises male members of this society, and two samples are drawn, one of very slim men and the other of overweight men. These give us two categories on the *weight* variable. The number of people in these samples who have had one or more heart attacks before their fiftieth year is ascertained, and so they are divided into two categories; 'have experienced at least one heart attack' and 'have not had a heart attack'. These give us two values for the second variable *heart attack history*. Note that I have been careful to call the two variables involved just 'variables', without identifying a dependent variable (DV) and an independent variable (IV). Although it is possible that excess weight does cause heart attacks, you must remember that the *chi*-square test is *only* a measure of association, and says nothing about causality. If we had manipulated people's weights, and *then* observed the heart attacks which followed, we could have called our weight variable the IV and the heart attack rate the DV. Even then though, we would still need some caution in interpreting our results. Just because we make people fat, and they then have heart attacks does not mean to say that it is the excess body weight which causes the attacks. It may be that we make them fat through asking them to eat plenty of fatty foods, or sweets, or by drinking lots of alcohol; it may be the *type* of food they eat which causes the heart condition. However, on the whole, we would be in a much stronger position for advocating weight reduction than if we just went by the results of the *survey* type of study, shown in table 1. All the survey tells us is that there is an *association* between the variables. It might even be that having a heart attack at an early age encourages people to 'eat, drink and be merry', and so become overweight. Our survey did not tell us anything about the *order* in which the events occurred, and it is this which is rather crucial for making predictions. Experimental work normally has something to say about the relative timing of events.

Returning to table 1, you can see just by inspection of the data that overweight people have more heart attacks than the thinnies. This is a nice clear-cut example – not at all like the sort of data which we tend to obtain in 'real-life'! However, it is useful to have a clear-cut example like this, in order to explain the way the *chi*-square test works. Conceptually it is fairly easy to grasp. In the example, 1000 men were studied; 500 fat and 500 thin. If there is no association between body weight and heart attacks, then we would expect by chance roughly equal numbers of heart attacks to occur in both groups. By a mind-blowing feat of mental arithmetic, you might conclude that the *expected* figure for each group would be about 250, i.e. half the fat men and half the thin ones having attack reports. Actually, you may have reasoned this way when you carried out your first eye-ball test on the data. Alternatively, you may have decided that 400 heart attacks just looks a lot more than 100, and left it at that, without calculating the rough estimate of what would be anticipated if the null hypothesis were true. The null hypothesis would state that there is no association between weight and heart attacks, and in mathematical terms, would suggest that the value of 500 attacks would be divided evenly into two, between the overweight and underweight men. The total number of men who didn't have heart attacks would also be evenly divided, so that overall, a contingency table drawn up on the basis of the null hypothesis would look like table 2.

Table 2. The null hypothesis for the heart attack data

Men	Have experienced heart attack(s)	Have not had a heart attack	Totals
Overweight	250	250	500
Underweight	250	250	500
Totals	500	500	1000

All right so far? Notice that the row and column totals have not changed, only the distribution of the numbers in the cells, now rearranged according to a theoretical expectation. The *chi*-square test works by taking each of the *obtained* values in the cells and comparing it with what would have been there if the null hypothesis were true. So we compare each of our *obtained* values of 400:100 and 100:400 with the figures of 250:250 and 250:250 which we would have *expected* to get under the null hypothesis. We find the difference between the two figures for every cell in the table, and the larger the differences are, the more our two distributions differ from each other. After we have obtained the differences (which is easy in simple *chi*-square, and especially when the samples are of equal size), we do a little squaring and dividing here and there, and the final result of our labours is a value for the statistic χ^2. The larger it is, the more likely the two distributions are to differ – but the amount of largeness required before the two can be considered *really* different has to be determined by looking up the values of the statistic in a table, as is the case with other kinds of statistical tests.

There is nothing magic about the fact that the *expected* hypothesis gives rise to the number 250 in all the cells. This is what we would expect if we knew absolutely nothing about the incidence of heart attacks, and assumed that there was no connection between them and weight. This may not always be the case though. We may know from previous research that there is a strong association between the two variables, and make our *expected* figures 400:100 on the basis of this knowledge. Our survey might have pulled in figures showing a 50:50 breakdown, and so we would wonder what was different about the samples we had just taken, and start to look for the existence of another variable which would explain the discrepancy. For instance it might be that some of the overweight men had taken up exercise, stopped smoking, started to take the drug Heartaid, etc., and so altered their tendency to suffer from heart attacks. Alternatively, we might have decided that the particular sample we had taken was in some way atypical. However, we would still be in the position of having two distributions, an *obtained* and an *expected* one, which, whatever the cause, appeared to differ.

Simple *chi*-square can also be used when the numbers making up each of the samples (overweight/underweight) are unequal. We might have had 600 overweight and 400 underweight men in our example. In this case, although the overall total is still 1000, we would not expect to get 250 (half 500) of each falling into the two heart attack categories. Instead, we would anticipate the values 300 and 200 respectively, these being half the two sample sizes. Unequal sample size poses no problems for *chi*-square, although you will find that the calculations are longer and more tedious, as the *expected* numbers for every single cell have to be obtained individually. Don't forget, though, that it is not permissible to change the original data into percentages (making calculations easier!), as this gives an incorrect value for the χ^2 statistic when evaluated with the original frequencies.

One-sample *chi*-square

Because we drew two samples (overweight and underweight men) in the *chi*-square example just given, that design also goes by the name '*chi*-square test for independent samples'. Sometimes, in carrying out an investigation, we need only draw one sample and observe certain characteristics which we can categorise. We can then compare them with those which we might expect on theoretical grounds, and by using theory alone, therefore not need to draw another sample for comparison purposes. This kind of *chi*-square analysis is called a *one-sample chi*-square, and is illustrated in the following example. University degrees are classified into five categories, from Class

Table 3. Science degree classifications obtained and theoretically expected results at Wetwang University.

	Degree category					
	I	IIi	IIii	III	Pass	Totals
Actual no. of students	13	17	20	23	27	100
Expected no. of students	20	20	20	20	20	100
Totals	33	37	40	43	47	200

I down to a Pass degree. At Wetwang University, during a lull in the Science Degree Day proceedings, Professor Egghead observes from the printed programme that there don't seem to be many good degrees being awarded at all. He imagines that theoretically there should be an equal number of students falling into each of the five categories.

Where does *chi*-square come in? Professor Egghead wants to know whether there is an unreasonable number of poor degrees (the *obtained* data) in comparison with the roughly equal numbers in each category expected theoretically (the *expected* data). Both distributions are shown in table 3. On a theoretical basis, the professor anticipated that the 100 students would be divided evenly into five groups, i.e. 20 in every degree class. In computing *chi*-square, we simply compare each of the *obtained* values of the one sample, 17, 20 etc., with the expected value of 20. Just as in simple *chi*-square, the larger the discrepancy, the more we can suspect that there is a real difference in existence, rather than a variation which can be attributed to chance. The discrepancy is shown in figure 2. Calculation of χ^2 on these particular numbers reveals a value of 5.8 which is not large enough to be significant – and so indicates that the discrepancy observed is not sufficiently large to be attributed to a real drop in standards.

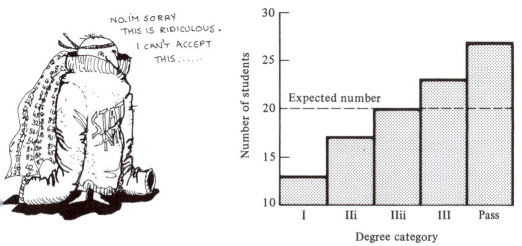

Figure 2. Bar diagram showing *obtained* and *expected* degree categories

Tests of goodness of fit

The point about this example is that only one sample of students was taken. It differs from the previous one in which two samples (over- and underweight men) were categorised and compared with each other. The computational steps for the one-sample case, with more than two categories, are almost the same; in schedule 13, instead of going through Steps 1–3 to obtain the *expected* categories, you can virtually start at Step 4, because the *expected* numbers can be calculated very simply. The only other thing which differs is the calculation of the degrees of freedom. With one-sample *chi*-square it is always the number of categories minus 1.

Complex *chi*-square

Complex *chi*-square is an extension of the simple 2×2 *chi*-square, and it refers to any sets of samples and categories which exceed four cells in size. For instance, if we had obtained three categories of people in the heart attack study – over, under and correct weight – we would have created a 3×2 contingency table. We might also have categorized heart attacks differently, and given that variable three values also – none, one and more than one. Now we would have a 3×3 contingency table, containing nine cells in all. We can make our tables as big as we like, but there are one or two snags which can arise. If the table gets very big, then we are more likely to obtain *expected* frequencies which are less than 5 in size. Sometimes this can be overcome by increasing the sample size. Another problem arises over the interpretation of significant results. Unfortunately, even if we know, from our calculated value of χ^2, that our distributions differ from each other, the statistic tells us nothing about precisely where in the table the crucial differences are to be found. Up to a point the eye-ball test helps – and particularly in smaller tables. If, for instance, in our degree results, we had obtained a significant difference, we could have guessed that it lay in the numbers of students at the extreme ends of the scale, as they show the biggest discrepancies from the value of 20. But it is much more difficult when there are many categories of different variables, because the value of *chi*-square might have arisen through several moderate differences, rather than one or two outstandingly large ones. There is a method for finding out where the differences lie, and it is described by R. Rosenthal and R. L. Rosnow in their *Primer of methods for the behavioral sciences* (New York, London: Wiley, 1975). Ironically, it comprises carrying out another *chi*-square test!

Note, by the way, that complex does not mean more difficult, but rather more tedious to calculate. The principle behind computation is exactly the same as that for simple *chi*-square. I am including here a table of data obtained yet again from the University of Wetwang Degree Day proceedings. It shows how the numbers would be presented in a formal manner, and provides the material for the steps of schedule 12.

Table 4. Degree classes obtained by students at Wetwang University

Subjects	Degree classification					Totals
	I	IIi	IIii	III	Pass	
Languages	5	10	20	35	30	100
Maths	35	40	80	25	20	200
Economics	0	10	10	20	20	60
Totals	40	60	110	80	70	360

If these data were presented in a formal report, the conclusion might be worded:

'The value of χ^2 obtained (74.696) when $df = 8$, is significant at the 0.001 level of probability. Therefore the null hypothesis can be rejected. It is concluded that there is a relationship between the different subjects studied and final degree classification.'

In a discussion of the data, it might tentatively be advanced that language and economics students showed a pattern of results which was negatively skewed, i.e. fewer obtained good degree classes, whilst the classes obtained by maths students approached normal distribution, although with a suggestion of a positive skew. This is a good example of an occasion when in writing up a report, good use could be made of illustrations to help the reader quickly and clearly understand the data.

Accuracy and *chi*-square

In schedule 12, you are asked to subtract the value of 0.5 from the observed frequencies. The incorporation of this step into the *chi*-square calculations is known as *Yates' correction*. It is a correction for continuity, which is sometimes omitted. However, it improves the accuracy of the test and has the effect of giving a slightly more conservative estimate of χ^2. It should always be included in calculations from a 2 × 2 contingency table, and is absolutely essential when samples are small, i.e. the total is less than 25.

Obtaining a value for χ^2 provides one of the rare occasions when you can include as many decimal places as you wish – during the computation. If you round off the decimals before you do the final addition, you risk introducing a substantial error into the total, and particularly when there are many cells involved. For once you can give free rein to your pocket calculator, and use its great capacity for instant accuracy without incurring the danger of it being labelled 'spurious'!

Degrees of freedom

As with the t test, you have to calculate the degrees of freedom (df) at the end of chi-square calculations in order to evaluate the particular χ^2 statistic which you have obtained. It is a little more complicated than it was for t tests, because instead of two lists of numbers, you have as many lists as you have columns, but each list is also sliced up into rows. In simple chi-square, provided that you know all the row and column totals (which is generally the case at the conclusion of data gathering!), you only need a single cell entry to be able to fill in all the other numbers of items in the cells. Degrees of freedom, you may remember, means how many items we need to know before the remainder are fixed. If you find it difficult to believe that in a 2 × 2 table you only need to know one value (i.e. $df = 1$) to be able to compute all the cells, you can prove it for yourself by filling in the numbers on table 5.

Table 5. Fill in the missing numbers

	Category 1	Category 2	Totals
Category A			10
Category B		2	10
Totals	18	2	20

The official way to obtain the df for any chi-square (not just the 2 × 2 variety) is to multiply the number of rows, minus 1, by the number of columns, minus 1. In a 3 × 2 table (see table 6) you will need two pieces of information only, as you can find out for yourself again. The 'official' way would be $(3 - 1) \times (2 - 1) = 2 \times 1 = 2$. In one-sample chi-square, which is really only a single list of numbers, the df is the number of categories you use, minus 1.

Table 6. An empty 3 × 2 contingency table. Find out how many numbers you need to know before you can fill in all the cells.

	Category 1	Category 2	Category 3	Totals
Category A				10
Category B				13
Totals	3	15	5	23

When filling in the numbers on tables 5 and 6, you may notice that it doesn't matter in which cells the starting numbers go. Once the essential values are fixed, and whichever cells they are in, the remainder are not free to vary.

Exercises

1 Decide which type of *chi*-square is appropriate for the following:
   (a) Boys and girls, and whether or not they pass an exam.
   (b) Men, women and children, and whether or not they manage to get into a lifeboat.
   (c) Men, women and children, whether they get into a lifeboat, cling to floating spars, or have to swim.
   (d) I suspect a coin of being weighted, and toss it 100 times.
   (e) I suspect a dice (or die, to be correct!) of being loaded, and throw it 200 times.
2 Of 500 customers going into two different supermarkets, 300 went into Bymor and 200 into Ripoff. Data from the checkout tills showed that in each shop, 150 customers had spent less than £1. Is there any suggestion that the two different sets of customers differ in their spending behaviour?
3 Lord Amulree, in an article on monastic infirmaries, provides data on the proportional incidence of sickness for varying periods of time. He compares figures from the Middle Ages with those published by the Ministry of Pensions and National Insurance in 1957–58. Use the *chi*-square test to determine whether the pattern of sickness has changed over the 500 year interval.

Sickness periods by days	Infirmarer's rolls	Ministry of Pensions and National Insurance Report
0–3 days	10.2%	3.8%
4–6 days	25.0%	21.5%
7–12 days	27.3%	33.2%
13–18 days	9.5%	16.4%
19–48 days	18.5%	17.5%
49–312 and longer	9.5%	7.6%

4 Four towns report the following numbers of cycles stolen over a period of a week: 51, 72, 33 and 44. Carry out a one-sample *chi*-square test, and decide whether there is a significant difference between the towns, in terms of cycle thefts.
5 In the example given earlier, concerning the science degree classifications at Wetwang University (table 3), Professor Egghead based his theoretical expectations on the belief that the same number of students would fall into each of the five categories. In fact exam results usually turn out to show a normal distribution. From what you know about the normal distribution, obtain a different set of *expected* results, and then see whether it differs significantly from the *obtained* results.
6 Obtain both one- and two-tailed probability levels, using table S6, for the following values of χ^2.
   (a) $df = 4$, $\chi^2 = 12$ (b) $df = 2$, $\chi^2 = 5$ (c) $df = 3$, $\chi^2 = 0$
   (d) $df = 1$, $\chi^2 = 12$ (e) $df = 5$, $\chi^2 = 20$ (f) $df = 6$, $\chi^2 = 10$.

13   The design of experiments

THE REPEATED MEASURES DESIGN – ALWAYS A FAVOURITE WITH SUBJECTS!

In this chapter I am going to consider more closely the different ways in which we obtain from experiments and surveys the sets of data which we will subsequently compare. You will get the most benefit from this material if you understand the steps we go through in carrying out an experiment (chapters 6 and 7). The particular statistical analysis carried out after the data have been collected is determined by the level of measurement attained by the scores, and whether they are paired off in any way. The different methods of matching either groups or individual scores come under the general heading 'experimental design'. However, many of the points made in this chapter will have some relevance to the gathering of material by non-experimental methods, e.g. through surveys or observational studies.

In their investigations, psychologists and other social scientists are hampered by two things (besides shortage of funds!). One is ethical considerations, and the other is the sheer complexity of human and animal behaviour. In an attempt to make the best of things, they have to make use of experimental designs which will overcome, to a very limited extent, these problems. These designs are described in this chapter, and I give illustrative examples from the social sciences, because social scientists constantly face problems which require more design ingenuity than those tackled by 'real' scientists. However, the designs I cover here are of use in most kinds of experimental work.

Examination nerves!

Before going any further, I am going to outline an experiment, so that you can use the framework to check that you have got the hang of all the terms used in connection with experimental work. The experiment concerns the effect of taking tranquillisers upon the examination performance of students, and the hypothesis is that the students will benefit from them, as evidenced by their higher exam marks. Before the exam, students who had requested tranquillisers were identified and located, and formed the experimental group. Students from the same year and discipline were also selected, and matched from records with students in the experimental group on such variables as previous exam results, IQ, gender, medical record and exam subject. These formed the control group. Thus there were two groups of subjects which were, as groups, indistinguishable on all the criteria used in matching. All subjects in the experimental group were given a tranquilliser two hours before their exam. The control group subjects were asked not to take any drugs before the exam, although both groups were permitted to take tea, coffee, mints etc., as they wished, and smokers were allowed to inhale their usual dose of nicotine.

Stop now – and answer the following questions:

1 What are the IV and DV in this experiment?
2 Which variables have been controlled?
3 Which relevant variables have *not* been controlled?
4 What criticisms of the experiment can you make?
5 Is the experimental hypothesis one- or two-tailed?
6 What is the null hypothesis?

Now for the results. Exam marks were obtained, and it was found that the experimental group – the students who had received tranquillisers – had marks which were significantly higher than those obtained by the control group. The difference was significant at the 0.05 level.

Stop again! Think!

7 Would the null hypothesis be accepted or rejected?
8 Which statistical test would be the most appropriate for these data?
9 What does the 0.05 level of significance mean? Now proceed . . .

We are now going to pull the experiment to pieces. Before *I* start the demolition job though, criticise it yourself. Main clue – do you think that the subjects in the experimental group were really well matched with those in the control group?

Where am I going? to exams of course. Why do you ask?

Confound that variable!

One of the major flaws in the experiment just described is apparent in the first sentence – 'students who had *requested* tranquillisers'. Although it is stated later that students comprising both groups are indistinguishable, in fact they are not. They are different in that the first group asked for drugs, whilst the second didn't. Worse is to come. Although the groups were matched on what the experimenter apparently considered to be the relevant variables, they did not appear to be matched on any personality characteristics. It might be that the students who asked for tranquillisers were completely different on an important personality dimension from those who didn't. When a variable – *any* variable, but the request for a drug in this example – alters consistently with the two groups, it is called a *confounding* variable. Usually, confounding variables go undetected at the stage of experimental design, and are particularly nasty because they do not affect the experimental and control groups equally, as 'nuisance' variables do. The variables which were uncontrolled in the tranquilliser/exam study, such as anxiety, fatigue, meals, are examples of nuisance variables, and considered to be fairly harmless if affecting both groups equally, which is the assumption made. Confounding variables alter *systematically* with the IV, and so may actually bring about a change in the DV which is wrongly attributed to the IV.

In the experiment just described, it might be that the students who asked for tranquillisers *believed* that their work would subsequently be better – and as we all know, such expectations can materially alter outcomes. The design of this experiment would be improved considerably if tranquillisers had been given to members of the experimental group without their knowledge – and if the group comprised students who had not requested the drug. Giving people drugs without their awareness is unethical, however, and as a consequence, much drug research is conducted the other way round. *Both* sets of subjects (who have already agreed to take a particular drug) are given what appears to be the drug, and what they are all led to believe *is* the drug. In fact only half the subjects, the experimental group, actually receive the drug, and the remainder are given an identical-looking inert substance, a *placebo*. In clinical drug trials the nurses who actually give out the drugs do not know who is getting what, either, although of course they will be aware that some patients will only be receiving placebos. This procedure is called the *double-blind*, and it is meant to ensure that the administering staff don't differentiate, even if unconsciously, between patients receiving different treatments. The point is that in a good experiment, the experimental and control groups should be indistinguishable, so that any difference in outcome can be truly attributed to the IV. If a confounding variable, rather than the IV, has created a significant result, this would have to be classed as a Type I error – if it was discovered!

Spot the confounding variables – examples

1 A gardener, wishing to compare two varieties of begonia, counts the flowers in ten plants of each type. He has placed all the pots of one variety on one side of the greenhouse, and the remainder on the other side. One side gets considerably much more sun than the other . . .

> *Confounding variable*: position in the greenhouse, and the subsequent effect of different amounts of sunlight. The two varieties should have been mixed together.

2 Professor Grimrap starts to run the first group of subjects in an experiment on anxiety and performance on a visual task. The last subject in the group attacks him, and as the work has to go on, his pretty assistant Miss Smile, runs the subjects who make up the second group.

> *Confounding variable*: experimenter. Even if Grimrap and Smile were not as different as their names would suggest, it is not good for one person to run one set of subjects and another the other group. Even when extreme care is taken to standardise the procedure and instructions to the subjects, the effect of an imposing-looking male, as opposed to a less-threatening female, cannot be entirely ignored. This is particularly important in view of the nature of the experiment – Professor Grimrap may arouse anxiety levels, whilst Miss Smile may prove to be a more attractive visual target than the experimental one! If the professor and his assistant had run equal numbers of subjects in each group, then the effect of their personalities (if any) could be regarded as a nuisance variable, affecting both groups equally, rather than a confounding variable having a different effect on each group.

A STICKY END FOR PROFESSOR GRIMRAP

3 An experiment is undertaken to judge the efficacy of two types of literature devoted to post-natal baby care. One batch of literature is distributed at Poshgrove clinic, and the other at the nearby Backstreet clinic. Changes in maternal attitude are compared for the two kinds.

Confounding variable: clinics – together with their staff and customers. Where the literature is distributed, and how, matters. Not only might the type of client at these places differ substantially and systematically, possibly as a result of clinic location, but the staff in the two places might also differ in their attitudes towards their clients, *and* towards the distribution of educational material. If all the Poshgrove clients, after receiving rather dry and technical information on baby care, had apparently heeded the literature, then the results might suggest that this format was superior to the comic strips distributed at Backstreet. However, it might really be that the effect of the literature was a function of the type of clients reading it. The Poshgrove ladies may well read, mark, and inwardly digest all the written information they receive, whilst the Backstreet clients might regard paper handouts as useful things for lighting the fire, or wiping the baby's bottom! The manner in which the clinical staff gave out the information might have had an effect, with the Poshgrove staff carefully making sure that each client received the information, and the overworked Backstreet staff first of all forgetting that they had to distribute the leaflets, and then, in their hurry to dispose of them, shoving handfuls out to all comers – including illiterate mothers!

What is to be done? Counterbalance!

When any variable is spotted as likely to influence the results of an experiment, we try to control its values if possible, and hold them constant for all values of the IV. However, it is usually impossible to control all such variables at once, and so what we must avoid is letting any particular variable exert its influence in a systematic manner, and thus give rise to a confounding error. The solution is a common-sense one. We try to arrange our experiment so that suspected confounding variables are spread equally across all experimental conditions. One particular way of doing this is known as *counterbalancing*.

105

Suppose we design an experiment in which subjects have to come to the lab. and learn something under one of two possible conditions. We suspect that time of day might influence their performance, but it is simply not practicable for us to run one single subject every day at 10 am – which would make 'time of day' into a strictly controlled variable. Instead, we will counterbalance 'time of day' so that it influences subjects in both groups equally. We will work with half our subjects undergoing both conditions (one subject in each condition) in the morning, and the remaining halves of the two groups in the afternoon. If we think that dividing the day into just two blocks is still not enough, because 'early' morning differs from 'late' morning for most of us, then we could alternate the two conditions throughout the entire day.

If the experimental condition is called A, and the control condition B, we emerge, when we alternate the two, with a particular type of design known as (and get ready for it!) the $ABAB$ design. There is one other design commonly used in counterbalancing, and it is especially useful when learning is involved and subjects are acting as their own controls. If the experiment consists of subjects learning two roughly similar sets of information, one under condition A and the other under condition B, we might feel that the first learning experience will affect the second for better or worse, and *systematically*, if we let all the subjects learn the material in the same order, AB AB AB. So we alternate the order and have half the subjects learn under condition B first. The design is thus known as the $ABBA$ design. If there are two conditions, and subjects have to make hundreds of responses under both, the $ABBA$ design is ideal, for it ensures that A comes before both A and B, and that B also occurs equally often before A and B. In the $ABAB$ design, you may observe, A never occurs before A, and B never before B. In these $ABAB$ and $ABBA$ designs the pattern is repeated *ad infinitum*, I should add. When we have finished running the experiment, the results from each of the A and B conditions are put together into two complete samples of A and B for statistical analysis. There are methods of analysis available which tell you whether in fact any 'order' effect has occurred – but they are rather beyond the scope of this book.

Randomisation

In the previous section, possible confounding errors were dealt with by systematic counterbalancing. This technique involves deliberate alternation of conditions, according to a previously chosen scheme. Another strategy is to distribute the values of the variable in question (in the last example, the two conditions) across the trials in a random manner – a technique known as *randomisation*.

For instance, if time of day was a possible confounding variable to be dealt with, as subjects turned up to take part in an experiment, they would be allocated to *either* the experimental *or* the control group condition by the experimenter tossing a coin or using a table of random numbers. In using the latter, the experimenter would take the sheet of numbers, and without looking in detail, place the point of a pin or pencil somewhere on the page. He or she might have decided beforehand that if an even number comes up the subject goes into the experimental group, and if an odd number, into the control group. Either way, forces of nature, and not undreamt-of biases of the experimenter, determine the victim's fate. (Note: it is wise not to alarm subjects unnecessarily by allowing them to witness random allocation procedures!)

Over the long run, it will be found that approximately half the subjects experience the experimental and half the control conditions. It is usual, towards the end, for experimenters to abandon coins, pins, pencils etc., and allocate the remaining subjects in such a way that the numbers participating in each condition are perfectly equal. *All* subjects were allocated according to a randomisation technique however, including the last ones. This is because it was chance effects determining the allocation of earlier subjects which settled the fates of the later ones, and not just the fact that they turned up later in the day (another potential source of bias).

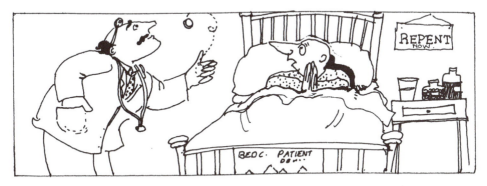

The word 'random', used in connection with selection procedures, does not mean haphazard, or even uncontrolled, but rather 'by chance'. As the subject draws near, the decision about his or her fate is not determined by biasing factors, but strictly according to chance, so that the probability of entering either group is the same.

When you think about it, it is really common-sense to take certain effects into account, and to attempt to prevent them from influencing one of your groups more than the other. Counterbalancing and randomisation are systematic attempts to deal with this potential source of error.

Are you related in any way?

One of the major considerations in planning an experiment and its subsequent analysis is whether or not the two samples you intend to compare are *related*, or *matched*, in some way. The statistical tests described earlier were of two sorts, besides being parametric and nonparametric. One kind was meant for samples derived from two separate (although at least generally similar) sources, and the other for samples which were matched. By this we mean that every score in one sample has a 'partner' in the other. It would make nonsense of the results to shuffle the order of one of the sets of scores if they had been individually matched with the other set. With the unrelated samples tests however (the Mann–Whitney and independent *t* tests), this is not the case, and the order of scores within the sample is quite arbitrary. This is underlined by the fact that these tests can be carried out on samples of unequal sizes.

Although statistical tests are mainly concerned with whether scores are paired off or not, it would not make sense, experimentally, to compare groups of scores which had come from very disparate sources. For instance, if you wanted to see whether a new teaching method helped children to acquire a larger vocabulary, you must make sure that the children forming the experimental and control groups were fairly similar. It would not be a very fair test if group *A* comprised children from a class for gifted children, whilst group *B* was made up of youngsters with reading problems! This seems perfectly self-evident, but we always have to be on the lookout for less-dramatic manifestations of this problem. Even comparisons between classes of children within the 'normal' range of academic ability, but with different home backgrounds, or between classes with different teachers, could be unfair. What kind of error does this constitute? The old confounding error – so as far as possible, the children in both groups must be equated. However, making sure that groups are generally similar before the experiment starts is not the same as matching. Matching always involves a careful pairing off of individuals or individual scores on the basis of one or more variables. You can easily tell whether matching has taken place in a design, or is up to the standard required for a paired statistical comparison, by taking the first score of one group, and asking yourself whether it has an *obvious* partner. If the answer is 'No', then the samples are not matched.

From a statistical point of view, whether or not groups are equated doesn't matter. Statistical analysis is completely divorced from the topic under consideration, and will simply tell you the probability of samples being drawn from the same parent population. However, tests for matched samples differ from those for unrelated scores in that they take into account the extra degree of matching. As you saw in exercise 2(d) (chapter 11), sets of scores can differ significantly when they are matched, but be regarded as indistinguishable when they are treated as unrelated data. So the statistics test just does its job according to the types of data fed in, and whether the samples are matched. To obtain matched scores, we normally follow one of two possible procedures. Either we can ask subjects to act as their own control, so that they each provide two scores, or else we pair individuals off on some basis, so that the one score each gives can be matched with its partner. These designs are called the *repeated measures* and *matched subjects* designs respectively.

The repeated measures design

As the name implies, subjects repeat their performance, but under slightly different conditions. If we suspect that order may act as a biasing variable, then we can combine the repeated measures design with an *ABBA* design, as shown in table 1.

Table 1

Subject	Condition *A*	Condition *B*	
1	First	Second	
2	Second	First	
3	First	Second	
4	Second	First	etc.

If we did not consider the order of conditions to be an important variable at all, then we could skip the counterbalancing entirely, and have each subject participate under identical conditions.

This kind of design, because it provides scores which will be compared from 'within' each subject, is sometimes called the *within subjects* design. The most serious

'CARROT OR STICK' RESEARCH IN THE CLASSROOM

problem associated with its use is that when subjects take part in experiments over a longish period of time (i) they start to understand the task requirements better and improve with practice, and (ii) they start to get bored and tired. It is traditional to assume that these *practice* and *fatigue effects* cancel each other out, and so do not create a confounding error which would cloud the effect of the IV. It is also possible for subjects to provide more than two scores, and their performance can even be analysed in such a way that any consistent trend they show will be discerned. Like the 'order' effects I mentioned earlier though, these advanced designs will not be covered in this text.

The repeated measures design, culminating in a 'matched' statistical analysis, is one of the neatest and most powerful of the simpler designs. Unfortunately, it cannot be used as often as we would wish, because in many experiments, when a subject has taken part once, he, she or it cannot participate again. Learning experiments are particularly vulnerable in this respect. It is not possible, for instance, to ask someone to learn certain items under noisy conditions, and then – perhaps the next day – learn the same material under quiet conditions. The test material can only be learned once, and even if the gap between sessions is quite long, a certain amount will have been retained, making learning quicker on the second occasion, whatever the experimental conditions. One way round this problem is to obtain two very similar sets of material for learning. However, this is not a perfect solution, for you never know what personal associations the material can trigger for the subjects, making the material of unequal difficulty for them.

Often, it is necessary to *debrief* subjects after an experiment – i.e. tell them what the whole thing was all about – and this provides another reason why subjects may not be able to participate in an experiment on a second occasion. It is particularly common in experiments undertaken by social psychologists, in which it is essential that subjects are not aware of the aspects of their behaviour which are under scrutiny. Once they have this awareness, then of course their behaviour alters. Not to tell subjects about the true purpose of an experiment (and often to deliberately mislead them) is a form of dishonesty, and many psychologists refuse to do this. However, some psychologists think that it is justifiable, and especially if subjects are informed of the true nature of the experiment immediately after they have participated. The work of Stanley Milgram (*Obedience to authority*, London: Tavistock, 1974), in which he persuaded subjects to administer what they thought were strong electric shocks to other subjects, is a source of much controversy. The problem of what constitutes unethical conduct can only be resolved by the individual at present, in the absence of any general guidelines for psychologists – in Britain, at least.

Finally, subjects may not survive to take part in a re-run of an experiment. In medical research rats and mice are commonly used to evaluate new drugs, or in studies of brain tissue and body organs. After the experimental treatment has taken place it is often necessary to kill the animal painlessly, in order to inspect the tissue to determine changes which have been brought about.

The matched subjects design

In the repeated measures design, every subject contributes two scores for analysis, each score going into a different sample. There is another kind of set-up which gives matched data suitable for related statistical tests, and it occurs when individual subjects are paired off precisely with a member of the other group. In order to get the pairing precise enough, it is common to get one group of subjects together, and then look round for partners for everyone. If you just took two groups of roughly equated subjects, and *then* tried to pair them off, you would be lucky if you managed to match up all the individuals involved, and so it is easier in the long run to look for individuals with specified characteristics from the outset.

The obvious choice for matched partners is to procure identical twins. We know that their genetic make-up is the same; most of their social background, and to a lesser extent their intelligence, personality and other psychological characteristics are also highly similar. Having procured specimens, we persuade the twins to take part in an experiment, each under different conditions. Twins are the experimental psychologist's delight, and this is increased no end if twins who have been raised in different households are found! Any differences between the twins can be attributed solely to upbringing and environmental influences, and so such twins figure prominently in the 'nature–nurture' arguments over relative contributions of heredity and environment which abound in psychology.

Unfortunately, for the psychologist not involved in nature–nurture work, or for the research in medical conditions for which purpose-built twin 'banks' have been established so that a ready supply of identical twins exists, twins do not appear all that frequently. It may be that they are wisely avoiding the vicinity of psychology departments! Therefore, although the use of identical twins for matched subjects designs is ideal, it is not normally practicable, and the less-satisfactory alternative of matching unrelated individuals on the basis of relevant variables must be employed. Often, members of the experimental group will have come to our attention because of some unusual condition they show, and so we would then attempt to find others who are similar in as many respects as possible, but who do not display the condition itself.

Work carried out on the effects of premature delivery, or low birth weight, upon later intellectual, physical and motor development contains some good examples of matched subject work. Infants born prematurely in the same hospital, and to mothers from the same population, can be matched with babies which are within the normal weight range. There is one aspect of this work though which makes it very difficult to draw any safe conclusions about the effects of low birth weight. This is that the factor or factors which helped to bring about the premature birth may often continue to exist after birth, usually to the detriment of the developing child. Social class and malnutrition are two such factors which can play an indirect and direct role respectively, on the developing foetus or child.

Of course, matching isn't restricted to experiments in social sciences. In any kind of work involving animals and inert materials, individual animals or specimens can be paired off with each other – once again, on the basis of important characteristics. For economists and geographers, whole communities can be matched for certain studies. In examining the regional incidence of diseases, epidemiologists (and there's a word which will impress your friends!) might compare communities, one which shows a high incidence of a particular malady, the other a low incidence. Differences between the two, likely to be causal factors, would then be sought. For ethical reasons the research must be done this way. It would not be possible to take two carefully matched towns, and then see if a high incidence of a particular disease could be induced in one of them!

The independent subjects design

The last kind of experimental design to be covered has already been used in many of the examples given earlier in the book. It is a very common one, in which results are derived from groups of subjects who have been roughly matched, *as a whole*. For instance, two groups of children at a school may be given two types of dental treatment – but it would previously have been ascertained that the children in each group had approximately the same number of fillings, used the same brands of toothpaste, and ate about the same quantity of sweets. Individuals would not be assessed with a view to pairing off though. If this were done, then the design would be a matched subjects one, rather than an independent subjects design. Sometimes this design is called a *between subjects* design; as I mentioned earlier, it provides data which are less likely to show a significant difference than matched design data – and particularly if the change in the DV is only a small or subtle one.

Summary

Statistical tests, besides being nonparametric or parametric, are also designed to analyse independent or matched sets of scores. Fitting into these *two* categories of tests are *three* types of design:

    1 Repeated measures (or *within* subjects)
    2 Matched subjects
    3 Independent subjects (or *between* subjects)

Groups 1 and 2, which generate paired scores, are suitable for matched tests, whilst data from the third group would be analysed using an independent (or unrelated) test. This information is also given on page 198.

14   Sampling

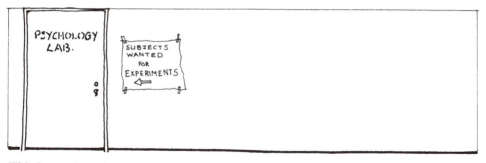

This is another chapter aimed primarily at life scientists, although the principles of sampling are universally applicable to scientific work of any description. Some knowledge of the content of chapters 6 and 7 will help you to appreciate the relevance of sampling, but it is not essential for an understanding of the information included in this chapter.

Generalisation

As life scientists we wish to understand and predict the behaviour of living organisms. Therefore we conduct experiments and surveys, and occasionally even find that yes, indeed, a certain variable does have a consistent effect upon something else. *So what?* This is the big question which confronts us at the conclusion of an experiment or study. Although we might have shown that something is the case for particular organisms in a particular environment, clearly the aim of our labours was not just to make detailed statements about single members of a species, or special groups of animals or plants. We hope to be able to apply our findings to *all* the animals belonging to the species under consideration (often *Homo sapiens*), and which live under roughly comparable conditions. This application of findings from the particular to the general is called *generalisation*, and it is an aim which underlies almost all scientific investigations, and whatever mode of enquiry is used.

The problem with generalisation lies in the fact that we *are* generalising. We can never be quite certain that our conditions apply to all other members of the species involved, for the simple reason that our study did not include all its members. We took a *sample*, and it is purely from this that we draw our conclusions. However, the validity and generalisability of our conclusions rely entirely upon how good our sample was. If it was poor, then the findings will be of very limited value, and will merely tell us about what happened when *organism X*, under *conditions Y*, was subject to *procedure Z*. We can't say very much about *species X*, or the likely effect of *Z* on that species under conditions other than *Y*. So it is important that we are careful to obtain good samples.

There's more to it than you think!

In principle, it sounds as though nothing could be simpler than taking a sample. After all, we 'sample' offerings of food and drink easily enough, and pronounce judgements on such offerings without hesitating over possible methodological difficulties. But in practice, *good* sampling is far from easy. You can see this from your own experience of sampling, if you give the matter some thought.

It is just possible that you visit your local pub fairly regularly (strictly for observer-participation studies, of course!), and so you will probably have noticed that during the evening at least one person will comment upon the state of the beer that night. Beer varies – the causes of this variation being perhaps best known and understood by publicans, but giving rise to seemingly endless speculation by the customers – and each visit to the pub provides an opportunity to obtain and 'test' a sample. You must realise intuitively that any one occasion does not necessarily provide a good indication of the 'usual' quality of the pub's beer, and inevitably the beer closely resembles water on the day your rival darts team visits to play you 'at home'! Individual samples, i.e. pints of beer, which are obtained daily over a period of weeks, will be combined to give a proper sample – a reasonably sized portion of the parent population, the pub's beer. In a sense a single pint of beer is a sample, but it is such a tiny one that it could not safely be used as a basis for sound judgements. Up to a point, the larger the sample, the better it is, for it is more likely to truly reflect the characteristics of the parent population. Exactly where the 'point' lies will be discussed later in this chapter.

THE TIME WHEN JUDGEMENTS ARE MADE CAN MATTER...

Suppose we take all the draught bitter sold at a particular pub over the course of a year as our parent population, and on the basis of sampling decide that we wish to make a pronouncement on its quality. (This could be the preliminary stage in the compilation of *The Statistician's Guide to Public Houses*!) First, we would decide upon an *objective* scheme for judging the quality of the samples. 'Objective' means something which is publicly examinable, as opposed to more private *subjective* feelings, which are unique to an individual. We could construct a five-point scale, ranging from 'undrinkable', 'fair', 'good' and 'very good' to 'superb', and spend some time sampling beer to decide which quality of taste will be put into which category. In important studies, when several people are involved in making judgements like this one, and on a rating scale specially constructed for the task, we like to be sure that they are all making comparable judgements. In other words, they have to be in agreement over how they will categorise the samples. When their agreement is good, we speak of high *inter-judge reliability*. When the judges are in agreement over the matter of categorisation, then the sampling procedure proper can begin.

Let's say that unknown to the judges, the parent population of beer overall would be judged 'good', and has a normal distribution. Samples collected over a reasonable time period will be combined to form a large overall sample, and in which we should find that judgements of 'good' will predominate. There will be several 'fairs' and 'very goods', but relatively few 'undrinkable' and 'superb' decisions. This proportion of comments reflects the underlying normal distribution, and will remain the same, whatever the size of the sample, once the first few judgements have been made. As the sample gets larger, the more it can be trusted to be representative, and after it displays a pretty solid looking normal distribution, further efforts are unnecessary.

The faith we can have in a sample isn't just a matter of knowing how large the sample is however. It also depends upon how well the items constituting the sample were chosen. If they were picked in such a way that every part of the variation which exists in the parent population has an equal chance of selection, then all is well. But if some parts of the population have a better chance than others, then the sample is not a good one, and becomes what we call *biased*. Just because items taken from a population keep having roughly the same value is not necessarily an indication of bias – provided the selection procedures were adequate. In the beer example just given, selection procedures were fine, and the many judgements of 'good' were a true reflection of the mean value. However, if all the daily beer samples had been taken right at the start of every evening, on the first few pints drawn, this would have constituted a poor sampling strategy which would probably have resulted in the researchers reaching the erroneous conclusion that the beer quality was mainly 'poor'. Sometimes, we take samples from populations about which a great deal is known. At other times, we may feel we know nothing about the characteristics of the parent population, and the whole point of taking a sample is to discover what it comprises. In this case we can't check the accuracy of our sampling by comparing the results with any 'expected' values, and the snag is that if the sampling strategy is a poor one, further samples will only add more poor data to the pile. Unfortunately there is no handy way of recognising a poor sampling procedure; basically, you need to think intelligently about the features of data collection which are likely to give rise to biased results – and then try to avoid them!

Poor samples can be disastrous. First of all, they can provide misleading information about the characteristics of a population and result in errors which are costly in terms of money or well-being. If I think, from the basis of talks to teachers, that this book is God's gift to students, and ask for a million copies to be printed, I would probably end up in the modern equivalent of the debtor's prison! The teachers who gave me their comments are friends – do you think that they form an unbiased panel of judges? And what about the bits of the book upon which they were basing their judgements? Did I wave the book open at random, or make sure that they saw all the best drawings and funniest cartoons?

In obtaining judgements about a book, or gauging the quality of a pub's beer, our main concern has been to draw one good sample of data. In both cases we were dealing with opinions, but we could draw single samples of virtually anything which provides some kind of numerical score.

Now we will look at sampling error in connection with statistical tests, when we normally draw two samples and compare them with each other. Let's return to the analogy of the biologist busy obtaining samples of water from ponds, who was described at length in chapter 6. As you may recall, he lost the labels off the test-tubes, and left the samples on the table. His colleague, who was unaware of the sources of samples, had to decide, on the basis of their constituents, whether they had come from one or two ponds. If the samples looked different, and contained the different micro-organisms, she would be able to conclude that they had been drawn from two separate ponds (populations). However, it might be that the field worker had in fact taken two water samples from one pond, but that one had been collected from near the mud at the bottom, whilst the other came from a place where a clear stream entered the pond. Would you expect the contents even to *look* the same in this case? Of course not, Neither sample is truly representative of the bulk of pond water, which is somewhere between the two extremes of muddy and clear. So the colleague, in deciding that the samples were drawn from two ponds, would be mistaken. By incorrectly rejecting the null hypothesis (which would have stated that the samples were derived from one source) she has committed a Type I or Type II error. Can you remember which one?

Similarly, poor sampling might lead to an erroneous conclusion of the other Type. If the biologist had obtained muddy water from the bottom of an otherwise clear pond, and compared it with water taken from a completely muddy one, it might be concluded that the samples came from the same source, when in fact they had been drawn from two ponds. This would constitute a Type II error (the null hypothesis has not been rejected), and the first example a Type I error. I hope you were able to work that out yourself!

These examples should help you to see why, if we are to generate data which is trustworthy and useful for generalisation and analysis, we should go about sampling very carefully.

What's the problem then?

I have already hinted that it is harder than it sounds to obtain 'good'– meaning 'representative' – samples. By taking samples in social sciences we mean obtaining scores or observations from people (samples of *events*) under certain conditions (samples of *environmental variables*) over a specified time period (samples of *time*). All these things vary – with tremendous consequences; and this is one of the reasons why work in social sciences is so much more complex than that of the physical sciences, in which inert substances do not vary appreciably in the 'normal' environment over a short period of time.

The people who turn up at the psychology lab door as potential subjects are a sample of human beings – but who knows what kind of sample they comprise? Almost certain to be biased, at any rate! It is often quite difficult to procure subjects for experimental work, and usually they have to be bribed in some way – by direct payment, reassurances that despite appearances they are contributing to a worthwhile experimental undertaking, or by repayment with baby-sitting offers, etc. Sometimes coercion even comes into it. There is an element of this in the requirements laid down by some psychology departments, that in order to satisfy university regulations students must participate in the staff's experiments for at least *x* hours per year. A considerable proportion of psychological research has been carried out in which students have been used as subjects, and psychologists face criticism on that score. Students are by no means typical members of the human race – or even of the society to which they belong, for that matter!

A LINE-UP OF 'NORMAL' SUBJECTS ...

Sometimes people volunteer for experiments because they need something. It might be money, it might be advice and help with some personal difficulty they are experiencing, or it might be because they need to alleviate their boredom or loneliness. Whatever the need, such people – and especially the ones who turn up without much persuasion – are probably particularly unlikely to form a good representative sample. It is not that having problems or being short of cash makes people 'abnormal' – it is just that these subjects are at the extreme end of the problem continuum, as evidenced by the fact that the severity of the factors is forcing the would-be subjects to take some action. Even people who volunteer for studies from the purest of intentions, i.e. who would like to make a contribution to scientific knowledge, have to be regarded as somewhat different from their fellow humans!

So, in recruiting people to take part in experiments, it is difficult to find representative members of the society under consideration. Even if we didn't have all the 'volunteer' and other sorts of bias creeping in, it would still be difficult, for we don't really have a very clear idea of what characteristics a 'typical' member of our society would show, or how to measure all the attributes which we ought to consider. And even when we know roughly what we are looking for, there still might remain the problem of actually finding the intended victims.

Suppose you want to conduct a market research study on the response of 'normal' schoolchildren from middle-class homes to some new-fangled toy you intend to develop. Having decided that 'normal' covers certain values of IQ, number of parents in the home, siblings, dogs and hamsters, scholastic achievements, pocket money, parental aspirations, etc., and that all the children you are interested in will be between ten and fourteen years old, how do you actually locate the ones you wish to interview? Just walk into the nearest school? It might be quite an unusual school though – perhaps one for subnormal children, or with a catchment area in a very well-to-do district. Clearly this is not satisfactory. If your marketing plan was aimed at *all* the children in the British Isles who fitted your requirements, then to obtain a representative sample you would have to obtain children from several locations throughout the country. And the first and most persistent agent operating against the selection of good samples rears its ugly head – the *cost*! Limitations of time, equipment and personnel usually boil down to financial restrictions, and exist in addition to all the other budgeting considerations which beset every research project.

Sampling

If we did have vast resources, and came up with a list of all the suitable schools to include in the parent population from which the sample will be drawn, we still have the problem of selecting individual schools from the list. Human nature being what it is, the research personnel, if left to their own devices, would no doubt opt for holidays in Cornwall, Wales or Scotland, and the matter would be decided. Not good enough! Some poor souls must be despatched to Salford, Battersea, Scunthorpe and other unattractive sounding places; in fact *most* of them must be, because these industrial areas, being fairly densely populated, will contribute more schools to the list than the rural areas. And after having arrived at the schools, do the researchers proceed to look for the quietest, most innocuous-looking creatures to interview, and shy away from those specimens which look as if they have stepped straight out of the pages of a comic? Again, if they had their own way, no doubt they would! Once more, this would be biasing the sample, and to avoid this, *all* children possessing the attributes listed must stand an *equal* chance of selection. The use of a school register and random number table would do the trick at this level.

Besides considerations of cost, there are other reasons why we are forced to use samples. Sometimes, our population may be of infinite size, and it would be impossible to scrutinize every member or item. If we are studying personality, or wish to measure it in some way, we cannot wait until people have lived their entire lives, and then assess *all* the characteristics they displayed during every moment. We have to give a person a 'test', i.e. take a sample of their reactions or behaviour within a limited time period and treat this as a sample from which we can generalise to much of the remainder of his or her life. But when you think that only a few hours goes into the test – if that – and that the results are meant to be generalised to a time period embracing months or years, your faith in such psychological tests and their results goes a little limp. It wouldn't even be so bad if test scores presented a true picture, but who, under close scrutiny from another person, behaves in an exactly typical fashion?

Another practical consideration, and one which influences final sample size, is that if we attempt to measure *all* members of a population – or even a substantial portion – limited resources mean that this may be done less well than if we had taken a smaller sample, perhaps using fewer, but more highly trained, personnel, or a more precise method of assessment. The more highly trained (and hence paid) the 'samplers' are,

Isn't he sweet!

PRESENTING ONESELF IN THE MOST FAVOURABLE LIGHT

the better they will carry out the task. I am sure that we can all imagine student leaflet distributors at work, stuffing old handfuls of literature into the letter boxes of empty houses, or behind bushes here and there! The more subjects a person has to interview or use in an experiment, as a general rule, the less likely he or she is to carry out the job carefully. The less well-trained people are, the less seriously they will take a study, and the less likely they are to understand the subtle nuances of the task in hand. So this all comes back to cost again, although there must be a point at which, even with all the financial resources one could wish for, it is still impossible or impracticable to tackle a complete population of subjects.

Finally, as I mentioned in the previous chapter, in some kinds of work – medical research, for instance – the experimental animals must eventually be killed so that their tissue can be studied. Obviously, it would be impossible and undesirable to work on a complete population of rats or mice; after the show was over, there would be no members of the parent population left to whom the results could be generalised! The whole point of sampling though, is that if a careful selection is made, it isn't necessary to go on adding to it, *ad infinitum*. From a *good* sample, generalisations can be made with some confidence.

Random sampling

In this section, I am going to outline the three main types of sample-drawing technique which are commonly used. Because all three methods are based on the principle of random selection, meaning that at the outset, all possible items included in the population have an equal chance of selection, they are known as *random sampling*. 'Random', in this context, does not mean 'haphazard', and in fact it means anything but haphazard! It doesn't mean selected according to the whims and foibles of the researcher, either. It implies a very careful pre-selection plan, which has been drawn up to ensure that all items in the parent population have the same chance of appearing in the sample.

1 Systematic sampling

The essence of this method is that each member of the population under study (for instance the inhabitants of a town) is given a number, and then a subgroup is taken for study. The term 'systematic' refers to the fact that the population has been numbered off according to some convenient system, such as an alphabetical list of names, class registers or consecutive house numbers. Any kind of complete listing which is available may be used. Random number tables are made up from long sequences of jumbled digits, in which all the numbers from 0 to 9 will, in the long run, appear equally often. Although single digits are used in table construction, we can use the tables for numbers greater than 10 by treating the digits as if they were grouped into units larger than our maximum required number. If our sample of people, objects or events was numbered 1 to 40, then we could obtain an order in which to use them in a study by reading the digits from the table off in pairs, giving a minimum value of 00 and a maximum of 99. From table S9 at the end of this book, in which the digits are already grouped in pairs, you would obtain the numbers:

19 90 70 99 00 20 21 14 68 86 14 etc.

The first pair of digits, 19, is below 40, and so the person with this number would start the ball rolling. The second person would be number 20, then 21, then 14, and so on, until everyone has been included. If the number of items in the list exceeds 100, then in this case, the digits would be put into groups of three, to obtain an order. We would find that our first number was now 199, the second 70, followed by 990 and 20. We can use random number tables to obtain a sample from a group of numbered items by taking the numbers from the table until we have obtained as many items as we wish our sample to comprise – e.g. fifty people from a population of a thousand. Quite often, researchers do not start at the top left-hand corner of the table to obtain the first number, but close their eyes and point to a number somewhere in the middle of the page. This then serves as the starting point.

2 Stratified sampling

This method can only be used when there is detailed knowledge of the population under study. Variables considered relevant to the sample are considered, and when the sample is taken it is made up of subgroups, each of which shows the vital factors, and in the same proportions as in the parent population. Different values of the variables involved are known as *strata*.

For example, if in a university there are twice as many undergraduates as postgraduates, and a sample of the entire student body is desired, then the eventual sample, if it is stratified, will include twice as many undergraduates as postgraduates also. Lists of students and a table of random numbers might be used, and when the correct number of items for one of the strata has been reached, then only items for the other would be drawn. In fact systematic sampling, as outlined above, would provide approximately the correct proportions in any case, if it were carried out properly.

The advantage of stratifying a population before taking a sample is that the chances of picking a deviant sample are smaller, and therefore estimates of population values are much more precise than is the case with a simple random sample of the whole population. The major limitation of stratified sampling is that it requires advance knowledge of the important factors within the population, and their relative proportions. Examples of factors which are often considered to be relevant are age, sex, social class, income and race.

3 Cluster sampling

This relies on the existence of natural groups, such as houses on a block, people in a family, or children in a class. These kinds of *blocks* or *clusters* are numbered, and from them a random sample is selected, the number used being mainly determined by the size of the sample required. Next, from within each cluster, subgroups are identified, and from one or more of these, the item for inclusion in the sample is taken. This method has the advantage of cheapness, in that by using only certain clusters, usually falling within a particular locality, subjects can be interviewed fairly conveniently, and the investigator does not need to travel miles and miles between each one. Unfortunately though, this very advantage is also its weakness, for if a particular cluster, from which several items were taken for inclusion in the sample, was unrepresentative in some way, then there will be a certain amount of systematic error present.

The man in the street

Students commonly believe that using the 'man in the street', perhaps selected 'at random' (e.g. by approaching every tenth passer-by), results in a better sample than if the more usual procedure of roping in all available and willing students is followed. Also, there is a kind of vague feeling that if 'real' people, as opposed to students, are to be used in a study, it is perfectly adequate to obtain people – literally – from the street outside. In fact these beliefs are just as likely to give biased samples of the 'general population' as the easier method of taking students from the dining room was. The only studies in which people walking the streets would make appropriate subjects would be those concerning things like the quality of the pavements, provision of litter bins, aesthetic appearance of street lights, or proposed zebra crossings. Any investigation involving people who have been plucked from their wanderings on the streets is going to miss out the tremendous proportion of humans who are at work all day, or on night shifts, in hospitals, schools, convents or prisons, at sea, and so on. As these absentees from the street never had much of a chance to be included in a sample, a sample made up roughly from 'men in the street' would in fact be very far from random!

The electoral roll in sample selection

If you are faced with the task of having to obtain hundreds of people to make up a sample which is supposed to be typical of the general population of Britain, you might wonder where on earth to start. Hopefully, you don't set about it the way some political opinion pollsters in the States did a few years ago. They had the bright idea of obtaining peoples' names from telephone directories. Can you spot the error there? They didn't – and that year the election predictions were fantastically awry. Only a select portion of the population has telephones, and especially a few years ago, it would be a portion tending to reflect a reasonable income and fairly high standard of living – together with certain political opinions, no doubt. The error of using phone directories as a source for names is a nice example of a procedure likely to give a very biased sample.

A much better way of obtaining names of people who reside in Britain, and one far less likely to result in a biased sample, is to use the electoral roll. It is a list of all voters, and there is a legal requirement that everyone over the age of eighteen should be included. Naturally, there will still be a few who escape the net – and you can bet that these people will show some form of bias, and probably in the opposite direction to the ones whose names appear in telephone directories. They will be the homeless, those making frequent (and perhaps speedy!) moves, the illiterate, and those who believe in ignoring official-looking documents. So no prizes for deciding that the electoral roll is not quite as unbiased a source of names as the keen researcher would like to have at his or her disposal. It would be particularly important to make sure that the 'oversights' were contacted in research involving things like housing conditions, rents or low income families.

The problem of sample size

A major decision which investigators must make is the number of subjects to include in a sample. This problem has no easy or general answer, and each solution depends upon a variety of factors which sometimes cannot be specified in advance. In general, there are three main considerations. The first is the kind of statistical analysis which is planned. This is a complex and controversial question. Often it is possible to demonstrate that a significant difference exists between experimental groups when each contains only a very small number of subjects. This is particularly the case when the IV has a dramatic effect upon the DV, or when fairly precise interval or ratio numbers are used to quantify a more subtle effect. On the whole, as an effect becomes more subtle, and thus harder to detect, larger groups of subjects are needed before populations of scores can be distinguished. Financial considerations often turn out to be a deciding factor in the long run.

Secondly, variability within the samples and results matters. On the basis of previous experience, the expected variability can be taken into consideration when an investigation is planned. In some types of research much greater variation is anticipated than in others, and so larger numbers of subjects would be used. *Single subject* designs have played an important part in psychology though, the classic example being the work of Ebbinghaus on memory – with himself as the sole subject!

Finally, traditions develop in research areas concerning the appropriate numbers for samples. The traditions are of course based on experience of work in a particular field, and this in turn will reflect the relative importance of the factors which have just been described.

Other kinds of samples

It is now realised that the sex, race and physical characteristics of an investigator may affect the kind of results obtained from subjects; this source of variation brings home the point that in social sciences, the people carrying out the studies are themselves part of a sample. This potential source of bias should be controlled (for instance by using only one investigator, or a variety of investigators who have been thoroughly trained in the use of standardised instructions and procedures), or it may be considered an IV in its own right and scrutinised accordingly.

When particular stimuli are presented to subjects, then for later generalisation the ones selected should be representative of those encountered in the population to which later reference will be made. In selecting objects for inclusion, a list of suitable samples may be drawn up, and from this, random samples for presentation to the subjects, or for use in the study, can be drawn. This is known as *stimulus sampling*.

When an investigator chooses particular values of an IV for an experiment, he or she is in effect taking a sample. Once again, if the findings are to be generalised, it is important to make sure that this *sampling of conditions* is done appropriately.

Finally, all investigations and measurements take place at a distinct point in time. How well the data from a sample can be generalised can depend upon when the sampling took place. The example I gave earlier, of the first pints of beer drawn in a pub being used as a basis for judgement of *all* the beer sold at that pub, provides an illustration of poor *time sampling*.

The general population

'General population' is a term to use with care. Strictly speaking, it means 'typical' members of a society – or at least, the 80% or so who fall into the central values of all the attributes which we take into consideration. Whilst the term doesn't apply to any group of people who are simply 'not students', neither does it refer to people walking about in towns and cities! To do a study on members of the general population would involve a great deal of careful pre-sampling planning, as I have already indicated.

Don't confuse the population of a country with the *statistical* meaning of a population though. The statistical concept refers to all members of a group of people, items or events sharing some quality – the population of a country refers to the people who actually live in a defined area.

THE BIASED AGENT

15 Correlation

ONE CAN ONLY SPECULATE ABOUT THE LINK BETWEEN TV AND THE BIRTHRATE

I shall now conclude the practical part of the book with *correlation*, a statistical technique which is unusual in that it can be used either in a descriptive capacity, or as a means of drawing inferences. It is not necessary to have read all the material which has appeared earlier in the text to be able to grasp what I cover in this chapter, although an understanding of the difference between descriptive and inferential techniques will help, and for the final section on probability, chapter 5 will provide a good foundation.

A measure of association

No doubt you will have come across the word 'correlation' before, and formed a rough idea that it means 'association', or 'going together'.

'Expenditure is correlated with income.'
'Cancer is correlated with cigarette consumption.'

Statements like these may be familiar to you, and they tell us that the more income you have, the more you spend, and the more cigarettes you smoke, the more likely you are to get cancer. Notice that in both cases we are being told that the *more* of one thing, then the *more* of another. Rather than use fairly vague words like 'more' or 'a little', mathematicians prefer to quantify things by using numbers, and so the mathematical technique of correlation was devised as a means of specifying precisely the extent to which two things (variables) are associated. The numbers used to express correlation, or extent of association, are called *correlation coefficients*. If two measures are in perfect association, i.e. a great deal of one thing is always accompanied by a great deal of another, and when one is absent or nearly so, then the other also has a low value, we have a *perfect positive* correlation, and the correlation coefficient which corresponds is the number +1. If on the other hand there is no association between two variables, then we speak of there being no correlation, and assign the number 0 to this situation.

As you may well have realised, most cases of paired variables are probably going to lie somewhere between the values of 0 and 1. That is, they will be 'a little bit', 'fairly' or 'very well' associated, rather than showing a perfect relationship. Any correlation which is less than perfect means that some of the pairs of scores from the two variables don't quite fit the general pattern. All the intermediate positions between 0 and 1 can be stated numerically, and this method is so satisfactory that it becomes easier, and more precise, to deal with numerical descriptions rather than the vaguer verbal labels.

Now let's look at another case of association. Suppose I say that there is a correlation between the weight of clothing I wear and the temperature outside. The two variables I am linking are weight of clothing and temperature – and clearly they are connected. However, they are not connected in such a way that an increase in one accompanies an increase in another, but just the opposite. This is *negative correlation*, and it describes circumstances in which the *more* there is of one variable, the *less* there is of the other. As the term 'negative' suggests, quantification of such an inverse relationship is indicated by using a minus sign before the coefficient, which will again be a figure between 0 and 1, but this time, −1 (minus 1), rather than 1 (plus 1). Intermediate cases of association are given values which lie between 0 and −1, so a correlation of −0.9 means that the two variables have a very clearly established negative association; of −0.5, that they are inversely related to a moderate degree; and of −0.2, that there is only a tendency towards an inverse relationship. The relative positions of correlation coefficients are shown on the straight line in figure 1.

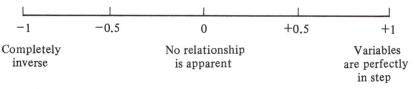

−1	−0.5	0	+0.5	+1
Completely inverse		No relationship is apparent		Variables are perfectly in step

Figure 1. The relative positions of various correlation coefficients

Next, we can look at the relationships between variables by means of diagrams, but first, it is necessary to understand how we draw ones which involve two variables. Taking two axes, and joining them in the traditional manner, at the bottom left corner, the horizontal axis (or abscissa) will be used for measuring one of the variables (A), whilst the vertical axis (or ordinate) will be for the other variable (B). Mathematicians would probably label the horizontal axis X and the vertical axis Y, but I shall stick to A and B. Figure 2 shows A and B labelled for two variables, 'size of garden' and 'annual income'. Each axis is divided up into the appropriate units of measurement for the two variables. It is standard practice to draw graphs and diagrams with the points of lowest measurement meeting in the bottom left-hand corner.

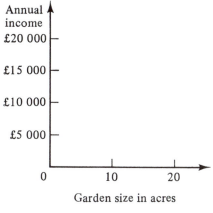

Figure 2. Axes labelled for correlation data

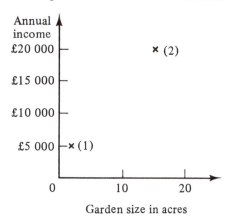

Figure 3. Labelled axes with two points plotted

125

Correlation

In correlation, we are always dealing with *paired* scores, and so values of the two variables taken together will be used to make a diagrammatic representation. Suppose our findings tell us that we have a person with an income of £5000 pa, and whose garden is 0.2 acres. A cross is marked on the diagram where imaginary lines drawn from the two axes, at these values, meet. It is shown on figure 3, where it has the number 1 beside it. Another person in our sample has an income of £20 000, and a garden of 15 acres. The point for this is labelled 2 in figure 3, and it lies where the imaginary line drawn across from £20 000 crosses that coming up from 15 acres. So, each point used in determining the correlation is plotted from all the pairs of scores included in the data, and by using the two scales in conjunction. A completed diagram for a case of positive correlation is shown in figure 4, where we *invariably* have more of A going with more of B.

Point x shows where there is hardly any of either A or B.
Point w where there is an intermediate amount of both A and B.
Point y where there is a good deal of both A and B.

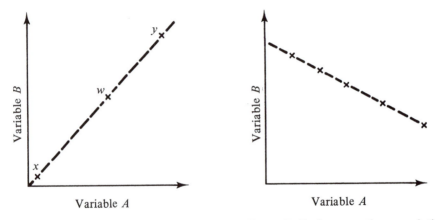

Figure 4. Perfect positive correlation   Figure 5. Perfect negative correlation

Now look at the picture which is presented by negative correlation, and shown in figure 5. A great deal of B goes with hardly any A. An imaginary line linking up the points plotted from a perfect negative correlation will always start high up on the left-hand side and slope down to the right.

What does a correlation of zero – no association – look like? You can't draw a line connecting up the points which have been plotted, because the measures on the two variables are so unrelated that all we see is a large cluster of points (forming a rough circle), as in figure 6. The point marked 1 shows where variables A and B both have high values; 2 is positioned where A is fairly high and B fairly low, and 3 where both A and B are low.

These diagrams, representing visually the association between two variables, are called *scattergrams*. When they are constructed, it is fairly unusual for points to lie in an exactly straight line, and so it is quite rare to see an actual line joining them all, as in figures 4 and 5. A more frequently met pattern consists of several of the points plotted lying *more or less* along a straight line. When such less-than-perfect associations are shown, it is possible to work out mathematically the exact angle at

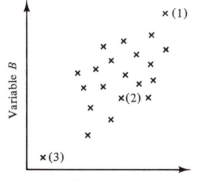

Variable *B*

Variable A

Figure 6. The cluster of points in zero correlation

which a line should be drawn in, so as to come closest to the majority of points. Such a line is called a *regression line*, or *line of best fit*. Unless you have actually gone through the appropriate calculations, it is better to leave the line out, rather than guess where it would go.

For the near perfect positive and negative correlations then, the points lie in virtually straight lines pointing up or down on the right, according to the relationship. As correlation becomes further removed from perfect, and the coefficient starts to approach 0, so the points get rather more spread out, and move through an oval shape (again pointing up or down), towards a circular shape – the stage at which even the most ardent optimist has to admit that no line is in the least bit evident! The shape of a circle is formed because most variables will tend to give values which are normally distributed. The central cluster of points on variable *A* will be halfway up on one axis, and of variable *B*, halfway along the horizontal axis. Extreme scores on either scale will be relatively rare, and on both variables together even rarer; they will be shown on the scattergram by points which lie in any of the four corners.

The shapes of scattergram patterns associated with the varying extents of different correlations are shown in figure 7.

When you write up any report which includes correlated scores, it is always best to include a diagrammatic representation of the results, in the form of a scattergram drawn on graph paper. In the case of non-perfect correlations, but in which a line of points is roughly discernible, it is best *not* to draw it in, unless its angle has been properly calculated.

Exercise

1 Draw scattergrams for the following pairs of numbers, and describe in words the degree of association you consider to exist between the paired variables.

(a)	*A*	*B*	(b)	*A*	*B*	(c)	*A*	*B*	(d)	*A*	*B*
	2	2		1	2		1	7		10	1
	4	4		2	2		2	5		8	2
	5	5		4	3		3	9		6	4
	9	9		4	4		5	4		4	5
	12	12		5	6		7	8		3	7
	13	13		7	7		2	3		0	10
							9	1			

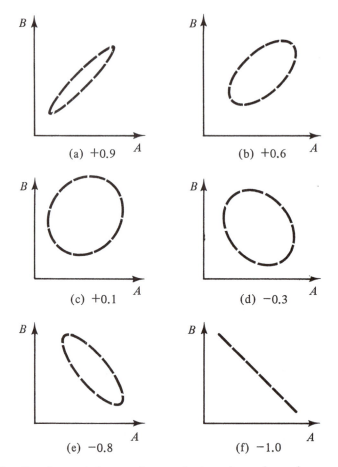

Figure 7. The direction and shapes of score clusters shown by various correlation values

Spearman's *rho*

Now we move on to the calculation of precise correlation coefficients from given sets of data. There are a few methods in existence for calculating correlation coefficients and, needless to say, the coefficients obtained from each are subject to slightly different interpretations; fortunately, for most of our work in social sciences, we do not need to be concerned with the mathematical subtleties. We shall start off by looking at a simple and quick method for obtaining a correlation coefficient, developed by Spearman, and giving the coefficient known as *rho*. *Rho* is pronounced like 'row' in 'rowing boat', and is the Greek version of the letter *r* – this letter of the alphabet having been chosen to indicate a correlation coefficient.

Step by step instructions for obtaining Spearman's *rho* are given in operation schedule 14. After you have completed the calculations, you should end up with a number between −1 and 0, or 0 and +1. If you obtain a coefficient which is larger than 1, you can be absolutely certain that you have made a mistake somewhere in your calculations, for the formula will work with *any* set of paired scores. Note also that the value of 6 which is used in Step 6 is unchanging, and does not alter with the size of sample.

In working out Spearman's *rho* you have to rank the scores, i.e. put them into order of size. This ranking operation crops up as a preliminary step in several statistical tests, and precise instructions are given in schedule 6. The value of Spearman's *rho* is then calculated from ranks, rather than from the original values of the two sets of scores. This means that it is quite possible to calculate a coefficient from data which are originally in the form of grades or ranks, and in fact Spearman's technique really comes into its own in this respect, for many of the more sophisticated methods of calculating a correlation coefficient require the variables to be given in rather more precise units than just grades (i.e. interval or ratio level of measurement must be achieved – for those of you who have read chapter 10).

An example of a graded scale would be one which measures political affiliation along a continuum. According to their beliefs, people could be assigned a position on the scale, ranging from, say, 0 to 10. Grades do not even need to be expressed numerically on the original scale though, and attitude measurement commonly involves pinpointing a person's opinions on a continuum ranging from 'strongly disagree' at one end through 'disagree', 'don't know' and 'agree' to 'strongly agree' at the other. Scales like this are called *Likert* scales, and in using any data from them to calculate Spearman's *rho*, the five degrees of opinion would be rated from 1 to 5.

Suppose you obtained data which, when plotted on a scattergram, showed a pattern similar to either of those shown in figure 8. When the plotted data points form a curved rather than straight line, we have a *curvilinear monotonic* relationship.

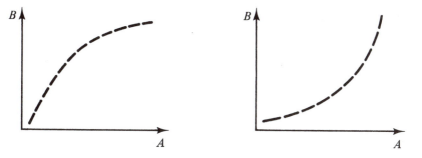

Figure 8. Examples of curvilinear monotonic relationships

Although variables *A* and *B* are both increasing or decreasing together (i.e. as in a positive correlation), the rate of change in the variables is not equal. In the left scattergram the fastest change in *A* is at higher values of *B*. Speed of change in variable *A* is indicated by the angle at which the line lies to the vertical *B* axis. It would of course be possible for variable *B* to change at a different rate from *A*. Can you work out what the scattergram would look like in that case? Such non-linear relationships do not mean that a correlation or association between the variables does not exist, and Spearman's *rho* can be calculated on scores showing a monotonic curvilinear relationship without any problems. However, if the curve in the line starts to change direction, as in figures 9(a) and 9(b), becoming arched or U-shaped, then even though there may still be a very orderly relationship between the two sets of scores, it is too complex for Spearman's *rho* to be used as a means of describing it.

Correlation

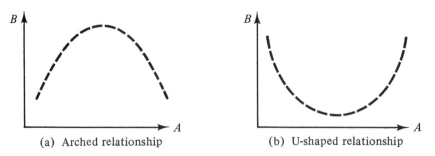

(a) Arched relationship (b) U-shaped relationship

Figure 9. Examples of arched and U-shaped relationships

Non-linearity means that correlation techniques must be selected with care. The easiest way of detecting it is usually by means of a scattergram, and so we have an excellent reason for inspecting the data in diagrammatic form fairly early in the proceedings. Maybe when you did exercise 1 you noticed how much easier it was to see a relationship from a diagram rather than a collection of numbers.

When describing a relationship between variables by means of a correlation, it is necessary to add two pieces of information to the value of the coefficient obtained. One is the number of paired scores used in the calculations, and the second is the likelihood of your having obtained a relationship accidentally, from the occurrence of chance factors. This last value is expressed by a probability, and I shall say more about this aspect in the final section of the chapter. Meanwhile, although the operation schedules include steps for obtaining a probability after *rho* has been obtained, don't worry about it when you carry out the next exercises.

Exercises

2 Calculate Spearman's *rho* for the four sets of scores given in exercise 1.

3 The manager of Beastly Breweries has just read a book on interpersonal communication, and he decides that maybe the recent decline in takings could be attributed to poor staff–customer interaction. He devises a means of assessing quality of interaction (by such things as gaze avoidance, proximity, attention) on a scale ranging from 0 to 35. In addition, in those pubs in which he has spent some time rating the quality of interaction, he also asks customers to describe the place on a six-point scale ranging from 'abominable' to 'superb'. He converts the verbal category to a number, and uses the median category obtained to describe each pub. So finally, he has the pairs of scores given in table 1 at his disposal.

Table 1

Public house	Quality of interaction	Customer assessment
Rose and Trilby	30	5
Dog and Pups	27	1
Magnificent Motel	5	0
Rusty Plough	22	4
Blink's Bar	20	2
Bent Walking Stick	12	0
King Canute	32	3

From the basis of a correlation coefficient, Spearman's *rho*, what conclusion do you think the manager would reach?

Pearson's product-moment

I have already told you that one of the great assets of Spearman's *rho* is that it can be used to calculate a correlation coefficient on data which are originally expressed only in grades. Therein lies its weakness though, for when a technique operates on grades rather than more precise scores, the lack of precision means that detailed mathematical tricks cannot be called into play, and sometimes, the lack of detail means that a subtle, even if definite, association is not discerned. However, when pairs of variables are both measured by means of scales which use precise numbers (the interval or ratio scales – like inches, minutes, grams), different methods of calculating a correlation coefficient become available. *Pearson's product-moment*, giving the statistic *r*, is one such method, and steps for obtaining it are given in schedule 15. Unfortunately, even with a calculator, it takes much longer to calculate than Spearman's *rho* – although many would say that this disadvantage is compensated by the fact that it supplies a more precise coefficient. However, there are also other snags attached to obtaining Pearson's *r*. Not only must we have scores in the form of precise numbers (and not, for instance, data from Likert scales), but certain other restrictions exist concerning the distributions of the scores involved. This is because the product-moment belongs to the group of statistical operations known as *parametric* techniques. More information on parametric techniques and tests, their strengths, weaknesses and the restrictions concerning their use, will be found in chapter 10.

Yet another drawback to Pearson's *r* is that it is not a meaningful figure if it has been obtained from a set of scores which shows any curvilinear relationship whatsoever. Thus if you are considering calculating a product-moment coefficient, it is essential to draw a scattergram and make sure that the data fall into an unambiguous linear pattern. Social scientists, who often work with variables which are expressed in ranks or grades along a continuum, and who often have cause to suspect the linearity of their data, will find that Spearman's *rho* is not only the correlation coefficient most appropriate for their data, but that it also gives a perfectly satisfactory degree of association.

Correlation

Exercises

4 Use a scattergram to decide what kind of relationship is shown by the following pairs of scores. Then state whether Pearson's product-moment or Spearman's *rho* would provide the more appropriate correlation coefficient.

(a)	Variable A	Variable B	(b)	Variable A	Variable B
	1	4		8	1
	3	5		7	3
	5	8		5	7
	5	11		3	11
	8	12		1	15
	11	14			
	4	4	(c)	Variable A	Variable B
	2	7		15	1
	7	10		14	3
	10	11		14	5
	13	12		10	8
	15	15		5	9
				2	11
				2	13
				1	14

(d)	Variable A	Variable B	(e)	Variable A	Variable B
	1	1		1	2
	4	2		8	5
	3	3		6	4
	6	3		11	6
	6	5		13	7
	8	5		15	8
	9	6			
	1	12	(f)	Variable A	Variable B
	7	7		2	2
	9	9		5	3
	6	9		9	4
	5	10		10	7
	7	11		11	10
	5	13		12	14
	3	12			
	2	14			

5 Calculate the Pearson product-moment *r* for the sets of scores in exercise 1.

Correlation and causation

It is commonly believed, when there is a strong correlation between two variables, and hence a high degree of association, that one of the variables *causes* the other. Don't let yourself be numbered among the many who fall into this trap!

ASSOCIATION DOES NOT MEAN CAUSATION.

In exercise 3, as you would see from the answer (you *have* done the exercise, haven't you?), the manager of Beastly Breweries was quite mistaken when he

132

concluded that the poor staff–customer interaction was responsible for the decline in alcohol sales – even though it seemed a plausible explanation. Let's look at some more situations taken from 'real life', to see how the common misconception that correlation can imply causation arises. The third example given below shows that variables which can be associated statistically may not necessarily interact at all.

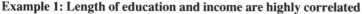

DON'T GET CAUGHT OUT BY CORRELATION

Example 1: Length of education and income are highly correlated

The correlation (which we assume to be a positive one) tells us that the more education a person receives, then the more money that person will earn. It seems plausible to deduce from this that it is education itself which directly determines income – but a moment's thought will reveal this to be an erroneous conclusion. It so happens that in our society, people who have studied longest tend to have the better paid jobs. However, it may be the responsibility attached to the job which determines pay, rather than training, although undoubtedly the latter will help! Intelligence is another factor to consider, particularly as our society tends to base its understanding of intelligence on academic (and hence educational) criteria. The so-called clever person, good at exams, staying longer at school and then proceeding to university, will tend to end up in a more highly paid job than a person who 'dropped out' of school at the first possible opportunity. In our society, education *does* play a part in determining income, but as this in turn is affected by such things as personal circumstances, intelligence and luck, it cannot be seen as the single, or even major determinant. The high correlation simply describes the relationship which exists at the time of measurement between the two variables, education and income.

Example 2: TV viewing and the birth rate are negatively correlated

This interesting phenomenon could generate some fascinating research. As an example of the correlation trap it is a little more transparent than the first one, for we would not seriously consider that mysterious rays emitted by television sets have contraceptive properties! We might speculate though, about people's activities when there is no TV available, and a massive bulge in the birth rate which occurred nine months after a wide-spread TV blackout in the States suggests that there is some connection between the two variables, albeit an indirect one! This example was of a negative correlation. A positive correlation which is frequently bandied around concerns the association between violence on TV and levels of aggression. It is quite clear that in the minds of many people there is a definite causal relationship here. In fact the relationship may or may not be direct, but it is certainly unlikely to turn out to be a simple one. As with TV and the birth rate, the problem provides good grist for experimental work and research, but cannot be solved on the basis of strong correlation alone.

Example 3: The strong correlation between left- and right-arm length

Perfectly true, but an example in which you can see quite clearly that the two variables do not interact at all, but were both determined by other factors, such as genetic make-up or diet, which affected both arms equally. You would laugh if someone suggested to you that the length of your left arm *determined* the length of your right arm. Yet this is exactly the kind of mistake people make when they impute any degree of causation to a correlation or association.

It might help you to avoid the trap if you remember the way in which a coefficient is calculated. The two columns of paired scores could have been written *either way round* for arithmetical purposes; there is absolutely nothing in the mathematical procedure which can tell us that the values in one of the columns in some way give rise to corresponding values in the other. So we obtain no more than a precise description of the relationship which exists between two sets of *numbers*. Variables might interact in a direct manner, there may be an indirect link (as for instance between ice cream sales and the number of fainting guardsmen, or as in the previous arm length example), or there may be no connection at all between them, any correlation obtained being coincidental. You must consider all these possibilities when interpreting a coefficient.

Exercise

6 Examine the variables described in the following correlational studies, and decide whether they interact directly, indirectly, or not at all.
  (a) The positive correlation between pints of beer sold in a pub and temperature centigrade.
  (b) The negative correlation between the number of people seen waiting at bus stops and the number of buses in evidence.
  (c) The slight positive correlation between premature births and later school difficulties.
  (d) The positive relationship between motorway accidents and aircraft accidents.
  (e) The negative correlation between orders for fresh milk taken by the local dairy, and the number of trifles appearing for sale in nearby shops.
  (f) The negative correlation found between the growth rate of a plant and the incidence of car horn-blowing in the nearby streets.

Misleading coefficients

I have already told you that it is incorrect to use Pearson's product-moment on curvilinear data, as it will give a misleading value of r. Of course there is absolutely nothing to stop you taking *any* set of paired scores and obtaining a coefficient from them, regardless of the shape they make on the scattergram. When you carry out the calculations there is no built-in warning device which indicates that you are violating assumptions, and that your final coefficient is misleading. It is up to you to know what assumptions underlie each kind of coefficient, and to respect them. Two more data patterns, besides linearity, provide aspects for consideration. One concerns *outliers* and the other *partial samples*.

Outliers were mentioned in chapter 2, when we looked at them in connection with dispersion. An outlier is an atypical extreme score. If, in correlation, one of the values of a pair of scores is atypical, then the position of the intersection between the two values on the scattergram will be away from the general line of points, as illustrated in figure 10. When the sample under consideration is small, the existence

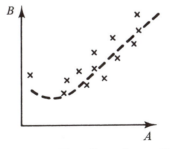

Figure 10. The effect of an outlier

of an outlier can have a very misleading effect on data interpretation. It might suggest that the data are really curvilinear (and in which case the product-moment would be an inappropriate technique to use), or, if included in the calculations, bring about a small coefficient, when in fact a strong linear relationship exists. So, should outliers be excluded from analysis on the grounds that chance events caused an atypical score, or included as valid data? There is no easy solution I'm afraid. If you exclude outliers you will be accused of 'fiddling' your results, but if you include them, you risk losing a strong relationship which may really exist (in other words, you commit a Type II error). If a strong relationship does emerge when outliers are ignored, then you must at least compensate for their omission from the coefficient calculations by mentioning such scores in your report, and giving an account of why you suspect each one arose. As the number of scores in a sample increases, so it becomes easier to judge whether outliers are either atypical scores, or indicative of a curvilinear relationship. If the former, they can be included in the analysis, for as part of a large sample they will not be able to exert as much influence on the coefficient obtained as they would if they were part of a small sample. Note: this is another reason why it is better to avoid basing correlations on small samples, if possible.

Correlation

Finally, we move on to partial sampling. If a researcher undertaking correlational studies chooses to work with scores taken from *only one end* of a range of values obtainable from a particular variable, he or she risks failing to detect an association which is really present – and once again we see a Type II error. The effect of this kind of restriction of range is best shown by means of an illustration. Figure 11(a) shows a scatter of points for the full range of variable *A* plotted against variable *B*, in which a rough line of correlation can be discerned. Clearly there is a fairly strong positive relationship between the two variables. However, if scores are taken only from the *middle* of the range of variable *A*, as shown in figure 11(b), then *exactly the same scores* give rise to the pattern shown by the dotted lines, which indicates to us that there is no correlation between the two variables.

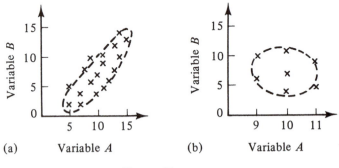

Figure 11.

On the other hand, if a researcher includes data from *both* extremes of a continuum, and ignores the intermediate range of scores, than a correlation coefficient will be obtained which is higher than that which would have been obtained from a complete set of data. This kind of misleading coefficient provides an excellent example of how to 'lie' with statistics!

Correlation and prediction

As correlation coefficients describe the relationship between two variables, then, regardless of whether or not one causes the other, we are able to use the technique to make predictions about scores. Suppose that there is a strong positive correlation between students' exam marks in chemistry and physics. The coefficient tells us that if students do well on one of the papers, then they will also do well on the other. The higher the coefficient is, then the more points on the scattergram will lie along a straight line, rather than form an ellipse. I mentioned earlier that when points only roughly form a line it is best to omit it rather than guess where it lies. You can find out precisely at which angle and where it lies by carrying out the appropriate mathematical procedures; the line of best fit calculated in this way is also called a *regression line*, and it will pass through or close to the maximum number of points plotted. It is by using such a line that we can find out what values of one variable will accompany certain values on the other, and the more clearly a line is formed by the scores (i.e. the higher the correlation coefficient), the more precise we can be about extrapolating from one variable to the other. Turn back to figure 3, and place a ruler so that it connects points 1 and 2. If a perfect correlation existed between income and size of garden, then *all* instances plotted on the scattergram would fall along the edge of the ruler, thus forming a regression line. Use it now to find out what garden size you would anticipate for someone known to earn £10 000 pa or £15 000 pa; what income would you anticipate for a person whose garden occupies half an acre? If there had not been a perfect correlation between garden size and income, but the points had fallen into a band, like the one shown in figure 7(a), then instead of being able to predict and state a single figure for garden size or income, we could only give a range of values likely to include the point we are estimating.

In education, exam marks are frequently used to predict performance over a period of time. For instance A-level results can be linked with performance at university; indeed the very system of making university entrance dependent upon A-level grades assumes that there is a distinct relationship between the two: students who do well at the A-level hurdles are considered likely to succeed in the university stakes.

Correlation and prediction are often used by psychologists in connection with personality and intelligence tests. The relationship between different test results might be examined, or between a test and some aspect of behaviour, education or a disorder. For instance extraverts (people who get high scores on paper and pencil tests designed to measure the 'sociability' aspect of personality) have been shown to take longer to acquire conditioned responses than introverts. A psychologist, knowing a person's extraversion score, might be able to predict the conditioning rate for that individual, or vice versa – predict the person's degree of extraversion from performance during conditioning procedures.

Still on the subject of measuring personality, and by means of paper and pencil tests, psychologists need to know whether a test which has been developed for a special purpose can be regarded as *reliable*. A reliable test is one in which the scores obtained by subjects are known to be consistent, and unlikely to change because of factors which are not connected with the test procedure. Assessing the reliability of tests is quite difficult for a number of methodological reasons, but all the methods involve carrying out correlations. If a high positive correlation is obtained, then the test under scrutiny can be regarded as reliable. Tests are also normally assessed for their *validity*. A valid test is one which measures what it is supposed to measure, and not something else! Again, correlation is the statistical technique which provides the backbone for this aspect of psychological test research and development. If intelligence were found to be directly related to head size, then to assess it by using a tape measure, and giving a rating in terms of units of length would be quite sufficient, and we would have a perfectly valid test of intelligence. Unfortunately, such a correlation does not appear to exist (perhaps the sayings 'too big for your boots', 'bossy boots' and 'clever clogs' indicate that we should concentrate on foot size, instead!), and as psychologists disagree over what intelligence *really* is, we don't have any test which at present is agreed on by one and all to be a valid measure of intelligence. Scores on IQ tests might correlate well with such things as subsequent exam performance, status and income, but this is probably because they all involve the same mental skills, i.e. they are correlated because they all have common elements.

The statistical technique of correlation is used for prediction in fields as diverse as economics, geography, town planning, sociology, medical and physical sciences, archaeology, biology and linguistics.

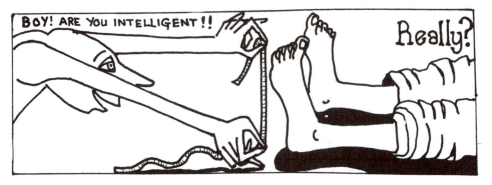

Correlation in experimental work

So far I have only discussed correlation as a descriptive technique, although several of the examples I have mentioned make it clear that a strong correlation is not simply a result of coincidence, but that either direct or indirect links exist between the variables. I have also emphasised that the existence of an association cannot be interpreted as implying a causal relationship – and I would now like to consider the extent to which correlation can be used in experimental work, when the whole aim is to discover laws of cause and effect. At the start of this chapter I quoted the example of the link between cancer and smoking. Another example is the possible link between dietary cholesterol and heart disease, and this provides an interesting example of the way in which correlation can be used in research. Although it appears that there is an association between heart disease and the fatty deposits on the walls of blood vessels, and the latter are connected with the type of fat included in the diet, researchers are plagued by the fact that despite a general positive correlation, there are always individuals who must be noted as outstanding exceptions. These exceptions illustrate the complexity of the matter and show that the association between diet and heart disease is not completely straightforward. However, in recent studies of dietary habits carried out on a wide range of human groups, the relationship between animal fat consumption and incidence of heart disease for societies taken *as a whole* turns out to be an extremely strong positive correlation. So even though it is still impossible to make a detailed prediction for any individual, our knowledge of existing associations means that we can predict *trends* within given societies.

Much of the controversy surrounding the issues of diet, smoking and diseases arises from the very fact that the evidence has been largely drawn from correlation studies, so that the argument can always be advanced that other factors, such as personality or physical make-up, are *really* the cause of the disorder. However, experiments can be designed in which the proposed linking factors are subject to scrutiny, and, still by means of correlational techniques, the various relationships become better understood. An improved understanding of the role of hereditary factors in schizophrenia has come about partly through correlational studies of the incidence of this mental disorder in related people – identical twins, fraternal twins, ordinary brothers and sisters, parents and children – when the extent of differing hereditary components can be scrutinised. Correlational studies have also provided the basis for many studies aimed at investigating the extent to which intelligence is acquired through hereditary factors, rather than as a result of early training or exposure to a stimulating environment. It is mainly because ethical considerations prevent direct manipulation of children and environments to produce dullards and geniuses that correlational studies – in which *existing* relationships are assessed – predominate. So although a *single* correlational study cannot throw any light on what causes what, several correlational studies built around the various variables thought to be involved can comprise a satisfactory experimental programme of investigation.

Probability and correlation

Much earlier in this chapter I told you that after the numerical value of a correlation has been determined, it is normal to state the number of pairs which were used in the calculations, and to give a probability value to your coefficient. These steps are carried out so that we (and other people) can know just how much confidence can be placed in a particular coefficient. It is fairly obvious, if a description is based on only five numbers, that such a small sample is not likely to be representative of the populations from which they were drawn, and that chance events, if they have occurred, will have a big influence on the evaluation. If something is coincidentally related in one pair of readings out of five, this comprises a fifth of the total sample, whereas the same coincidence would only affect one-hundredth of the sample if there had been a hundred pairs of measures. A simple practical exercise will give you good insight into the role of chance in correlation.

Take a piece of paper and tear it into eight pieces, each piece about the size of a bus ticket. Number the pieces 1 to 4, twice. You should now have four sets of paired numbers. Divide the papers into two sets, each containing four different numbers, turn them over and shuffle them. Now take a clean piece of paper and head two columns *A* and *B*. Without looking at the numbers on the papers, draw one from the first pile, write its number down on column *A*, and then draw a number from the second pile. This number will go into the corresponding *B* column. Do this three times more, without putting any numbers back, taking numbers from alternate piles, and pairing them off in the two columns. Now pretend that these numbers are material for a correlation coefficient, and inspect them. Their order may be quite haphazard – without any discernible pattern – or there might be evidence of some sort of trend in the two columns (either separately, or looked at in conjunction with each other). You know yourself that the numbers were selected at random, and that there was no link of any sort between the first and second numbers of each pair, yet there is a reasonable chance that just by coincidence you have obtained a good positive or negative correlation. The order in which the pairs of numbers emerged would not matter, but the pairs themselves would have to be either 4/4, 3/3, 2/2 and 1/1 for a perfect positive correlation, or 4/1, 3/2, 2/3 and 1/4 for a negative one. There is just a very slight chance that one of these sets of pairing may have occurred. On a slightly bigger scale then, perhaps you can see that positive and negative correlations can be partially determined by chance factors, and that some kind of allowance must be made for this. The larger the sample, the less likely it is that a positive or negative

Correlation

correlation will be attributable to such chance elements. Fortunately, stating the chance element which will be associated with any particular correlation coefficient derived from variously sized sets of scores is quite simple – a matter of looking up the probability values on the appropriate table. In this book, table S7 is for use with Spearman's *rho*, and table S8 for Pearson's *r*. The only information you need in order to ascertain the possible role of chance factors (called the *level of significance*) for a stated coefficient value is the number of pairs of scores making up a sample. The minimum level of significance which is acceptable, before an association can be regarded as a 'real' one, is the one in twenty, or 5% level, which was mentioned in connection with the acceptability of statistical test results in chapter 8. Exactly the same levels apply, the one in a hundred (1% or 0.01) and one in a thousand (0.1% or 0.001) levels being regarded as stronger evidence of a relationship than the 5% (0.05) level.

In addition, as in looking for a difference between two samples and using a test for analysis, in correlation we also need to state in advance whether we are establishing a one- or two-tailed hypothesis (see chapter 7). If we predict *either* a positive *or* a negative correlation, our prediction is directional, i.e. one-tailed; if we are more vague, and merely say we expect a significant correlation in *either* direction, then our hypothesis is two-tailed. Needless to say two-tailed hypotheses are relatively rare in correlational studies!

Exercises

7 Give one-tailed probability levels for the following values of Spearman's *rho*.
   (a) $N = 7, r_s = 0.84$ (b) $N = 9, R_s = -0.6$ (c) $N = 10, r_s = 0.65$
   (d) $N = 11, r_s = -0.91$ (Take the value as lying between those for $N = 10$ and $N = 12$.)
   (e) $N = 20, r_s = 0.58$ (f) $N = 28, r_s = 0.30$
8 Using Pearson's *r*, and one-tailed values, what coefficients would be required for significance at the 0.05 level when (a) $N - 2 = 8$, (b) $N - 2 = 6$, (c) $N - 2 = 30$, (d) $N - 2 = 15$, and at the 0.01 level with Spearman's *rho* when (e) $N = 5$, (f) $N = 8$, and (g) $N = 20$?

16 In the last analysis . . .

In this chapter I shall provide some hints for writing experimental reports which will be particularly useful to social science students. Then we move on to material of a more light-hearted nature, which I imagine you will be able to appreciate without having read the entire book beforehand. I hope it provides evidence that people can emerge from scientific and statistics courses with unbroken spirits!

General guidelines for report writing

There are really only four vital questions to bear in mind:

WHY?
HOW?
WHAT?
SO WHAT?

The key to successful report writing lies in answering them in an appropriate manner. The first point to bear in mind is that there is no single format which is regarded as 'correct' by everyone. Rather there are many variations, and almost everyone (including your teacher or lecturer) has his or her favourite.

It is through writing and presenting reports that most scientific communication takes place, and so it is important that you learn to deal adequately with this aspect of your course. Listed below are some general guidelines on writing style.

1 Use complete sentences in reports, and do not present material in note form.
2 Avoid using the first person (either singular or plural) in your writing.
3 Although the convention has, until recently, been to use the masculine pronoun in writing about a person of unspecified sex, it is increasingly acceptable (and desirable) to either include the female pronoun and its derivatives, or write in a way which avoids mentioning gender. For instance, 'When the subject arrived, he was asked to . . .' could become either 'When subjects arrived, they were asked to . . .' or, 'On arrival, subjects were asked to . . .'.
4 Avoid using slang expressions.
5 It is quite acceptable to use the abbreviations *S, E, DV* and *IV* for subject, experimenter, dependent variable and independent variable respectively.

Always make the attempt to write up your report as soon as possible after you have conducted the work – and certainly within days, rather than weeks. Otherwise you will confirm for yourself the amazing rapidity with which unrehearsed and un-organized material is forgotten.

In the last analysis . . .

Sections of reports

1 Title

This should indicate in a precise manner the nature of the topic being investigated. Take care over the detail of whether you call the report an 'experiment', 'survey' or just an 'investigation', for each term implies a slightly different kind of study.

2 Abstract (or summary)

Although it is rather inconvenient when you are actually writing your report, the custom established for papers published in academic journals is that the summary appears at the beginning! It is done so that potentially interested readers can quickly discover whether they wish to read the main body of the article, without having to wade through it all, looking for a summary towards the end. It should comprise a very brief statement – no longer than 100 words – of what you did, the method you used, and what you found.

3 Introduction

In this section, attempt to answer the following questions:
    (a) What is the general nature of the problem?
    (b) What have other people had to say about the problem, and why are their findings open to doubt, ambiguous, or in some way inadequate?
    (c) Why is this particular experiment being undertaken?
    (d) What is your experimental hypothesis – and is it one- or two-tailed? If you like, you can also state the null hypothesis at this point.

4 Method

Use the past tense throughout this section. There are several sub-headings which are commonly used in the 'Method' section. These include:

(a) Subjects
Mention the number of subjects who participated – or 'ran' – in the experiment, their sex, ages and general educational background or occupations. Include any other *relevant* information concerning the subjects here. Were the subjects volunteers, or selected according to some criteria?

(b) Apparatus
If your apparatus has a recognised technical name, state it, and give a very brief description of its purpose; if not, describe it as accurately as possible, using diagrams where necessary.

(c) Procedure

Describe what happened, very carefully, and – **note this** – what *actually* happened, not what should have happened! You should provide enough information for a reader to be able to go away and carry out an exact replication of your experiment.

If the experiment included specific instructions given to the subjects, then put these in this section, as a direct quotation. If the instructions are very long, then write them out on a separate sheet of paper, which is headed 'Appendix I. Instructions to subjects' and put this right at the back of the report. In the 'Procedure' section, state 'The exact instructions which were given to subjects are included in Appendix I.' An appendix is an extra bit, providing information which not everyone might want, but which would certainly be needed by someone who took a serious interest in your findings, and perhaps wished to replicate the experiment precisely.

If the seating arrangement of the experimenter and subject(s), or subject and apparatus, is not straightforward, use diagrams to convey the information. Such diagrams do *not* need to be backed up by long verbal descriptions.

(d) Experimental design

Make a formal statement of the design used in the experiment, and the statistical analysis which is planned. If you decided beforehand which level of significance you would accept as the minimum, then give it here. There should also be reference to all procedures used to identify, isolate or control all variables considered relevant to the study.

5 Results

This section should contain a condensed version of the data you obtained in your experiment. The original, or 'raw' data are those observations which you made during the experiment, and will only be included in this section in unchanged form if they are fairly brief. The reader wants to see fairly swiftly what happened, and so it is the usual practice to put raw data into an appendix at the back, and to include only 'derived' data – such as descriptive summaries, means, standard deviations, etc., often in the form of a table, in this section. Derived data include figures, graphs, statistics and summaries compiled from the raw data. Any or all of these can be given in this section, but the main criterion to be met is that a reader should be able to understand quickly what the results were, without having to read any other part of the report.

It is not correct to include statistical calculations, formulae or details of computation in this section. Again, all this type of clutter should be tucked away in an appendix at the back, where it is available, should a reader wish to refer to it.

It is quite common, and acceptable, to open your 'Results' section with the following statements . . .

'Raw data are included in Appendix I, and statistical calculations in Appendix II. A summary of the mean reaction times obtained from subjects in the experimental and control groups is shown below in table 1. The difference in reaction times between the two groups was significant at the 0.05 level ($t = 2.56$; $df = 10$; independent t test, two-tailed hypothesis) and the null hypothesis was rejected. It was concluded that . . .'

All tables, figures and graphs should have a title, and in the case of diagrams, there should be labels so that the information they convey can be quickly assimilated by the reader. Take care over the detail of whether a figure is a graph, histogram, scattergram or whatever – they are all slightly different.

In the last analysis . . .

Although brevity is the keynote throughout this section, take care to include *all* results (summarised if necessary) to which reference is made in the next section – the 'Discussion'.

6 Discussion

Use the past/present/future tenses as appropriate.

The first question which needs answering is 'To what extent do your results support the experimental hypothesis?' It is normal to start this section off by repeating the main *verbal* findings and conclusions which you gave in the 'Results', but omitting details of the statistical test used, statistic value and *df*. Do your findings suggest any further hypotheses which could be investigated experimentally? Are there any faults in the design of the experiment (which were not evident at the design stage) which could or should be eliminated?

The second question to deal with, if your experimental hypothesis was not supported, is 'Why not?' In this section you can suggest reasons as to why the experiment didn't work, and again, suggest outlines for future experiments which might clear the problem up.

To conclude, and possibly in the form of a brief 'Conclusions' subsection, which must not be confused with the 'Summary' or 'Abstract', make an attempt to provide an answer to the original problem which was described in the 'Introduction', and spell out the ways in which your experiment and findings have moved our knowledge along from that point.

In the 'Discussion' section it is quite acceptable to present conclusions which you have drawn which were *not* anticipated in the original formulation of the problem and its likely outcomes.

7 References

Give detailed references of all work you mention in your report. There are several standard ways to present references, and I am giving just one of them below. If you mention 'Watson (1913)' somewhere in the body of your report (or in an essay), then the reference should appear in the correct place in an alphabetical listing:

Watson, J. B. Psychology as a behaviorist views it. *Psychol. Rev.*, 1913, 20, 158–177

and for the book 'Woodworth and Sheehan (1964)',

Woodworth, R. S., and Sheehan, M. R. *Contemporary schools of psychology.* (3rd ed.) New York: Ronald Press, 1964.

Whichever system of referencing you use, stick to it throughout the whole list. If you quote the results of a survey or experiment from a text book, rather than from the original article, then list the name of the investigator, but follow it with the source of your information:

Goldstein (1957), as reported in Hilgard, E. R., Atkinson, R. C., and Atkinson, R. L. *Introduction to Psychology.* (6th ed.) New York: Harcourt, Brace, Jovanovich, 1975.

Although references seem unnecessary, and are a bore to compile and write out, it is useful to acquire the habit of keeping tabs on information you refer to fairly early in your scientific career. Also, when it comes to revision time, you may well need to find the sources of your material quite rapidly, and it is extremely frustrating to have to waste time searching out long-forgotten items.

144

The language of report writing

Now that we have dealt with the structure of scientific reports, it is time to examine in more detail the language of which they are composed. The following phrases are examples of technical vocabulary commonly used in reports – together with their 'real-life' equivalents.

Introduction

It is generally agreed that . . .	We decided during the coffee break . . .
It has long been known that . . .	I have lost the original reference!
It would appear to be consistent with previously reported findings to speculate that . . .	My excuse for doing this work is . . .
In a pilot study . . .	We started to carry out the experiment, but it was a disaster, and so we were forced to make a fresh start.
A survey showed that . . .	I asked a couple of the secretaries what their views were.

Method

The experimental animals were randomised.	The rats all escaped from their cages one day.
The procedure used was based on that first developed by Smith (1968).	We have just pinched Smith's idea.
Subjects were permitted to familiarise themselves with the task.	It took ages, and many trials, before we realised that the subjects hadn't understood the instructions properly.
Subjects were trained to the appropriate criterion.	I can't remember exactly what the subjects had to do.

Results

Some subjects were found to have unexpectedly long reaction times.	Some subjects went to sleep during this long and boring experiment.
Computer analysis of the data was conducted by Dr Bloggs.	I haven't the faintest idea what he does with my data, but I don't ask questions!
The results shown in table 2 were adjusted to allow for variations arising from errors in the sampling technique.	I fiddled my results.
However, when plotted on a log scale, the effect is apparent.	The last resort in order to present hopeless data in an impressive way.
. . . was nevertheless significant.	. . . was the only minor deviation from complete randomness in the entire experiment.
Typical results are shown.	The best results are shown.

The results show a clear trend in the predicted direction which might be expected to reach significance with a larger sample.

Our supply of subjects dried up,
or,
I couldn't be bothered to run any more.

Nonparametric statistics were felt to be highly appropriate for analysing these data.

We couldn't interpret the complex patterns of statistics which emerged from a computer-run parametric analysis.

Discussion

The results corresponded well with theoretical predictions.

Whilst I was running the experiment I worked out what sounded like good predictions.

It might be argued that . . .

I have a really good answer for this criticism, so shall raise it now.

Further work is required to elucidate this finding.
(Personal communication)

I don't understand the results of the experiment.
(according to this chap I met in the pub . . .)

It is hoped that this study will stimulate further work in the field.

That is about the only respect in which this report might be useful!

These phenomena would seem to be worthy of further investigation.

The whole area is rubbish, but I am committed to it for two more years.

Acknowledgements

I would like to acknowledge the assistance of Bill Smith, and valuable advice from Dr Bloggs.

Bill Smith did all the work, and Bloggs explained what it meant.

. . . and my wife for her speedy and efficient typing.

I had to have the Department Secretary retype her manuscript.

'IT IS GENERALLY AGREED THAT . . .'

Some observations on the diseases of *Brunus edwardii* (species nova)

These extracts are taken from a paper which appeared in *The Veterinary Record*, 1 April 1972. My thanks go to the editor of the journal for kindly agreeing to my reproducing part of the paper in this book. The authors of the paper are D. K. Blackmore, D. G. Owen and C. M. Young. Notice how only the most formal style of writing is used throughout the paper, as is correct for scientific prose.

Summary

The correct specific and generic terminology for *Brunus edwardii* is discussed, and the results given of a survey involving 1599 complete specimens and 539 miscellaneous appendages. These results indicate that primary infectious agents do not occur, and that the species is safe for children to handle. Suggestions as to the future role of the profession in relation to this species are made.

Introduction

For more than a century, the species *Brunus edwardii* has been commonly kept in homes in the UK and other countries in Europe and North America. Although there have been numerous publications concerning the behaviour of individuals (Milne, 1924, 1928; *Daily Express* (numerous editions)), there have been no serious scientific contributions, and a careful search of the literature, using abstracting journals and computerised data retrieval systems, has failed to reveal any comprehensive survey of the diseases of these creatures. A few of the previous publications include references to certain disease syndromes, and Milne (1928) refers to obesity associated with the excessive intake of honey, and to psychological disturbances associated with territorial disputes with Tiggers, Heffalumps and even small children. One publication (Bond, 1958) concerning a certain individual known as Paddington, refers to the animal receiving treatment from medical practitioners without a veterinary qualification. These records emphasise two disturbing factors, firstly, the obvious need for treatment of diseased individuals, and secondly, the infringement of the Veterinary Surgeon's Act of 1966 that would presumably be involved if such animals were treated by any person not on the Veterinary Register.

Commonly-found syndromes included coagulation and clumping of stuffing, resulting in conditions similar to those decribed as 'bumblefoot' and ventral rupture in the pig and cow respectively, alopecia, and ocular conditions which varied from mild squint to intermittent nystagmus and luxation of the eyeball. Micropthalmus and macropthalmus were frequently recorded in animals which had received unsuitable ocular prostheses.

The following case notes illustrate the complexity of both the causes and resulting manifestations of disease in the species.

Case 1. A six-month-old bear, owned by a four-year-old male, was found to be suffering from acute dyslalia, torticollis and loss of one lower limb. The general condition of the animal was good, with a normal pelage. The injury had been the result of disputed ownership. The dumbness was the result of a ruptured acoustic membrane, and complete renewal of the voice box was necessary. This involved laparotomy, removal of the damaged organ from the surrounding viscera, and

Case 1. Torticollis and loss of limb

careful positioning of the replacement so that the acoustic membrane faced ventrally to prevent the development of muffled speech.

Case 2. A young bear owned by a child of six months was found to be suffering from 'soggy ear' when removed from the owner's cot one morning. Oedema of the pinna was a commonly occurring condition in bears belonging to children under 18 months age, who slept with an ear clamped firmly in their mouths. Treatment consisted in removal from the owner, lavage and drying in an airing cupboard.

Case 3. A ten-year-old bear, which had been owned successively by three siblings. The normal yellow coat colour had changed to a dirty grey, there was extensive alopecia which had progressed to 'threadbareness' over the ears, nose and limb extremeties. The axillary and inguinal seams were weak, resulting in an intermittent dislocation of limbs, but there was no herniation of stuffing. Old age, and persistent handling with transport by one limb were the main reasons for the chronic debility, for which there is no satisfactory treatment.

Case 3. Alopecia, discoloration

Case 4. A sixteen-year-old bear, with an asymmetrical expression and obvious emotional disturbance, was found at the back of a cupboard. After the removal of superficial dust, the coat condition was seen to be good, but the animal had a permanent squint, due to careless replacement of the right eye with a shoe button.

Case 4. Lopsided squint

Tracing of the case history revealed that this bear had suffered recurrent ocular prolapse, which had progressed to total rupture of the filamentous orbital attachments, and the loss of the eye. It was hoped that a new owner might be found for this animal, and that with newly-matched eyes, his expression and psychological state might improve.

Case 5. An aged, cobweb-covered bear, found in an attic. Its general condition was poor, with loss of forelimb, and hernation of stuffing. The frontal seam was ruptured, exposing a rusted voice box with helical weakness. The animal was heavily infested with commensals, which included a pair of *Mus musculus* with two generations of young, a total of 23 individuals . . . Treatment of this case included vigorous shaking, dusting with pyrethrum, a stuffing transfusion, and a forelimb graft.

Case 5. Attic bear and mice

Pet ownership surveys have shown that 63.8% households are inhabited by one or more of these animals, and that there is a statistically significant relationship between their population and the number of children in the household. The public health

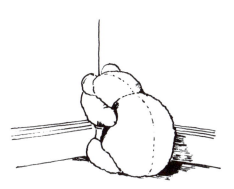

A case of emotional disturbance, hypertension

implications of this fact are obvious, and it is imperative that more be known about their diseases, particularly zoonoses or other conditions which might be associated with their close contact with man . . .

The importance of avoiding the use of colloquial names in scientific contributions has been stressed by Keymer *et al.* (1969), but previous publications have apparently used the term 'teddy bear'. Preliminary studies have suggested that this term might include several different strains, if not species. However, it was found that teddy bears will accept cutaneous, and even limb grafts from other bears without showing signs of rejection. These findings suggest that all teddy bears are genetically homozygous and of the same species. We therefore consider the correct generic and specific terminology to be *Brunus edwardii*.

Materials and methods

(*i*) *Source of material for survey.* A total of 1598 specimens of *Brunus edwardii* was examined. Of the 1600 owners approached, 1599 agreed to examination of their bear, and the majority were able to provide a comprehensive case history. One specimen was eventually unavailable, as it was in quarantine because its owner was affected with rubella.

A further 539 miscellaneous appendages were made available for examination by nurseries, schools and children's hospitals in the London area. These specimens were in a dilapidated condition, but careful grafting restored 136 intact bears, with only one surplus ear, which has been stored in liquid nitrogen for future use.

(*ii*) *Examination technique.* Examinations were carried out as quickly as possible, because many owners were reluctant to be parted from their bears for very long. No restraint was necessary, as the bears showed no apprehension and were obviously used to being handled. An attempt was made to record body temperature, but this was abandoned, as all specimens appeared to be homoiothermic. Each bear was given a thorough external examination, and data were collected on approximate age, weight, condition and colour of coat and physical disabilities. Stuffing and internal condition were assessed by careful palpation. Where necessary, radiographs were taken, and biopsies obtained to identify the stuffing material. Sub-cutaneous and deeper tissues often protruded from superficial abrasions, and where necessary, a small seam incision was made, a sample taken, and the opening sutured with Coates Machine twist 30, using a standard Millwards darning needle. Voice boxes, where present, were tested by percussion and auscultation.

In the last analysis . . .

The psychological state of the bear was assessed by the facial expression, and also by investigating the case history with special reference to the frequency and duration of association with children.

Results of the survey

Classification of the results of the survey carried out on 1598 intact specimens, plus miscellaneous appendages was attempted, but almost all cases were of multi-factorial aetiology, and it was impossible to determine the primary agent. Similar lesions appeared at many sites, making systematic tabulation of results impracticable. No primary pathogens were isolated, and the predominant cause of pathological change was external mechanical trauma, which was either severe and sudden in onset, causing loss of limbs and appendages, or more insidious, giving rise to chronic wear and tear.

Commonly-found syndromes included coagulation and clumping of stuffing, resulting in conditions similar to those described as bumblefoot and ventral rupture.

Discussion

This survey has revealed many facts of interest to both the comparative pathologist and the clinician. It is with considerable relief that it can be recorded that *Brunus edwardii* appears to be resistant to any pathogenic organisms and cannot, therefore be affected by any zoonotic condition. However, this species can be involved in a variety of commensal relationships, as was described in Case 5 . . .

Teddy bears can act as transitory mechanical vectors of human pathogens. Although superficial contamination with rubella virus has no direct effect on the bear, the unskilled treatment of carrier teddies can result in serious secondary disease. Examples found included a singed integument caused by over-heating during decontamination in a domestic oven, and coat discolouration due to treatment with an unsuitable disinfectant.

True diseases of *Brunus edwardii* can therefore be classified as either traumatic or emotional. Acute traumatic conditions, characterised by loss of appendages, are often the result of disputed ownership. Chronic traumatic conditions are usually associated with normal wear and tear, and are not necessarily detrimental, as there appears to be a statistical relationship between the presence of such lesions, the lack of emotional disturbance, and the affection given by the owner.

Emotional disturbances are either apparent or inapparent. Apparent emotional disturbances are recognised by changes in facial expression, and in almost all cases the condition is the result of unskilled remedial surgery. Inapparent emotional disturbances are not fully understood, but seem to be related to the fact that an unloved teddy is an unhappy teddy. Few adults (except perhaps the present authors) have any real affection for the species, and as children mature, their teddy bears may be neglected and relegated to an attic or cupboard, where severe emotional disturbances develop.

The authors consider it significant that *B. edwardii* appears to be classless in both the taxonomic and socio-economic sense.

References

Bond, M. (1958). *A bear called Paddington*. Collins, London.
Milne, A. A. (1924). *When we were very young*. Methuen & Co. Ltd. London.
Milne, A. A. (1928). *The house at Pooh Corner*. Methuen & Co. Ltd. London.

Operation schedules

Lots of small steps.
—No problem!

Operation schedule 1. The mean

Data requirements

Numbers used to calculate a mean must be of at least interval status (see chapter 10).

Example

Six rose bushes bear the following numbers of flowers: 5, 26, 13, 12, 19, 21. The mean number of flowers per bush will be calculated.

Step 1: List the numbers in a vertical column.

5
26
13
12
19
21

Step 2: Add the numbers together.

$5 + 26 + 13 + 12 + 19 + 21 = 96$

Step 3: Count the number of items making up the list, to obtain N.

The list comprises 6 items; $N = 6$.

Step 4: Divide the total of Step 2 by the value of N fouhd in Step 3.

$$\frac{96}{6} = 16$$

The mean number of flowers per bush is **16**.

Abbreviations

The formula for calculating the mean is

$$\frac{\Sigma X}{N},$$

where X = the individual score, N = the total number of scores.

     Σ = the sum of (pronounced 'sigma'),

The symbol $\bar{X}$ (pronounced 'bar X') is often used to represent the mean. If the means of lists which had been labelled A or Y had been found, then the means would be denoted by the symbols $\bar{A}$ and $\bar{Y}$, respectively.

Operation schedule 2. The median

Data requirements

Can be used with all types of numbers, except those of *nominal* status.

Example

The median of the numbers 13, 21, 12, 4, 26, 19.

Step 1: List all the scores in ascending order, in a straight line.

    4   12   13   19   21   26

Step 2: Count the number of items making up the list to determine where the mid-point will lie. It will lie on a whole number if the list comprises an odd number of items, and something-and-a-half if the list is even-numbered.

There are 6 items on the list; the mid-point of 6 is $3\frac{1}{2}$.

Odd-numbered lists only
Step 3: Count along the items from the left-hand side until you arrive at the number lying in the position found to be at the mid-point in Step 2. *This is the median.*

Even-numbered lists only
Step 3: Count along the list until you arrive at the item which is in the position of the number with the $\frac{1}{2}$ added on.

    4   12   13

13 is in the third position.

Step 4: Take the value arrived at in Step 3, and add to it the value of the next number to the right from the original list. Add the two numbers together and divide by two. *This gives the median.*

$$\frac{13 + 19}{2} = \frac{32}{2} = 16$$

Check: If Steps 3 and 4 are re-calculated, but the counting started on the right-hand side rather than the left, the median should have the same value.

Abbreviations

As the median is obtained by counting, no symbols are used to describe its computation. The symbol for the median itself is *Md*.

Operation schedule 3. The mean deviation

Data requirements

Scores must be of at least interval status.

Example

The mean deviation of the numbers 5, 26, 13, 12, 19, 21.

Step 1: Count the number of items on the list, to obtain N.

There are 6 items on the list, and so $N = 6$.

Step 2: Find the mean of the numbers.

$$\frac{5 + 26 + \cdots + 21}{6} = \frac{96}{6} = 16$$

Step 3: Compare each score with the mean. Subtract whichever value of the two is smaller from the larger. Record a value of 0 when a score has the same value as the mean.

$$16 - 5 = 11 \quad 16 - 13 = 3 \quad 19 - 16 = 3$$
$$26 - 16 = 10 \quad 16 - 12 = 4 \quad 21 - 16 = 5$$

Step 4: Add together the differences found in Step 3.

$$11 + 10 + 3 + 4 + 3 + 5 = 36$$

Step 5: Divide the value obtained in Step 4 by the value found in Step 1.

$$\frac{36}{6} = 6$$

The mean deviation for the set of scores is **6**.

Formula

$$\frac{\Sigma|X - \bar{X}|}{N}$$

where X = the individual score $\quad$ | | = find the difference
$\quad\quad\quad \bar{X}$ = the mean for all the scores $\quad \Sigma$ = the sum of
$\quad\quad\quad N$ = the number of scores in the list

Operation schedule 4. The standard deviation

Data requirements

Scores must be of at least interval status.

Example

The standard deviation of the numbers 18, 20, 22, 24, 26.

Step 1: Count the number of items on the list, to obtain N.

There are 5 scores making up the list, and so $N = 5$.

Step 2: Find the mean for the scores.

$$\frac{18 + 20 + 22 + 24 + 26}{5} = \frac{110}{5} = 22$$

Step 3: Subtract the mean (Step 2) from every observation.

$$18 - 22 = -4 \quad 22 - 22 = 0 \quad 26 - 22 = +4$$
$$20 - 22 = -2 \quad 24 - 22 = +2$$

Step 4: Square each of the differences obtained in Step 3.

$$(-4)^2 = 16, (-2)^2 = 4, (0)^2 = 0, (+2)^2 = 4, (+4)^2 = 16$$

Step 5: Obtain the *sum of the squares* by adding together all the squared differences obtained in Step 4.

$$16 + 4 + 0 + 4 + 16 = 40$$

Step 6: Subtract 1 from the number of observations in the group (Step 1).

$$5 - 1 = 4$$

Step 7: Divide the sum of squares (Step 5) by the value found in Step 6, to obtain the *variance estimate*.

$$\frac{40}{4} = 10$$

Step 8: Take the square root of the variance estimate, found in Step 7.

$$\sqrt{10} = \textbf{3.16}$$

Operation schedules

Note

These steps are the ones normally followed in obtaining a standard deviation when a *sample* is used. They will give a slightly larger value than that obtained by the method appropriate for a *complete population*, and which is rarely used. To obtain the standard deviation of a complete population, instead of subtracting the value of 1 from the number of items on the list (Step 6 above), you simply divide the sum of squares by the actual number of items, N, making up the list (Step 1).

Formulae

(a) for a sample estimate

$$\sqrt{\left(\frac{\Sigma(X - \bar{X})^2}{N - 1}\right)}$$

where X = the individual score
$\bar{X}$ = the mean of the scores

(b) for the population value

$$\sqrt{\left(\frac{\Sigma(X - \bar{X})^2}{N}\right)}$$

N = the number of scores used
Σ = the sum of

Operation schedule 5. The standard deviation (alternative method)

It is more convenient to use this method of obtaining the standard deviation when you have large sets of numbers, or when the mean is an 'awkward' number – for instance with several decimal places. The method will give precisely the same result as that given in schedule 4.

Example

The standard deviation of the sample 18, 20, 22, 24, 26.

Step 1: Count the number of items on the list, to obtain N.

There are 5 items on the list, and so $N = 5$ for this sample.

Step 2: Find the total of the scores.

$18 + 20 + 22 + 24 + 26 = 110$

Step 3: Square each of the original observations.

$18^2 = 324, \ 20^2 = 400, \ 22^2 = 484, \ 24^2 = 576, \ 26^2 = 676$

Step 4: Add together the squares obtained in Step 3, to get the *uncorrected sum of squares*.

$324 + 400 + 484 + 576 + 676 = 2460$

Step 5: Take the total of the scores (Step 2), and square it.

$110^2 = 12\,100$

Step 6: Divide the squared total (Step 5) by the number of items in the list (Step 1), to get the *correction term*.

$\dfrac{12\,100}{5} = 2420$

Step 7: Subtract the correction term (Step 6) from the uncorrected sum of squares (Step 4), to obtain the *corrected sum of squares*.

$2460 - 2420 = 40$

Step 8: Divide the corrected sum of squares (Step 7) by the number of observations (Step 1) minus 1, or the number of observations in the case of numbers comprising a population rather than a sample. This gives the *variance estimate* or the *variance* respectively.

$$\frac{40}{5-1} = \frac{40}{4} = 10$$

Step 9: Take the square root of the value obtained in Step 8.

$$\sqrt{10} = 3.16$$

The value of the standard deviation for the sample is **3.16**.

Formulae

(a) for a sample estimate

$$\sqrt{\left(\frac{\Sigma X^2 - \dfrac{(\Sigma X)^2}{N}}{N-1}\right)}$$

where X = the individual score

ΣX^2 = the sum of the squared scores

$(\Sigma X)^2$ = the square of the sum of the scores

(b) for a population value

$$\sqrt{\left(\frac{\Sigma X^2 - \dfrac{(\Sigma X)^2}{N}}{N}\right)}$$

ΣX = the sum of the scores

N = the number of scores used

Operation schedule 6. How to rank sets of scores

The purpose of ranking is to give your scores a number, according to their size. It is rather like 'numbering off', with the smallest score normally given the number 1.

Example

Rank the scores 10, 15, 13, 22, 21, 9, 22, 14, 8, 14, 12, 17, 22, 22, 9, 14.

Step 1: On a piece of scrap paper, write the scores down in order of size, and starting off with the smallest at the left-hand side.

8 9 9 10 12 13 14 14 14 15 17 21 22 22 22 22

Step 2: Count the number of scores which are to be ranked.

The group comprises 16 scores.

Step 3: Below each score, write a number. Start at the left with number 1 and proceed to number off each score until you finish with the final score at the right-hand side. The final score should have the same number as that found in Step 2.

8 9 9 10 12 13 14 14 14 15 17 21 22 22 22 22
1 2 3 4 5 6 7 8 9 10 11 12 13 14 15 16

Step 4: Look along the top line of the numbers for any which are the same. These are called *tied*, and their ranks, on the bottom line, must reflect the fact.

There are two scores of 9, three of 14 and four of 22.

Step 5: If there are two numbers in a tie, then the rank given to these two will be halfway between; i.e. the ranks will not be a whole number, but something-and-a-half. Three tied numbers will each take the value of the middle rank, i.e. a whole number, as will any uneven numbered group of tied scores.

The two values of 9 tie for ranks 2 and 3, and each will take the value $2\frac{1}{2}$. The three values of 14, occupying ranks 7, 8 and 9, will each take rank 8. The four values of 22, taking ranks 13, 14, 15 and 16, will each have the rank value of $14\frac{1}{2}$.

Operation schedules

Step 6: When all the ranks are sorted out, arrange the scores and the ranks in two vertical columns, headed 'Score' and 'Rank' respectively.

Score	Rank
8	1
9	$2\frac{1}{2}$
9	$2\frac{1}{2}$
10	4
12	5
13	6
14	8
14	8
14	8
15	10
17	11
21	12
22	$14\frac{1}{2}$
22	$14\frac{1}{2}$
22	$14\frac{1}{2}$
22	$14\frac{1}{2}$

Hint

In several nonparametric tests and Spearman's *rho* calculations you have to work with the ranks, rather than the actual scores. It is easy to get ranks and scores muddled, and particularly when you are working with more than one set of scores. You can avoid this by writing the ranks out in a different coloured pen, so that they can be distinguished at a glance.

Operation schedule 7. The Wilcoxon matched-pairs signed ranks test

Data requirements

Scores must be paired off in some way, and of at least ordinal status.

Example

The Wilcoxon test can be carried out on the rating scores obtained for the two brands of washing up liquid, Gresego and Kwikclene (see pages 68–70). The null hypothesis (H_0) is that

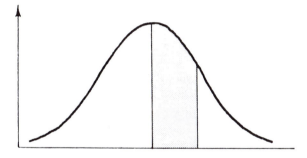

Table S1. Percentage area under the standard normal curve from the mean 0 to *z* scores

z	0.00	0.01	0.02	0.03	0.04	0.05	0.06	0.07	0.08	0.09
0.0	00.00	00.40	00.80	01.20	01.60	01.99	02.39	02.79	03.19	03.59
0.1	03.98	04.38	04.78	05.17	05.57	05.96	06.36	06.75	07.14	07.53
0.2	07.93	08.32	08.71	09.10	09.48	09.87	10.26	10.64	11.03	11.41
0.3	11.79	12.17	12.55	12.93	13.31	13.68	14.06	14.43	14.80	15.17
0.4	15.54	15.91	16.28	16.64	17.00	17.36	17.72	18.08	18.44	18.79
0.5	19.15	19.50	19.85	20.19	20.54	20.88	21.23	21.57	21.90	22.24
0.6	22.57	22.91	23.24	23.57	23.89	24.22	24.54	24.86	25.17	25.49
0.7	25.80	26.11	26.42	26.73	27.04	27.34	27.64	27.94	28.23	28.52
0.8	28.81	29.10	29.39	29.67	29.95	30.23	30.51	30.78	31.06	31.33
0.9	31.59	31.86	32.12	32.38	32.64	32.89	33.15	33.40	33.65	33.89
1.0	34.13	34.38	34.61	34.85	35.08	35.31	35.54	35.77	35.99	36.21
1.1	36.43	36.65	36.86	37.08	37.29	37.49	37.70	37.90	38.10	38.30
1.2	38.49	38.69	38.88	39.07	39.25	39.44	39.62	39.80	39.97	40.15
1.3	40.32	40.49	40.66	40.82	40.99	41.15	41.31	41.47	41.62	41.77
1.4	41.92	42.07	42.22	42.36	42.51	42.65	42.79	42.92	43.06	43.19
1.5	43.32	43.45	43.57	43.70	43.82	43.94	44.06	44.18	44.29	44.41
1.6	44.52	44.63	44.74	44.84	44.95	45.05	45.15	45.25	45.35	45.45
1.7	45.54	45.64	45.73	45.82	45.91	45.99	46.08	46.16	46.25	46.33
1.8	46.41	46.49	46.56	46.64	46.71	46.78	46.86	46.93	46.99	47.06
1.9	47.13	47.19	47.26	47.32	47.38	47.44	47.50	47.56	47.61	47.67
2.0	47.72	47.78	47.83	47.88	47.93	47.98	48.03	48.08	48.12	48.17
2.1	48.21	48.26	48.30	48.34	48.38	48.42	48.46	48.50	48.54	48.57
2.2	48.61	48.64	48.68	48.71	48.75	48.78	48.81	48.84	48.87	48.90
2.3	48.93	48.96	48.98	49.01	49.04	49.06	49.09	49.11	49.13	49.16
2.4	49.18	49.20	49.22	49.25	49.27	49.29	49.31	49.32	49.34	49.36
2.5	49.38	49.40	49.41	49.43	49.45	49.46	49.48	49.49	49.51	49.52
2.6	49.53	49.55	49.56	49.57	49.59	49.60	49.61	49.62	49.63	49.64
2.7	49.65	49.66	49.67	49.68	49.69	49.70	49.71	49.72	49.73	49.74
2.8	49.74	49.75	49.76	49.77	49.77	49.78	49.79	49.79	49.80	49.81
2.9	49.81	49.82	49.82	49.83	49.84	49.84	49.85	49.85	49.86	49.86
3.0	49.87	49.87	49.87	49.88	49.88	49.89	49.89	49.89	49.90	49.90

Source: F. C. Powell, *Cambridge mathematical and statistical tables*, page 71, 1976. Cambridge University Press.

the two sets of scores do not differ, and the experimental hypothesis (H_1 or H_A), is that Gresego gives better results than Kwikclene.

Subject	Rating		Subject	Rating	
	Gresego	Kwikclene		Gresego	Kwikclene
1	8	5	6	7	6
2	7	5	7	9	5
3	9	2	8	6	5
4	7	6	9	5	6
5	8	9			

Step 1: The data will be paired off, but in doing so, it does not matter which column comes first. Subtract each number in the first column from its partner in the second. Record the differences, being sure to note the sign.

$8 - 5 = +3, 7 - 5 = +2, \ldots, 5 - 6 = -1$

The differences are: $+3, +2, +7, +1, -1, +1, +4, +1, -1$

Step 2: Rank the differences according to size, and giving the smallest difference rank 1. Do not rank any values of 0 which occur. Ignore the signs during the ranking procedure. (See schedule 6 for ranking instructions.)

Differences	+3	+2	+7	+1	−1	+1	+4	+1	−1
Ranks	7	6	9	3	3	3	8	3	3

Step 3: Add the *ranks* for all the differences which are positive, and all the negative differences. Keep the two totals separate.

Positive difference ranks $7 + 6 + 9 + 3 + 3 + 8 + 3 = 39$
Negative difference ranks $3 + 3 = 6$

Step 4: Whichever total of the two obtained in Step 3 is the smaller is the value of the test statistic T.

$T = \mathbf{6}$

Step 4: To determine N, in order to decide whether a given value of T is significant using table S2, count the number of pairs of scores used, but subtract any pairs whose difference was found to be 0 in Step 1.

There are 9 pairs of scores, and no values of 0. $N = 9$.

Operation schedule 7a. Evaluation of Wilcoxon's *T* statistic

Example

The data analysed using Wilcoxon's test, in schedule 7 will be evaluated for significance, using table S2. From the data, $T = 6$, and $N = 9$.

Step 1: Decide whether the experimental hypothesis (H_1) was a one-tailed or two-tailed hypothesis.

In the experiment on washing up liquid, it had been hypothesised that scores from Gresego would be higher than those from Kwikclene. Therefore H_1 is a one-tailed hypothesis.

Table S2. Critical values of *T* for the Wilcoxon matched-pairs signed ranks test. *T* must be **equal to or less than** the stated value to be significant

	Level of significance for one-tailed test					Level of significance for one-tailed test			
	0.05	0.025	0.01	0.005		0.05	0.025	0.01	0.005
	Level of significance for two-tailed test					Level of significance for two-tailed test			
N	0.10	0.05	0.02	0.01	*N*	0.10	0.05	0.02	0.01
5	1	—	—	—	28	130	117	101	92
6	2	1	—	—	29	141	127	111	100
7	4	2	0	—	30	152	137	120	109
8	6	4	2	0	31	163	148	130	118
9	8	6	3	2	32	175	159	141	128
10	11	8	5	3	33	188	171	151	138
11	14	11	7	5	34	201	183	162	149
12	17	14	10	7	35	214	195	174	160
13	21	17	13	10	36	228	208	186	171
14	26	21	16	13	37	242	222	198	183
15	30	25	20	16	38	256	235	211	195
16	36	30	24	19	39	271	250	224	208
17	41	35	28	23	40	287	264	238	221
18	47	40	33	28	41	303	279	252	234
19	54	46	38	32	42	319	295	267	248
20	60	52	43	37	43	336	311	281	262
21	68	59	49	43	44	353	327	297	277
22	75	66	56	49	45	371	343	313	292
23	83	73	62	55	46	389	361	329	307
24	92	81	69	61	47	408	379	345	323
25	101	90	77	68	48	427	397	362	339
26	110	98	85	76	49	446	415	380	356
27	120	107	93	84	50	466	434	398	373

Source: F. Wilcoxon and R. A. Wilcox, *Some rapid approximate statistical procedures*, page 28, table 2, 1964. New York: Lederle Laboratories. Reproduced with the permission of American Cyanamid Company

Step 2: Locate the appropriate value for *N* in table S2, using the column headed *N*.

Opposite *N* = 9, you should read the values 8 6 3 2.

Step 3: Move along the row until you arrive at the tabled value which is equal to or just larger than the value of *T* which you have just obtained.

The second value of 6 is equal to the *T* just obtained.

Step 4: Read the appropriate significance level off from the top of the column reached in Step 3. Take the one- or two-tailed probability level stated, according to the decision made in Step 1.

The obtained value of 6 is significant at the 0.025 level for a one-tailed hypothesis.

Step 5: State the conclusion.

The results were significant at the $p = 0.025$ level, using Wilcoxon's test ($N = 9$, $T = 6$; one-tailed hypothesis). Therefore the null hypothesis can be rejected, and it is concluded that the performance of Gresego was superior to that of Kwikclene.

Note

If the obtained value of T falls between tabled values, both of which are significant, then the most conservative (i.e. the *least* significant, and with the *highest* value of p) is quoted.

Operation schedule 8: The sign test

Data requirements

The scores must be paired off in some way, but can be the simplest type of data (i.e. nominal).

Example

The data derived from the washing up experiment and analysed in schedule 7 will be used once more.

Subject	Rating		Subject	Rating	
	Gresego	Kwikclene		Gresego	Kwikclene
1	8	5	6	7	6
2	7	5	7	9	5
3	9	2	8	6	5
4	7	6	9	5	6
5	8	9			

Step 1: Put the data into a table, as above. It does not matter which column of scores comes first. Mentally subtract each value in the second column from its partner in the first. If the answer is positive, give the pairs a plus ($+$) sign, and if negative, a minus ($-$) sign. Note 0 if the two values are equal.

S	Gresego	Kwikclene	Sign	S	Gresego	Kwikclene	Sign
1	8	5	$+$	6	7	6	$+$
2	7	5	$+$	7	9	5	$+$
3	9	2	$+$	8	6	5	$+$
4	7	6	$+$	9	5	6	$-$
5	8	9	$-$				

Step 2: Count the number of times the less frequent sign occurs, to obtain the statistic *S*.

The minus signs are less frequent, and occur twice. So $S = 2$.

Step 3: Count the total number of pluses and minuses, to obtain *N*. (Note that any differences of 0 will not be included in *N*.)

There are 9 signs, and so $N = 9$.

Step 4: Decide whether your test comprises a one- or two-tailed test.

The hypothesis under consideration is a one-tailed hypothesis.

Table S3. Critical values of *S* for the sign test. *S* must be **equal to or less than** the stated value to be significant

	Level of significance for one-tailed test				
	0.05	0.025	0.01	0.005	0.0005
N					
	Level of significance for two-tailed test				
	0.10	0.05	0.02	0.01	0.001
5	0	—	—	—	—
6	0	0	—	—	—
7	0	0	0	—	—
8	1	0	0	0	—
9	1	1	0	0	—
10	1	1	0	0	—
11	2	1	1	0	0
12	2	2	1	1	0
13	3	2	1	1	0
14	3	2	2	1	0
15	3	3	2	2	1
16	4	3	2	2	1
17	4	4	3	2	1
18	5	4	3	3	1
19	5	4	4	3	2
20	5	5	4	3	2
25	7	7	6	5	4
30	10	9	8	7	5
35	12	11	10	9	7

Step 5: Use table S3 to evaluate the statistic *S* (from Step 2), in conjunction with *N* (determined in Step 3). The table is used in just the same manner as table S2 for the Wilcoxon test (see schedule 7a).

Opposite the value 9, we read 1, 1, 0, 0, —. Our obtained value of $S = 2$ exceeds all these tabled values, and so we conclude that as the probability exceeds that given for the 0.05 level, one-tailed test, our results are not significant.

Step 6: State the conclusion.

The results of the analysis were nonsignificant ($S = 2$, $N = 9$, sign test), and so the null hypothesis cannot be rejected. It is concluded that the two washing up liquids do not differ in their performance.

Operation schedule 9. The Mann–Whitney U test

Data requirements

Scores need to be of at least ordinal status.

Example

The results gathered whilst investigating a new memorising technique, described in chapter 1, will be used for analysis. They are:

Set 1:   30, 35, 45, 50, 75, 80 (the unaided group)
Set 2:   45, 50, 58, 62, 69, 70 (the aided group)

The experimental hypothesis was two-tailed, and the null hypothesis states that there will be no difference between the two sets of scores.

Step 1: Put the two sets of scores into two vertical columns, with a good gap between them. If one of the lists is smaller than the other, put it first, and call it 'list A'. If the lists are the same size, then it doesn't matter which comes first. Call the second list 'list B'.

List A	List B
30	45
35	50
45	58
50	62
75	69
80	70

Step 2: Count the number of scores in each list, to obtain N_A and N_B. Then multiply the two values together. This gives $N_A N_B$.

$N_A = 6$, $N_B = 6$; $N_A N_B = 6 \times 6 = 36$

Step 3: Take the number of scores in list A, and add the value of 1.

$6 + 1 = 7$

Step 4: Multiply the value found in Step 3 by the number of scores in list A, and divide the answer by 2.

$$\frac{7 \times 6}{2} = \frac{42}{2} = 21$$

Step 5: Rank all the numbers in both groups (see schedule 6 for ranking procedure), **taking both sets of numbers together**, and giving the smallest score rank 1. Write the ranks out in two more columns, headed R_A and R_B, and put each to the immediate right of the original lists of scores A and B.

List A	R_A	List B	R_B
30	1	45	$3\frac{1}{2}$
35	2	50	$5\frac{1}{2}$
45	$3\frac{1}{2}$	58	7
50	$5\frac{1}{2}$	62	8
75	11	69	9
80	12	70	10

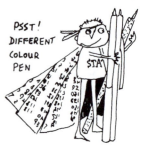

PSST!
DIFFERENT
COLOUR
PEN

Step 6: Add the **ranks** which were given to the items on list *A* (i.e. R_A)

$1 + 2 + 3\frac{1}{2} + 5\frac{1}{2} + 11 + 12 = 35$

Step 7: Add the value found in Step 2 to that found in Step 4, and subtract the value of Step 6.

$36 + 21 - 35 = 22$

Step 8: Subtract the value of Step 7 from the result of Step 2.

$36 - 22 = 14$

Step 9: The values of Steps 7 and 8 give two values for the statistics *U* and *U'* (pronounced 'U prime'). The smaller value will be *U*, and the larger *U'*.

$U = 14$ and $U' = 22$

Step 10: Use the two values of N_A and N_B, found in Step 2, in conjunction with table S4 (overleaf), to determine whether the obtained value of *U* is significant. If *U* is equal to or smaller than the critical values listed, then the null hypothesis can be rejected. Two significance levels are given in the table, for the 0.05 and 0.01 probabilities (two-tailed), and the 0.025 and 0.005 probabilities (one-tailed tests).

Looking in the table at the point where $N_A = 6$ and $N_B = 6$ intersect, we read off the two critical values of 5 and 2. Our value of *U* (14) exceeds both numbers, and so we cannot reject the null hypothesis.

Step 11: State the conclusion.

The results of the analysis were nonsignificant ($U = 14$, $N_A = N_B = 6$; Mann–Whitney *U* test), and so the null hypothesis cannot be rejected. It is concluded that the scores obtained from subjects who were using the memory aid do not differ from those obtained by subjects without the aid.

Note

A useful check is to rework all the calculations, but call the original list *A*, list *B*. You should obtain precisely the same values for *U* and *U'*. Again, the smaller of the two values is labelled *U*, and evaluated.

Formulae

The formula for *U* is *either*

$$N_A N_B + \frac{N_A(N_A + 1)}{2} - \Sigma R_A$$

$$or\ N_A N_B + \frac{N_B(N_B + 1)}{2} - \Sigma R_B$$

where N_A = the number of items in list *A*
N_B = the number of items in list *B*
R_A = the sum of the ranks given to items in list *A*
R_B = the sum of the ranks given to items in list *B*

Operation schedules

Table S4. Critical values of U for the Mann–Whitney test. For each value of N_A and N_B there are two numbers. The top one is the value of U which **must not be exceeded** for significance at the 0.005 level for a one-tailed test (0.01, two-tailed test); the lower one gives the value for the 0.025 level for a one-tailed test (0.05, two-tailed)

N_B	1	2	3	4	5	6	7	8	9	10	11	12	13	14	15	16	17	18	19	20
N_A																				
2	—	—	—	—	—	—	—	—	—	—	—	—	—	—	—	—	—	—	0	0
	—	—	—	—	—	—	—	0	0	0	0	1	1	1	1	1	2	2	2	2
3	—	—	—	—	—	—	—	—	0	0	0	1	1	1	2	2	2	2	3	3
	—	—	—	—	0	1	1	2	2	3	3	4	4	5	5	6	6	7	7	8
4	—	—	—	—	—	0	0	1	1	2	2	3	3	4	5	5	6	6	7	8
	—	—	—	0	1	2	3	4	4	5	6	7	8	9	10	11	11	12	13	14
5	—	—	—	—	0	1	1	2	3	4	5	6	7	7	8	9	10	11	12	13
	—	—	0	1	2	3	5	6	7	8	9	11	12	13	14	15	17	18	19	20
6	—	—	—	0	1	2	3	4	5	6	7	9	10	11	12	13	15	16	17	18
	—	—	1	2	3	5	6	8	10	11	13	14	16	17	19	21	22	24	25	27
7	—	—	—	0	1	3	4	6	7	9	10	12	13	15	16	18	19	21	22	24
	—	—	1	3	5	6	8	10	12	14	16	18	20	22	24	26	28	30	32	34
8	—	—	—	1	2	4	6	7	9	11	13	15	17	18	20	22	24	26	28	30
	—	0	2	4	6	8	10	13	15	17	19	22	24	26	29	31	34	36	38	41
9	—	—	0	1	3	5	7	9	11	13	16	18	20	22	24	27	29	31	33	36
	—	0	2	4	7	10	12	15	17	20	23	26	28	31	34	37	39	42	45	48
10	—	—	0	2	4	6	9	11	13	16	18	21	24	26	29	31	34	37	39	42
	—	0	3	5	8	11	14	17	20	23	26	29	33	36	39	42	45	48	52	55
11	—	—	0	2	5	7	10	13	16	18	21	24	27	30	33	36	39	42	45	48
	—	0	3	6	9	13	16	19	23	26	30	33	37	40	44	47	51	55	58	62
12	—	—	1	3	6	9	12	15	18	21	24	27	31	34	37	41	44	47	51	54
	—	1	4	7	11	14	18	22	26	29	33	37	41	45	49	53	57	61	65	69
13	—	—	1	3	7	10	13	17	20	24	27	31	34	38	42	45	49	53	57	60
	—	1	4	8	12	16	20	24	28	33	37	41	45	50	54	59	63	67	72	76
14	—	—	1	4	7	11	15	18	22	26	30	34	38	42	46	50	54	58	63	67
	—	1	5	9	13	17	22	26	31	36	40	45	50	55	59	64	69	74	78	83
15	—	—	2	5	8	12	16	20	24	29	33	37	42	46	51	55	60	64	69	73
	—	1	5	10	14	19	24	29	34	39	44	49	54	59	64	70	75	80	85	90
16	—	—	2	5	9	13	18	22	27	31	36	41	45	50	55	60	65	70	74	79
	—	1	6	11	15	21	26	31	37	42	47	53	59	64	70	75	81	86	92	98
17	—	—	2	6	10	15	19	24	29	34	39	44	49	54	60	65	70	75	81	86
	—	2	6	11	17	22	28	34	39	45	51	57	63	69	75	81	87	93	99	105
18	—	—	2	6	11	16	21	26	31	37	42	47	53	58	64	70	75	81	87	92
	—	2	7	12	18	24	30	36	42	48	55	61	67	74	80	86	93	99	106	112
19	—	0	3	7	12	17	22	28	33	39	45	51	57	63	69	74	81	87	93	99
	—	2	7	13	19	25	32	38	45	52	58	65	72	78	85	92	99	106	113	119
20	—	0	3	8	13	18	24	30	36	42	48	54	60	67	73	79	86	92	99	105
	—	2	8	14	20	27	34	41	48	55	62	69	76	83	90	98	105	112	119	127

Source: J. G. Snodgrass, *The numbers game*, table C.7, 1978. Oxford University Press

Operation schedule 10. The *t* test for related samples

Data requirements

1 The pairs of scores must be related to each other.
2 The scores must be of at least interval status.
3 The scores in each group must be normally distributed.
4 The two sets of scores must have similar variances.

Example

A family of hares challenges a family of tortoises to a race. The tortoises agree, provided that the hares wear lead boots. It so happens that each family comprises eight individuals; the parents and one grandparent, children aged 7, 6, 5, 3 years, and baby. Thus individuals can be paired off for statistical comparison purposes. The tortoises also stipulated that performance for both families taken as a whole should be used for judging purposes, not, for instance, a count-up of the number of winners in each family. The time to complete the course is measured in hours and minutes, but as the adjudicator, Statman, isn't too good with a time clock, it is decided to round each time up to the nearest complete hour. No one stated who the likely winners would be; the hypothesis is thus a two-tailed one. The results appear overleaf.

Operation schedules

Individual	Hare times (hr)	Tortoise times (hr)
Granny	15	14
Dad	4	4
Mum	9	10
Offspring 1	9	8
Offspring 2	10	10
Offspring 3	10	9
Offspring 4	12	10
Baby	17	15

Step 1: Count the number of pairs of scores involved. This gives N.

There are 8 pairs of scores. $N = 8$.

Step 2: Subtract 1 from the value of N (Step 1). This gives the *df*.

$$df = 8 - 1 = 7$$

Step 3: Multiply the values from Steps 1 and 2 together.

$$8 \times 7 = 56$$

Step 4: Find the mean for each set of scores.

$$\text{Hare mean time} = \frac{15 + 4 + 9 + 9 + 10 + 10 + 12 + 17}{8} = \frac{86}{8} = 10.75 \text{ hr}$$

$$\text{Tortoise mean time} = \frac{14 + 4 + 10 + 8 + 10 + 9 + 10 + 15}{8} = \frac{80}{8} = 10 \text{ hr}$$

Step 5: Subtract the smaller of the two values found in Step 4 from the larger, to give the difference between the two means.

$$10.75 - 10 = 0.75$$

Step 6: Subtract each score in the second column from its partner in the first. Note the signs $(+ \text{ or } -)$.

$15 - 14 = +1$	$10 - 10 = 0$
$4 - 4 = 0$	$10 - 9 = +1$
$9 - 10 = -1$	$12 - 10 = +2$
$9 - 8 = +1$	$17 - 15 = +2$

Step 7: Square each difference found in Step 6, and total the values.

$$1^2 + 0^2 + (-1)^2 + \cdots + 2^2 + 2^2 = 1 + 0 + 1 + 1 + 0 + 1 + 4 + 4 = 12$$

Step 8: Add up the differences found in Step 6, **taking sign into account**.

$$1 + 0 + (-1) + 1 + 0 + 1 + 2 + 2 = 6$$

Step 9: Square the value found in Step 8, and divide by N (Step 1).

$$\frac{6 \times 6}{8} = 4.5$$

Step 10: Subtract the value found in Step 9 from that of Step 7, and divide by the value which was found in Step 3.

$$\frac{12 - 4.5}{56} = \frac{7.5}{56} = 0.1339$$

168

Step 11: Take the square root of the value obtained in Step 10.

$\sqrt{0.1339} = 0.366$

Step 12: Divide the value of Step 5 (the difference between the two means) by that found in Step 11. This gives the value of *t*.

$$t = \frac{0.75}{0.366} = 2.049$$

Step 13: Find the significance of *t*, using table S5 (overleaf), and the *df* obtained in Step 2. The obtained *t* must exceed the values stated on the table for significance at the various probability levels.

Opposite *df* = 7, we read the values 1.895, 2.365, 2.998, 3.499, and 5.408. Our value of 2.049 exceeds the first value, which is significant at the 0.05 level **for a one-tailed test only**. Although the hares immediately claimed that all along they had known that *they* would win, and so a one-tailed evaluation was appropriate, Statman ruled that in the absence of a written statement beforehand, the hypothesis was two-tailed. So the null hypothesis could not be rejected; a draw was declared and everyone retired to the Bull and Bush, exhausted!

Note

The tortoises were sorry that they had stipulated that family times should be taken as a whole. Although the hares were sickened over their failure to establish a one-tailed hypothesis, the tortoises were equally dismayed, during the 'post-mortem', to realise that when matched animals were compared, their family could boast five winning times, as opposed to the hares' one winning time!

Formula

$$t = \frac{|\bar{X} - \bar{Y}|}{\sqrt{\dfrac{\Sigma D^2 - \dfrac{(\Sigma D)^2}{N}}{N(N-1)}}}$$

where $\bar{X}$ = the mean of the first list

$\bar{Y}$ = the mean of the second list

D = the difference between each pair of *X* and *Y* scores

N = the number of pairs of scores

$| \; |$ = the difference

ΣD^2 = the squared differences, totalled

$(\Sigma D)^2$ = the differences, totalled then squared

Take care not to confuse these.

169

Operation schedules

Table S5. Critical values of *t*. *t* must be **equal to or more than** the stated value to be significant

df	Level of significance for one-tailed test				
	0.05	0.025	0.01	0.005	0.0005
	Level of significance for two-tailed test				
	0.10	0.05	0.02	0.01	0.001
1	6.314	12.71	31.82	63.66	636.6
2	2.920	4.303	6.969	9.925	31.6
3	2.353	3.182	4.541	5.841	12.92
4	2.132	2.776	3.747	4.604	8.610
5	2.015	2.571	3.365	4.032	6.869
6	1.943	2.447	3.143	3.707	5.959
7	1.895	2.365	2.998	3.499	5.408
8	1.860	2.306	2.896	3.355	5.041
9	1.833	2.262	2.821	3.250	4.781
10	1.812	2.228	2.764	3.169	4.587
11	1.796	2.201	2.718	3.106	4.437
12	1.782	2.179	2.681	3.055	4.318
13	1.771	2.160	2.650	3.012	4.221
14	1.761	2.145	2.624	2.977	4.140
15	1.753	2.131	2.602	2.947	4.073
16	1.746	2.120	2.583	2.921	4.015
17	1.740	2.110	2.567	2.898	3.965
18	1.734	2.101	2.552	2.878	3.922
19	1.729	2.093	2.539	2.861	3.883
20	1.725	2.086	2.528	2.845	3.850
21	1.721	2.080	2.518	2.831	3.819
22	1.717	2.074	2.508	2.819	3.792
23	1.714	2.069	2.500	2.807	3.767
24	1.711	2.064	2.492	2.797	3.745
25	1.708	2.060	2.485	2.787	3.725
26	1.706	2.056	2.479	2.779	3.707
27	1.703	2.052	2.473	2.771	3.690
28	1.701	2.048	2.467	2.763	3.674
29	1.699	2.045	2.462	2.756	3.659
30	1.697	2.042	2.457	2.750	3.646
40	1.684	2.021	2.423	2.704	3.551
60	1.671	2.000	2.390	2.660	3.460
120	1.658	1.980	2.358	2.617	3.372
240	1.645	1.960	2.326	2.576	3.291

Source: Powell, page 72

Operation schedule 11. The *t* test for unrelated samples

Data requirements

1 The scores must be of at least interval status.
2 The scores in each group must be normally distributed.
3 The two sets of scores must have similar variances.

Example

A driver is able to follow two routes home, but is unsure which is the quicker, and so records his journey time each day. On alternate weeks he follows the Spaghetti Junction Special route (S) and the Traffic Light Trail (T) route, and obtains a mean score for the week. He started and finished with an S week, thus getting an uneven number of times for comparison. The null hypothesis states that there is no difference in time between the two journey speeds. The data, in minutes, are given below.

Week	Mean S route times (min)	Week	Mean T route times (min)
1	32	2	24
3	35	4	28
5	36	6	30
7	37	8	32
9	36	10	35
11	42		

Step 1: Count the number of scores in each set, to obtain N_S and N_T; then add the two together.

$N_S = 6$, $N_T = 5$, $6 + 5 = 11$

Step 2: Divide the total obtained in Step 1 by N_S and N_T multiplied together.

$$\frac{11}{6 \times 5} = \frac{11}{30} = 0.3667$$

Step 3: Add the scores in list S.

$32 + 35 + 36 + 37 + 36 + 42 = 218$

Step 4: Square every score in the S group, and total all the squares.

$(32)^2 + (35)^2 + (36)^2 + (37)^2 + (36)^2 + (42)^2$
$= 1024 + 1225 + 1296 + 1369 + 1296 + 1764 = 7974$

Step 5: Square the value obtained in Step 3, and then divide the result by the value of N_S (Step 1).

$$\frac{(218)^2}{6} = \frac{47\,524}{6} = 7920.667$$

Step 6: Subtract the value found in Step 5 from that of Step 4.

$7974 - 7920.667 = 53.333$

Step 7: Add the scores in list T.

$24 + 28 + 30 + 32 + 35 = 149$

Operation schedules

Step 8: Square every score in the *T* group, and total all the squares
$$(24)^2 + (28)^2 + (30)^2 + (32)^2 + (35)^2$$
$$= 576 + 784 + 900 + 1024 + 1225 = 4509$$

Step 9: Square the value obtained in Step 7, and then divide the result by the value of N_T *(Step 1).*
$$\frac{(149)^2}{5} = \frac{22\,201}{5} = 4440.2$$

Step 10: Subtract the value found in Step 9 from that found in Step 8.
$$4509 - 4440.2 = 68.8$$

Step 11: Add together the values of Steps 6 and 10.
$$53.33 + 68.8 = 122.133$$

Step 12: Subtract 2 from the value of Step 1. This gives the *df.*
$$11 - 2 = 9, \ df = 9$$

Step 13: Divide the value of Step 11 by the *df* (Step 12), and then multiply the result by the value of Step 2.
$$\frac{122.13}{9} \times 0.3667 = 13.57 \times 0.3667 = 4.976$$

Step 14: Take the square root of the value obtained in Step 13.
$$\sqrt{4.976} = 2.231$$

Step 15: Obtain the mean of list *S* (Step 3 divided by N_S), and for list *T* (Step 7 divided by N_T). Then subtract the smaller from the larger.
$$\text{mean of list } S = \frac{218}{6} = 36.333, \ \text{mean of list } T = \frac{149}{5} = 29.8$$
$$36.333 - 29.8 = 6.533$$

Step 16: Divide the value of Step 15 by that of Step 14 to obtain *t.*
$$\frac{6.533}{2.231} = \mathbf{2.928}$$

Step 17: Evaluate the significance of *t*, using table S5, and the *df* obtained in Step 12. The obtained *t* value must exceed the values stated on the table for significance.

Opposite *df* = 9, we read the values 1.833, 2.262, 2.821, 3.250, and 4.781. Our value of 2.928 just exceeds that of the third along, 2.821, and so reading the probability level off from the top of the column, we conclude that it is significant at the 0.02 level for a two-tailed test. The null hypothesis can be rejected.

Step 18: State the conclusion.

The time taken to travel route *T* was found to be less than that for route *S*. The difference was significant at the $p = 0.02$ level (two-tailed *t* test; $t = 2.928$, $df = 9$).

Formula

$$t = \frac{|\bar{X} - \bar{Y}|}{\sqrt{\left\{ \frac{\left(\Sigma X^2 - \frac{(\Sigma X)^2}{N_X} \right) + \left(\Sigma Y^2 - \frac{(\Sigma Y)^2}{N_Y} \right)}{(N_X + N_Y - 2)} \right\} \cdot \left\{ \frac{N_X + N_Y}{(N_X)(N_Y)} \right\}}}$$

where $\bar{X}$ = the mean of the first group of scores, list X

$\bar{Y}$ = the mean of the second group of scores, list Y

$|\ |$ = the difference between the two

ΣX^2 = the sum of the squared values on list X

ΣY^2 = the sum of the squared values on list Y

$(\Sigma X)^2$ = the square of the total of list X

$(\Sigma Y)^2$ = the square of the total of list Y

N_X = the number of scores in list X

N_Y = the number of scores in list Y

$\cdot$ = multiply

Operation schedule 12. Simple *chi*-square

Data requirements

1 Data must be in frequency form, i.e. counted, rather than scores.
2 Entries in each cell must be independent.
3 The *expected* number for each cell must not be less than 5.

Example

One hundred and fifty-six boys and two hundred and four girls were asked whether they liked vanilla slices. Ninety-four boys said that they did, and one hundred and seventy-five girls. The remainder did not like them. Is there any evidence that there is a sex difference in preference for vanilla slices?

Step 1: Plot the data into a large 2 × 2 table. The number in each cell is the *observed* frequency. Obtain row and column totals, and a grand total (N).

	Column 1 Like slices	Column 2 Dislike slices	Totals
	Cell A	Cell B	
Row 1 Boys	94	62	156
	Cell C	Cell D	
Row 2 Girls	175	29	204
Totals	269	91	360

Step 2: Multiply the row 1 total with the column 1 total, and divide the answer by the overall total, N. This gives the *expected* frequency for cell A.

By multiplying the row and column totals relating to each cell together, and dividing the answer by the overall total, N, you obtain the *expected* frequencies for each cell. Write the value obtained for each cell below the *obtained* frequency (with a different coloured pen).

Operation schedules

Cell A: $\dfrac{156 \times 269}{360} = 116.6$

Cell B: $\dfrac{156 \times 91}{360} = 39.4$

Cell C: $\dfrac{204 \times 269}{360} = 152.4$

Cell D: $\dfrac{204 \times 91}{360} = 51.6$

Step 3: Find the difference between each *observed* and *expected* frequency for each cell, always taking the smaller from the larger. Then, for each cell value, subtract 0.5.
Cell A: $116.6 - 94 - 0.5 = 22.1$
Cell B: $62 - 39.4 - 0.5 = 22.1$
Cell C: $175 - 152.4 - 0.5 = 22.1$
Cell D: $51.6 - 29 - 0.5 = 22.1$

Step 4: Square each of the cell values obtained in Step 3, and divide the answer by the *expected* frequency for that particular cell.

Cell A: $\dfrac{(22.1)^2}{116.6} = 4.189$ Cell B: $\dfrac{(22.1)^2}{39.4} = 12.396$

Cell C: $\dfrac{(22.1)^2}{152.4} = 3.205$ Cell D: $\dfrac{(22.1)^2}{51.6} = 9.465$

Step 5: Add together the four values obtained in Step 4 to get χ^2.
$4.189 + 12.396 + 3.205 + 9.465 = \mathbf{29.255}$

Step 6: Evaluate the value of χ^2, using table S6. In a simple *chi*-square test the *df* will always be 1.

The obtained value of 29.25 exceeds the tabulated value of 10.83 which is significant at the 0.001 level (two-tailed test). The null hypothesis can be rejected.

Step 7: State the conclusion.

A *chi*-square test carried out on the data obtained was significant at the 0.001 level ($\chi^2 = 29.254$, $df = 1$), and so it is concluded that there is a difference between the sexes in liking for vanilla slices.

Formula

The formula for *chi*-square, in which Yates' correction is incorporated, is

$$\chi^2 = \sum \frac{(O - E - 0.5)^2}{E}$$

where E = the *expected* frequencies
O = the *observed* frequencies
Σ = the sum of

Table S6. Critical values of χ^2. χ^2 must be **equal to or more than** the stated value to be significant

| | Level of significance for one-tailed test | | | |
	0.05	0.025	0.005	0.0005
	Level of significance for two-tailed test			
df	0.1	0.05	0.01	0.001
1	2.706	3.841	6.635	10.83
2	4.605	5.991	9.210	13.82
3	6.251	7.815	11.34	16.27
4	7.779	9.488	13.28	18.47
5	9.236	11.07	15.09	20.52
6	10.64	12.59	16.81	22.46
7	12.02	14.07	18.48	24.32
8	13.36	15.51	20.09	26.12
9	14.68	16.92	21.67	27.88
10	15.99	18.31	23.21	29.59
11	17.28	19.68	24.73	31.26
12	18.55	21.03	26.22	32.91
13	19.81	22.36	27.69	34.53
14	21.06	23.68	29.14	36.12
15	22.31	25.00	30.58	37.70
16	23.54	26.30	32.00	39.25
17	24.77	27.59	33.41	40.79
18	25.99	28.87	34.81	42.31
19	27.20	30.14	36.19	43.82
20	28.41	31.41	37.57	45.31

Source: Powell, page 73

175

NOT ALL EXPERIMENTS ARE UNPLEASANT FOR THE SUBJECT...

Operation schedule 13. Complex *chi*-square

Data requirements

Data must be in frequency form, i.e. counted, rather than actual scores.
Entries in each cell must be independent.
The *expected* number for each cell must not be less than 5.

Example

The different degree classifications obtained by finalists at Wetwang University (page 99) provide material for a complex *chi*-square analysis. The null hypothesis states that there is no difference between the three groups in terms of the proportions obtaining the different classifications.

Step 1: Put the data for the three groups of students and five degree classes into a 3×5 contingency table. The numbers in each cell stand for the numbers of students obtaining the particular degree and degree class, and are the *observed* frequencies.

Add together the numbers *across* the rows to get row totals, and *down* the columns to give column totals. The row and column totals added together should agree, and that total will be the overall total, N. Leave plenty of space in the table, for you will later be writing the *expected* values in each cell.

Subjects	Degree classification					Totals
	I	IIi	IIii	III	Pass	
Languages	5	10	20	35	30	100
Maths	35	40	80	25	20	200
Economics	0	10	10	20	20	60
Totals	40	60	110	80	70	360

Step 2: To compute the *expected* frequency for individual cells, follow this procedure. Take the row sum and the column sum which intersect at the cell, and multiply the two values together. Then divide the answer by the grand total, N.

For the top left-hand cell, Languages, and a class I degree, it will be

Row 1, Col. 1: $\dfrac{100 \times 40}{360} = \dfrac{4000}{360} = 11.111$

Don't round off the decimal places at less than three.

Row 2, Col. 1: $\dfrac{200 \times 40}{360} = 22.222$

Row 3, Col. 1: $\dfrac{60 \times 40}{360} = 6.667$

Row 1, Col. 2: $\dfrac{100 \times 60}{360} = 16.667$

Row 2, Col. 2: $\dfrac{200 \times 60}{360} = 33.333$

Row 3, Col. 2: $\dfrac{60 \times 60}{360} = 10.000$

Row 1, Col. 3: $\dfrac{100 \times 110}{360} = 30.556$

Row 2, Col. 3: $\dfrac{200 \times 110}{360} = 61.111$

Row 3, Col. 3: $\dfrac{60 \times 110}{360} = 18.333$

Row 1, Col. 4: $\dfrac{100 \times 80}{360} = 22.222$

Row 2, Col. 4: $\dfrac{200 \times 80}{360} = 44.444$

Row 3, Col. 4: $\dfrac{60 \times 80}{360} = 13.333$

Row 1, Col. 5: $\dfrac{100 \times 70}{360} = 19.444$

Row 2, Col. 5: $\dfrac{200 \times 70}{360} = 38.889$

Row 3, Col. 5: $\dfrac{60 \times 70}{360} = 11.667$

GROUGH!

... WELL, NOT AT THE TIME OF PARTICIPATION

Operation schedules

Step 3: When the *expected* values have been calculated, put each one into the table, below the appropriate *obtained* frequency. Check that they all exceed 4.

Subjects	Degree classification					Totals
	I	IIi	IIii	III	Pass	
Languages	5	10	20	35	30	100
	11.111	**16.667**	**30.556**	**22.222**	**19.444**	
Maths	35	40	80	25	20	200
	22.222	**33.333**	**61.111**	**44.444**	**38.889**	
Economics	0	10	10	20	20	60
	6.667	**10.000**	**18.333**	**13.333**	**11.667**	
Totals	40	60	110	80	70	360

Step 4: To obtain the values which will be added together to get χ^2, the following procedure must be undertaken for each cell. The difference between the *obtained* and *expected* frequency for every cell is found, i.e. by subtracting the smaller value from the larger. This is then squared, and the value divided by the *expected* frequency for that particular cell.

Row 1, Col. 1: $\dfrac{(11.111 - 5)^2}{11.111} = \dfrac{(6.111)^2}{11.111} = \dfrac{37.344}{11.111} = 3.361$

Row 2, Col. 1: $\dfrac{(35 - 22.222)^2}{22.222} = \dfrac{(12.778)^2}{22.222} = \dfrac{163.277}{22.222} = 7.348$

Row 3, Col. 1: $\dfrac{(6.667 - 0)^2}{6.667} = \dfrac{(6\ 667)^2}{6.667} = \dfrac{44.449}{6.667} = 6.667$

Row 1, Col. 2: $\dfrac{(16.667 - 10)^2}{16.667} = \dfrac{(6.667)^2}{16.667} = \dfrac{44.449}{16.667} = 2.667$

Row 2, Col. 2: $\dfrac{(40 - 33.333)^2}{33.333} = \dfrac{(6.667)^2}{33.333} = \dfrac{44.449}{33.333} = 1.333$

Row 3, Col. 2: $\dfrac{(10 - 10)^2}{10} = \dfrac{(0)^2}{10} = \dfrac{0}{10} = 0$

Row 1, Col. 3: $\dfrac{(30.556 - 20)^2}{30.556} = \dfrac{(10.556)^2}{30.556} = \dfrac{111.429}{30.556} = 3.647$

Row 2, Col. 3: $\dfrac{(80 - 61.111)^2}{61.111} = \dfrac{(18.889)^2}{61.111} = \dfrac{356.794}{61.111} = 5.838$

Row 3, Col. 3: $\dfrac{(18.333 - 10)^2}{18.333} = \dfrac{(8.333)^2}{18.333} = \dfrac{69.439}{18.333} = 3.788$

Row 1, Col. 4: $\dfrac{(35 - 22.222)^2}{22.222} = \dfrac{(12.778)^2}{22.222} = \dfrac{163.277}{22.222} = 7.348$

178

Row 2, Col. 4: $\dfrac{(44.444 - 25)^2}{44.444} = \dfrac{(19.444)^2}{44.444} = \dfrac{378.069}{44.444} = 8.507$

Row 3, Col. 4: $\dfrac{(20 - 13.333)^2}{13.333} = \dfrac{(6.667)^2}{13.333} = \dfrac{44.449}{13.333} = 3.334$

Row 1, Col. 5: $\dfrac{(30 - 19.444)^2}{19.444} = \dfrac{(10.556)^2}{19.444} = \dfrac{111.429}{19.444} = 5.731$

Row 2, Col. 5: $\dfrac{(38.889 - 20)^2}{38.889} = \dfrac{(18.889)^2}{38.889} = \dfrac{356.794}{38.889} = 9.175$

Row 3, Col. 5: $\dfrac{(20 - 11.667)^2}{11.667} = \dfrac{(8.333)^2}{11.667} = \dfrac{69.439}{11.667} = 5.952$

Step 5: Obtain the value of χ^2 by adding all the values obtained in Step 4.
$$3.361 + 7.348 + 6.667 + \ldots + 9.175 + 5.952 = \mathbf{74.696}$$

Step 6: Obtain the *df* which will be needed to evaluate χ^2. It will always be the number of rows minus 1 multiplied by the number of columns minus 1, unless you are using the steps for a one-sample *chi*-square, when the *df* is always the number of cells minus 1.
$$df = (3 - 1)(5 - 1) = 2 \times 4 = 8$$

Step 7: Use table S6 to evaluate the significance of the χ^2 value obtained.
When $df = 8$, we read off the values 13.36, 15.51, 20.09 and 26.12. Our value exceeds all these, and so we conclude that it is significant at the 0.001 level for a two-tailed test.

Step 8: State the conclusion.
The different degree classifications for finalists in languages, maths and economics were analysed, using *chi*-square. The value of χ^2 was found be significant at the 0.001 level ($\chi^2 = 74.696$, $df = 8$), and so it was concluded that the proportions of students obtaining the five classes of degree vary substantially between subjects.

Note

The test only tells us that the numbers come from distributions having different shapes. We have to decide how the shapes differ, and where the most substantial discrepancies lie by inspection of the data. In addition, take care over the interpretation of this significant result. We cannot say that 'brighter' students take maths etc., for the results may be dependent upon factors other than students' abilities, such as departmental marking policies. *Chi*-square is only a measure of association.

Formula

$$\chi^2 = \sum \frac{(O - E)^2}{E}$$

where E = the *expected* frequencies
$\quad\quad\quad O$ = the *observed* frequencies
$\quad\quad\quad \Sigma$ = the sum of

Maud has a garden of roses
And lilies fair on a lawn;

Operation schedule 14. Spearman's *rho*

Data requirements

1 Scores must be of at least ordinal status.
2 Scores for comparison must be paired off in some manner. Usually they will have been obtained from one source, but this may not always be the case.
3 When plotted on a scattergram, the points can be in a linear or slightly curved pattern.

Example

It was noted that residents at the Heyshott Asylum frequently referred to Tennyson's poem *Maud*. Enquiries revealed that those patients most seriously afflicted with insanity (as assessed by the Heyshott Lunacy Scale, HLS) appeared to have read the poem rather often. All inmates were given a rating on the HLS, and asked how many times they had read *Maud*. The results were then used to obtain Spearman's *rho*.

Subject	HLS score	Maud readings
1	10	0
2	100	4
3	125	4
4	45	15
5	90	23
6	170	45
7	165	61

Because the staff anticipated that degree of insanity would be positively associated with number of *Maud* readings, they have established a one-tailed prediction.

Step 1: Draw a scattergram for the two sets of data; the vertical axis measuring one variable, and the horizontal axis the other.

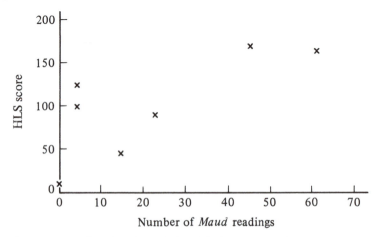

Figure 1. Scattergram showing the relationship between HLS scores and number of *Maud* readings

Step 2: Now cast the data into a table with seven columns. These will be:

S The label for each subject, animal or source of paired scores, using numbers or letters of the alphabet.

A The scores on one variable.

B The scores on the second variable.

R_A The scores from A, given ranks (see schedule 6).

R_B The scores from B, given ranks.

D Each value in list R_B subtracted from its partner in R_A.

D^2 Each value in D squared.

S	A	B	R_A	R_B	D	D^2
1	10	0	1	1	0	0
2	100	4	4	$2\frac{1}{2}$	$1\frac{1}{2}$	$2\frac{1}{4}$
3	125	4	5	$2\frac{1}{2}$	$2\frac{1}{2}$	$6\frac{1}{4}$
4	45	15	2	4	-2	4
5	90	23	3	5	-2	4
6	170	45	7	6	1	1
7	165	61	6	7	-1	1

Step 3: Count the number of paired scores in the sample, to obtain N.
There are 7 pairs of scores; $N = 7$.

Step 4: Multiply N by its own value, twice, and then subtract its own value.
$(7 \times 7 \times 7) - 7 = 343 - 7 = 336$

Step 5: Total the values in column D^2.
$0 + 2\frac{1}{4} + 6\frac{1}{4} + 4 + 4 + 1 + 1 = 18\frac{1}{2}$

Step 6: Multiply the value obtained in Step 5 by the number 6; then divide the result by the value found in Step 4.
$$\frac{18.5 \times 6}{336} = \frac{111}{336} = 0.3304$$

Step 7: To find *rho*, subtract the value of Step 6 from the number 1. Retain the sign. The result should always lie between -1 and $+1$.
$1 - 0.3304 = \mathbf{+0.6696}$

Step 8: Evaluate the significance of *rho*, using table S7. Follow the numbers along the row opposite the appropriate N, to find the value of *rho* which must be exceeded for the various significance levels given.
When $N = 7$, we read 0.714, 0.786, 0.893 and 0.929 for the one-tailed significance levels. Our obtained value of *rho*, 0.6696, does not exceed any of these, and so the null hypothesis cannot be rejected.

Operation schedules

Step 9: State the conclusion.

From the results of a correlation carried out on the number of times a patient had read the poem *Maud*, and their rating on the HLS, it was found that there did not appear to be a significant association between the two variables ($rho = +0.67, N = 7$). However, the association was positive, and the relationship may be found to be a significant one if a larger sample were used.

Formula and abbreviations

Spearman's *rho* is sometimes written ρ or r_s. The formula used for calculations is

$$r_s = 1 - \frac{6\Sigma D^2}{(N^3 - N)}$$

where ΣD^2 = the squared values of the differences between the ranked scores, totalled
N = the number of paired scores

Table S7: Critical values of Spearman's *rho*. *Rho* must be **equal to or more than** the stated value to be significant

	Level of significance for one-tailed test			
	0.05	0.025	0.01	0.005
	Level of significance for a two-tailed test			
N	0.1	0.05	0.02	0.01
5	0.900	1.000	1.000	—
6	0.829	0.886	0.943	1.000
7	0.714	0.786	0.893	0.929
8	0.643	0.738	0.833	0.881
9	0.600	0.683	0.783	0.833
10	0.564	0.648	0.746	0.794
12	0.506	0.591	0.712	0.777
14	0.456	0.544	0.645	0.715
16	0.425	0.506	0.601	0.665
18	0.399	0.475	0.564	0.625
20	0.377	0.450	0.534	0.591
22	0.359	0.428	0.508	0.562
24	0.343	0.409	0.485	0.537
26	0.329	0.392	0.465	0.515
28	0.317	0.377	0.448	0.496
30	0.306	0.364	0.432	0.478

N = the number of paired scores used.
Treat a negative value of *rho* as if it were positive, when using the table, but when interpreting it don't forget that it will indicate an *inverse* relationship. Source: Snodgrass, table C.6

Operation schedule 15. The Pearson product-moment correlation (*r*)

Data requirements

1 Scores for comparison must be paired off in some manner. Usually they will have been obtained from the same source, but this may not always be the case.
2 The relationship between the two variables must be a linear one. This can be assessed from a scattergram.
3 The scores must be of at least interval status.
4 The scores must be normally distributed.
5 The two sets of scores must have similar variances.

Example

A schoolgirl, recently annoyed by the antics of her small sisters, vowed that she would never inflict siblings on any child she might have when she was older. Curious to know her classmates' opinions, she asked six of them how many children they thought was a good number to have, and compared this with the number of children under the age of fifteen actually in each one's family.

Bearing in mind her own experiences, she imagined that the more siblings a person had, the fewer they would think was desirable! Thus she has predicted a negative correlation: this directional prediction constitutes a one-tailed hypothesis. The data she collected are given below:

Subject	No. of children in own family	No. of children thought ideal
Christine	1	5
David	2	3
Eric	3	4
Lynne	4	2
Margaret	4	1
Tom	5	1

MOST PARENTS HOLD THE SAME VIEW ABOUT THE IDEAL NUMBER OF CHILDREN

Operation schedules

Step 1: Draw a scattergram for the two sets of data, the vertical axis measuring one variable, the horizontal the other. At this stage, check for linearity.

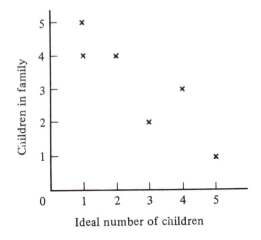

Figure 2. Scattergram showing the relationship between the number of children in a young person's family and the number that they would consider to be 'ideal'

Step 2: Now cast the data into a table, with six columns. These will be:
- S The label for each subject, animal or source of paired scores, using numbers or letters of the alphabet.
- A The scores on one variable (and which are added to give ΣA).
- A^2 Each A score squared (and which added gives ΣA^2).
- B The scores on the second variable (and which are added to give ΣB).
- B^2 Each B score squared (and which added gives ΣB^2).
- AB Each A score multiplied by its matching B score. (Added gives ΣAB)

Add all the columns, apart from the first one. This is a good stage to check that the data meets all the requirements other than linearity.

Subject	A	A^2	B	B^2	AB
C	1	1	5	25	5
D	2	4	3	9	6
E	3	9	4	16	12
L	4	16	2	4	8
M	4	16	1	1	4
T	5	25	1	1	5
	19	71	16	56	40

Step 3: Count the number of scores which are paired off, to get N.
There are 6 pairs of scores; $N = 6$.

Step 4: Multiply the total of the column for A^2 by N to obtain $N\Sigma A^2$.
$71 \times 6 = 426$

Step 5: Obtain $(\Sigma A)^2$ by squaring the total of the column for A.
$19 \times 19 = 361$

Step 6: Subtract the value of Step 5 from that found in Step 4.
$426 - 361 = 65$

Step 7: Multiply the total of the column for B^2 by N to obtain $N\Sigma B^2$.
$56 \times 6 = 336$

Step 8: Obtain $(\Sigma B)^2$ by squaring the total of the column for B.
$16 \times 16 = 256$

Step 9: Subtract the value of Step 8 from that found in Step 7.
$336 - 256 = 80$

Step 10: Multiply together the values obtained in Steps 6 and 9.
$65 \times 80 = 5200$

Step 11: Take the square root of the value found in Step 10.
$\sqrt{5200} = 72.111$

Step 12: Multiply the total of the column for AB by the value of N (Step 3).
$40 \times 6 = 240$

Step 13: Multiply together the totals of the columns for A and B.
$19 \times 16 = 304$

Step 14: Subtract the value of Step 13 from that of Step 12, making sure you keep the appropriate sign.
$240 - 304 = -64$

Step 15: Divide the value of Step 14 by the value of Step 11, to get r.
$$r = \frac{-64}{72.111} = \mathbf{-0.8875}$$

Step 16: Evaluate the significance of r, using table S8. First obtain the value of $N - 2$, which will be used for the table, by subtracting 2 from the value of N found in Step 2.
$6 - 2 = 4$

Opposite $N - 2 = 4$, we read the values 0.729, 0.811, 0.9172 and 0.9741 for the 0.05, 0.025, 0.005 and 0.0005 probability levels (one tailed hypothesis). Our value of 0.8875 exceeds that of 0.811 given for the 0.025 level, but not the figure of 0.9172 for the 0.005 level. Therefore we conclude that we have a negative correlation, which is significant at the 0.025 level.

Step 17: State the conclusion

From the results of the correlation carried out on the number of children in a young person's family, and the number of children they considered ideal, a significant negative association was found ($r = -0.887$, $N = 6$, $p = 0.025$). It was concluded that the more siblings there are in a family, the less likely a child of school-age is to appreciate their numbers, whilst only children appeared to consider brothers or sisters more of an asset!

Table S8 Critical values of Pearson's *r*. *r* must be **equal to or more than** the stated value to be significant

| | Level of significance for one-tailed test | | | |
	0.05	0.025	0.005	0.0005
	Level of significance for two-tailed test			
$N - 2$	0.10	0.05	0.01	0.001
2	0.9000	0.9500	0.9900	0.9999
3	0.805	0.878	0.9587	0.9911
4	0.729	0.811	0.9172	0.9741
5	0.669	0.754	0.875	0.9509
6	0.621	0.707	0.834	0.9241
7	0.582	0.666	0.798	0.898
8	0.549	0.632	0.765	0.872
9	0.521	0.602	0.735	0.847
10	0.497	0.576	0.708	0.823
11	0.476	0.553	0.684	0.801
12	0.457	0.532	0.661	0.780
13	0.441	0.514	0.641	0.760
14	0.426	0.497	0.623	0.742
15	0.412	0.482	0.606	0.725
16	0.400	0.468	0.590	0.708
17	0.389	0.456	0.575	0.693
18	0.378	0.444	0.561	0.679
19	0.369	0.433	0.549	0.665
20	0.360	0.423	0.537	0.652
25	0.323	0.381	0.487	0.597
30	0.296	0.349	0.449	0.554
35	0.275	0.325	0.418	0.519
40	0.257	0.304	0.393	0.490
45	0.243	0.288	0.372	0.465
50	0.231	0.273	0.354	0.443
60	0.211	0.250	0.325	0.408
70	0.195	0.232	0.302	0.380
80	0.183	0.217	0.283	0.357
90	0.173	0.205	0.267	0.338
100	0.164	0.195	0.254	0.321

Source: Powell, page 69

Formula

The formula for Pearson's r is:

$$r = \frac{N\Sigma AB - (\Sigma A)(\Sigma B)}{\sqrt{\{[N\Sigma A^2 - (\Sigma A)^2][N\Sigma B^2 - (\Sigma B)^2]\}}}$$

where N = the number of pairs of scores
ΣAB = the sum of the products of the paired scores.
ΣA = the sum of the scores on one variable
ΣB = the sum of the scores on the second variable
ΣA^2 = the sum of the squared scores on the A variable
ΣB^2 = the sum of the squared scores on the B variable

Table S9   Random numbers

19	90	70	99	00	20	21	14	68	86	14	52	41	52	48	87	63	93	95	17	11	29	01	95	80
65	97	38	20	46	85	43	01	72	73	03	37	18	39	11	08	61	74	51	69	89	74	39	82	15
51	67	11	52	49	59	97	50	99	52	18	16	36	78	86	08	52	85	08	40	87	80	61	65	31
17	95	70	45	80	72	68	49	29	31	56	80	30	19	44	89	85	84	46	06	59	73	19	85	23
63	52	52	01	41	88	02	84	27	83	78	35	34	08	72	42	29	72	23	19	66	56	45	65	79
60	61	97	22	61	49	64	92	85	44	01	64	18	39	96	16	40	12	89	88	50	14	49	81	06
98	99	46	50	47	12	83	11	41	16	63	14	52	32	52	25	58	19	68	70	77	02	54	00	52
76	38	03	29	63	79	44	61	40	15	86	63	59	80	02	14	53	40	65	39	27	31	58	50	28
53	05	70	53	30	38	30	06	38	21	01	47	59	38	00	14	47	47	07	26	54	96	87	53	32
02	87	40	41	45	47	24	49	57	74	22	13	88	83	34	32	25	43	62	17	10	97	11	69	84
35	14	97	35	33	68	95	23	92	35	56	54	29	56	93	87	02	22	57	51	61	09	43	95	06
94	51	33	41	67	13	79	93	37	55	14	44	99	81	07	39	77	32	77	09	85	52	05	30	62
91	51	80	32	44	09	61	87	25	21	13	80	55	62	54	28	06	24	25	93	16	71	13	59	78
65	09	29	75	63	20	44	90	32	64	53	89	74	60	41	97	67	63	99	61	46	38	03	93	22
20	71	53	20	25	73	37	32	04	05	56	07	93	89	30	69	30	16	09	05	88	69	58	28	99
01	82	77	45	12	07	10	63	76	35	19	48	56	27	44	87	03	04	79	88	08	13	13	85	51
53	43	37	15	26	92	38	70	96	92	82	11	08	95	97	52	06	79	79	45	82	63	18	27	44
11	39	03	34	25	99	53	93	61	28	88	12	57	21	77	52	70	05	48	34	56	65	05	61	86
40	36	40	96	76	93	86	52	77	65	99	82	93	24	98	15	33	59	05	28	22	87	26	07	47
99	63	22	32	98	18	46	23	34	27	43	11	71	99	31	85	13	99	24	44	49	18	09	79	49
58	24	82	03	47	24	53	63	94	09	74	54	13	26	94	41	10	76	47	91	44	04	95	49	66
47	83	51	62	74	22	06	34	72	52	04	32	92	08	09	82	21	15	65	20	33	29	94	71	11
23	05	47	47	25	07	16	39	33	66	18	55	63	77	09	98	56	10	56	79	77	21	30	27	12
69	81	21	99	21	29	70	83	63	51	70	47	14	54	36	99	74	20	52	36	87	09	41	15	09
35	07	44	75	47	57	90	12	02	07	54	96	09	11	06	23	47	37	17	31	54	08	01	88	63
55	34	57	72	69	33	35	72	67	47	82	80	84	25	39	77	34	55	45	70	08	18	27	38	90
69	66	92	19	09	49	41	31	06	70	05	98	90	07	35	42	38	06	45	18	64	84	73	31	65
90	92	10	70	80	65	19	69	02	83	67	72	16	42	79	60	75	86	90	68	24	64	19	35	51
86	96	98	29	06	92	09	84	38	76	63	49	30	21	30	22	00	27	69	85	29	81	94	78	70
74	16	32	23	02	98	77	87	68	07	66	39	67	98	60	91	51	67	62	44	40	98	05	93	78
39	60	04	59	81	00	41	86	79	79	47	53	53	38	09	68	47	22	00	20	35	55	31	51	51
15	91	29	12	03	57	99	99	90	37	75	91	12	81	19	36	63	32	08	58	37	40	13	68	97
90	49	22	23	62	12	59	52	57	02	55	65	79	78	07	22	07	90	47	03	28	14	11	30	79
98	60	16	03	03	31	51	10	96	46	54	34	81	85	35	92	06	88	07	77	56	11	50	81	69
39	41	88	92	10	96	11	83	44	80	03	92	18	66	75	34	68	35	48	77	33	42	40	90	60
16	95	86	70	75	85	47	04	66	08	00	83	26	91	03	34	72	57	59	13	82	43	80	46	15
52	53	37	97	15	72	82	32	99	90	06	66	24	12	27	63	95	73	76	63	89	73	44	99	05
56	61	87	39	12	91	36	74	43	53	13	29	54	19	28	30	82	13	54	00	78	45	63	98	35
21	94	47	90	12	77	53	84	46	47	85	72	13	49	21	31	91	18	95	58	24	16	74	11	53
23	32	65	41	18	37	27	47	39	19	65	65	80	39	07	84	83	70	07	48	53	21	40	06	71
00	83	63	22	55	34	18	04	52	35	99	01	30	98	64	56	27	09	24	86	61	85	53	83	45
87	64	81	07	83	11	20	99	45	18	45	76	08	64	27	48	13	93	55	34	18	37	79	49	90
20	69	22	40	98	27	37	83	28	71	69	62	03	42	73	00	06	41	41	74	45	89	09	39	84
40	23	72	51	39	10	65	81	92	59	73	42	37	11	61	58	76	17	14	97	04	76	62	16	17
73	96	53	97	86	59	71	74	17	32	64	63	91	08	25	27	55	10	24	19	23	71	82	13	74
38	26	61	70	04	33	73	99	19	87	95	60	78	46	75	26	72	39	27	67	53	77	57	68	93
48	67	26	43	18	87	14	77	43	96	99	17	43	48	76	43	00	65	98	50	45	60	33	01	07
55	03	36	67	68	72	87	08	62	40	24	62	01	61	16	16	06	10	89	20	23	21	34	74	97
44	10	13	85	57	73	96	07	94	52	19	59	50	88	92	09	65	90	77	47	25	76	16	19	33
95	06	79	88	54	79	96	23	53	10	48	03	45	15	22	65	39	07	16	29	45	33	02	43	70
68	15	54	35	02	42	35	48	96	32	95	33	95	22	00	18	74	72	00	18	22	85	61	68	90
58	42	36	72	24	58	37	52	18	51	90	84	60	79	80	24	36	59	87	38	67	80	43	79	33
95	67	47	29	83	94	69	40	06	07	46	40	62	98	82	54	97	20	56	95	27	62	50	96	72
98	57	07	23	69	65	95	39	69	58	20	31	89	03	43	38	46	82	68	72	33	78	80	87	15
56	69	47	07	41	90	22	91	07	12	71	59	73	05	50	08	22	23	71	77	13	13	92	66	99

Source: Powell, page 55

Answers

SOME CALCULATIONS ARE MORE TEDIOUS THAN OTHERS

Chapter 1

1 Using statistics tests, the results of evaluating the scores are:

Experiment 1: There is such a clear-cut difference between the sets of scores that we can be almost 100% certain that the memory technique works.

Experiment 2: The two groups appear to be reasonably different – it seems we can have some faith in the memory technique.

Experiment 3: There appears to be very little difference between the two groups, and we must conclude that the memory aid does not have a beneficial effect.

Experiment 4: The group using the new technique are definitely poorer at recall than the control group – the memory 'aid' not only fails to aid recall, but actually appears to impair it!

Later, you will learn about the statistical tests used to arrive at these conclusions. Meanwhile, ask yourself how you arrived at your decisions – and whether they agreed with the 'statistical' ones. Did you glance through the numbers, getting a 'feel' for the scores, or did you work out averages? You might also have looked at the total spread of scores, i.e. considered the lowest and highest in each group, and determined the extent of any overlapping which occurred. There will be more about averages and spreads anon.

2 (a) The man should use descriptive statistics. He won't tell his wife what the ten cars cost individually, but present her with an average; maybe with an indication of the type of price variation which exists. Of course, he has selected his 'examples' carefully, so that the price of his intended purchase compares very favourably with the average price.

(b) They could use descriptive statistics (averages) to arrive at a typical journey time for each route, and then inferential techniques to decide whether the two sets of journey times really differed.

(c) Descriptive statistics. The five days' weight loss would be averaged, and would be presented in such a way that the average would be seen to be equal to that of the two days' weight gain.

(d) Descriptive and inferential techniques. Average yields of tomatoes could be obtained for each bush, together with an indication of the range of variation encountered. Inferential techniques could then be used to compare the descriptive statistics obtained for the two sets of plants.

(e) Descriptive statistics. An average would be obtained for each 'sample' shelf, possibly with the range of cost. Estimation for the other shelves would then be on the basis of the averages, but taking a high value, rather than a low one, which might result in an overall under-estimation.

Chapter 2

1 (a) 27.6   (b) 370.4   (c) 3.5875 – rounded off to 3.59, because means are usually given to one decimal place more than the original data   (d) 21   (e) 74.9   (f) 60.

2 Comments: (a) Quite well. (b) Not too well. The scores seem to have higher and lower values rather than be around the mean. (c) As for (b). (d) The scores are evenly spread, the 40 being balanced by the 0, and·with the mean in the centre of the group. (e) A disaster. No score is anywhere near 74.8. (f) Another disaster!

3 (a) Yes. (b) and (c) Just about. (d) As the scores are so widely spread, the value of the mean as a descriptive statistic is dubious. (e) No.

4 (a) Mean 12.5. No. It is rather a high value, when most of the scores are 10. There are only two 'typical' scores, 10 and 20. This is not near either. (b) Mean 10.142 857 – rounded off to 10.14. There is only one atypical value fairly close to 10, and so this figure, or the mean, would both be appropriate. (c) Again we have a single atypical score, but this time so wildly different that it raises the mean to 10.396. Better to give a value of 10 in this case, and indicate that there is one atypical score which has not been included in the computation of the mean. (d) 14.58 – fine.

5 (a) 28 (b) 381 (c) 385 (d) 3.4 (e) 20 (f) 60

6 5(a) and 1(a): They are so similar that it doesn't really matter. 5(b) and 1(b) Again, close, but neither value particularly good. 5(d) and 1(c), also 5(e) and 1(d): Median and means very close in values, but not ideal descriptive figure. 5(f) and 1(f): Both figures are as poor.

7 (a) Mean 13.7, median 13, mode 13. (b) Mean 13.7, median 13.5, no mode. (c) Mean 14.583, median 15, modes 10 and 19. (d) Mean 21.69, median 23, mode 25.

8 (a) All the averages are close, so none would be too misleading, although the shape of the distribution is too 'flat' to be labelled normal, with any confidence. (b) The distribution is again a rather flat one, and the values of the mean and median should only be used with qualifying statements. (c) This is a bimodal distribution, and so both modes must be given. There is no score which resembles the mean or median. (d) This is a skewed distribution. The modal value is probably the best to give, and perhaps the median.

10 A – normal; B – negatively skewed; C – positively skewed; D – bimodal.

11 From the way the data are grouped it is not possible to obtain precise values for the mean, median and mode. As the distribution is skewed, an indication of all three would be relevant. The mode will be in the block 60–79; the median at the top end of 40–59; the mean, whose approximate value can be calculated from the mid-point of each block (i.e. 1×10, 8×30 etc.) will be around 57.

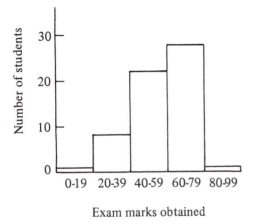

Obviously not a stats exam!

Exam marks obtained

Figure 1. The distribution of students' exam marks

Answers

Chapter 3

1 (a) 3.33 (b) 8.86 (c) 6.4 (d) 0.83

2 (a) Range 14 – fine. (b) Range 22 – a well-scattered bimodal distribution. (c) Range 22 – a poor measure, as there is an outlier, and without it the range would only be 4. (d) Range 4 – fine.

3 Mode 1, median 1.5, range 51, mean deviation 12.2. The mode, range and mean deviation are fairly appropriate, but the median and mean are not good descriptive statistics to use, as the distribution is skewed. Best to give *all* the measures of central tendency.

4 (a) 112, 18.67, 4.32 (b) 586, 83.71, 9.15 (c) 330, 66, 8.12 (d) 14, 1.167, 1.080

5 The standard deviations are all larger than the mean deviations. They would be larger still if $N - 1$ instead of N were used.

6 (a) 4.73 (b) 9.88 (c) 9.08 (d) 1.128.

7 (a) Normal distribution, mean, median and mode all 5. SD 0.707, range 2. (b) Normal distribution, mean, median and mode all 4. SD 2.05, range 8. (c) Bimodal distribution, modes 0 and 10, range 10. SD not appropriate.

8 (a) SD 0.739 (b) SD 2.16.

Chapter 4

2(a) No. The official name for a distribution with this shape is *rectangular*. (b) Positively skewed (c) Near enough to normal (d) Bimodal (e) Negatively skewed

3 Fairly different, as we know that 68% will vary between 12 and 20.

4 (a) About 1.14 dwarfs, i.e. 1. A score of 8 is two SDs below the mean, and so in a normal curve only 2.28% would have scores below this. Our sample comprises 50, so we halve the percentage. (b) and (c) 12 and 20 are both one SD away from the mean. We would expect 15.87% to be below and above these values, i.e. about 7.93, or 8 dwarfs from the sample below and 8 above. (d) 28 is three SDs above the mean. 0.13% would be expected, so in our sample of only 50 we would not anticipate anyone obtaining this score.

5 In a sample of 100 we would expect to find 0.13 in the extreme position of three SDs above the mean. To get one score in this portion then, 0.13 has to be multiplied by 8, to give 1.04. So a sample of 100, multiplied by 8 becomes 800. Our original sample comprised 50, so we would have to multiply it sixteenfold before we might expect to come across such a very very kind dwarf!

6 That his sample is not typical (assuming that the test had been properly constructed). This sample shows a skewed distribution. Alternatively, the dwarfs might have been deceiving him by presenting themselves in a favourable light – a ploy not uncommon in human subjects!

7 Mean pie consumption is 1000 pies. 1600 pies is three SDs above the mean, and so this consumption would only be anticipated on 0.13% of occasions – provided the pies were available, of course!

8 (a) 22.5 and 7.5 inches (b) £650 and £350 (c) 12 and 4.8 seconds (d) 95 and 65 elephants.

9 Although Ms Wink has a slightly lower mean, she shows greater variability of performance. She will have good days which are much better than Ms Sweetie's good days, but on the other hand, her 'off' days will be worse. Ms Scrooge's decision will rather depend on whether she prefers consistency to variability.

10 (a) Mean 60; 65.03, 70.06, 75.09, 54.97, 49.94, 44.91
   (b) Mean 7; 9.25, 11.50, 13.75, 4.75, 2.50, 0.25

11 (a) 33   (b) 62   (c) 58   (d) 48   (e) 46

12 All values are rounded off to whole numbers: (a) 100   (b) 31   (c) 16   (d) 7   (e) 26
(f) 29   (g) 33   (h) 38

13 (a) 0.75%   (b) 3.01%   (c) 35.94%   (d) 50%   (e) 81.59%   (f) 92.92%   (g) 99.55%

14 (a)   0   (b)   +0.44   (50% + 17%)   (c)   +2.41   (50% + 49.2%)   (d)   +0.70
(50% + 25.8%)   (e) −0.44 (50% − 17%)   (f) −2.33 approx. (50% − 49%)
Remember for (e) and (f) that the tabled values only cover 50% of the distribution, from the
mean upwards. Percentages will be the same, but the z scores need a minus sign before them,
to indicate that they are below the mean.

15 (a) 68   (b) 95.44   (c) virtually 50   (d) 0.13   (e) 15.74 (13.59 + 2.15)   (f) 15.86 (twice
7.93)   (g) 74.92 (36.43 + 38.49)   (h) 2.28 (50 − 47.72).

16 (a) 6.68%   (b) 78.88%   (c) 0.09% The number of applicants for Brillia in Never-Never
Land would be 30.85% of 30 million i.e. 9 255 000

17 (a)   34.13%   of   10 000 = 3413   (b)   34.13%   of   10 000 = 3413   (c)   95.44%   of
10 000 = 9544   (d) 99.74% of 10 000 = 9974.

Chapter 5

2 (a) 3.3%   (b) 1%   (c) 66%   (d) 5%   (e) 0.1%   (f) 0.2%   (g) 100%   (h) 10%

3 (a) 0.033   (b) 0.01   (c) 0.66   (d) 0.5   (e) 0.05   (f) 0.001   (g) 0.002   (h) 0.1

Chapter 6

1 (a) Domestic cats kept in Britain. (b) IQ scores of adult or teenage people. (c) A population
of virtually infinite size, all raindrops. (d) All tinned sardines – or perhaps, to name a
sub-population, all tinned sardines of a particular brand. (e) All adult/teenage males/females
of a particular nationality. (f) In the early morning, it is likely that the third person you saw
would be an adult, and perhaps more specifically, someone going to work. Therefore we might
hazard a guess at teenage/adult males/females in employment, resident in a particular town or
locality. (g) Again, in broad terms, humans, but in the late afternoon less likely to be
commuters. Shoppers, people out walking, jogging, taking dogs for walks, children playing,
etc., would all make up a likely afternoon population. (h) Responses on a particular task;
sub-population, responses after alcohol intake. (i) Population, cemeteries; sub-population,
London cemeteries; sub-sub-population, Victorian London cemeteries. (j) Population,
women; sub-population, female members of Royal families.

Chapter 7

1 (a) IV = punishment; DV = child's personality; one-tailed
(b) IV = number of heads; DV = quality of intellectual output; one tailed
(c) IV = presence or absence of someone; DV = affection; one-tailed
(d) IV = presence or absence of someone; DV = thoughts of that person; one-tailed
(e) IV = stone movement; DV = amount of moss present; one-tailed
(f) DV = quality of laughter; IV = order of laughter; one tailed

2 (a) one-tailed   (b) two-tailed   (c) two-tailed   (d) one-tailed   (e) two-tailed   (f) one-
tailed

4 (a) one-tailed   (b) null   (c) two-tailed   (d) one-tailed   (e) null   (f) two-tailed   (g) one-
tailed   (h) two-tailed   (i) one-tailed   (j) one-tailed

Answers

Chapter 9

1 The IV is the type of washing up liquid used. It has two 'values', either Gresego or Kwikclene. The DV is the rating score given for each performance in washing up by the person who carried out the operation, and to each of the two separate performances. The experimental hypothesis is that Gresego scores will exceed those from Kwikclene (i.e. G scores $> K$ scores). This is a one-tailed hypothesis. The null hypothesis is that the ratings for the performance of the two washing up liquids will *not* differ, i.e. that their numerical scores have been derived from only one parent population, not two separate, distinguishable, ones.

2 (a) The ranks of the less frequently occurring sign give $T = 3$. When $N = 8$, the null hypothesis can be rejected, and the significance level quoted is $p \le 0.025$. (b) $T = 9$, $N = 10$. Significant at the 0.05 level, one-tailed test.

3 (a) $p \le 0.025$ (b) $p > 0.05$ (i.e. nonsignificant) (c) $p \le 0.005$ (d) $p \le 0.01$ (e) $p \le 0.025$ (f) $p > 0.05$ (i.e. nonsignificant) (g) $p \le 0.025$ (h) $p \le 0.05$

4 (a) $p \le 0.05$ (b) $p > 0.05$ (i.e. nonsignificant) (c) $p \le 0.01$ (d) $p \le 0.02$ (e) $p \le 0.05$ (f) $p > 0.05$ (i.e. nonsignificant) (g) $p \le 0.05$ (h) $p > 0.05$ (nonsignificant)

5 (a) $N = 8$, $S = 2$ (nonsignificant) (b) $N = 10$, $S = 2$ (nonsignificant)

6 (a) $p \le 0.05$, one-tailed; $p > 0.05$ (nonsignificant), two-tailed (b) nonsignificant, both one- and two-tailed (c) $p \le 0.025$, one-tailed; $p \le 0.05$, two-tailed (d) $p < 0.005$, one-tailed; $p \le 0.01$, two-tailed (e) $p \le 0.025$, one-tailed; $p \le 0.05$, two-tailed (f) $p \le 0.0005$, one-tailed; $p \le 0.001$, two-tailed (g) $p \le 0.05$, one-tailed; $p > 0.05$ (nonsignificant), two-tailed (h) This could only be significant at the $p \le 0.05$ level for a one-tailed test. N is too small to obtain a higher significance level.

7 $U = 1$, $U' = 34$, $N_O = 7$, $N_U = 5$; one-tailed, $p \le 0.005$; two-tailed, $p \le 0.01$

8 (a) $U = 3\frac{1}{2}$, $U' = 31\frac{1}{2}$; $N_A = 5$, $N_B = 7$; one-tailed, $p \le 0.025$; two-tailed, $p \le 0.05$
(b) $U = \frac{1}{2}$, $U' = 120\frac{1}{2}$; $N_A = N_B = 11$; one-tailed, $p \le 0.005$; two-tailed, $p \le 0.01$
(c) $U = 10\frac{1}{2}$, $U' = 14\frac{1}{2}$; $N_A = N_B = 5$; the value is too large to be significant, even with a one-tailed test.

9 (a) $p > 0.05$, nonsignificant (b) $p > 0.05$, nonsignificant (c) $p \le 0.025$, one-tailed; $p \le 0.05$, two-tailed (d) $p \le 0.025$, one-tailed; $p \le 0.05$, two-tailed (e) $p \le 0.005$, one-tailed; $p \le 0.01$, two-tailed (f) $p > 0.05$, nonsignificant

10 (a) Wilcoxon (b) Mann–Whitney (c) Wilcoxon (d) Wilcoxon (e) Wilcoxon

Chapter 10

(a) nominal (b) ratio (c) ordinal (d) ratio (e) ordinal (The Beaufort scale is over a century old, and the intervals developed were based on personal observation, and calculated according to the effect the wind was creating and its estimated speed. Thus on land, a force 4 breeze moves small branches; at sea, a force 8 (fresh gale) causes 'smacks to make for harbour'! An ordered system, but not precise enough to be categorised at higher level than ordinal.) (f) ordinal (g) ordinal, although some psychologists treat IQ scores as interval (h) ordinal (i) ratio (j) nominal

Chapter 11

1 (a) related (b) independent (c) independent, unless people were matched on a one-to-one basis, using variables such as height or weight (d) unrelated, unless, again, there is some basis for pairing the scores off (e) related.

2 (a) $t = 2.493$ (b) $t = 6.240$ (c) $t = 3.602$ (d) $t = 1.6804$. The value of t is smaller, and thus less likely to be significant, when the data are not matched.

3 (a) $t = 2.493$; $df = 12$ (i) $p \leqslant 0.025$ (ii) $p \leqslant 0.05$
(b) $t = 6.240$; $df = 12$ (i) $p \leqslant 0.0005$ (ii) $p \leqslant 0.001$
(c) $t = 3.602$; $df = 6$ (i) $p \leqslant 0.01$ (ii) $p \leqslant 0.02$
(d) $t = 1.6804$; $df = 12$ (i) not significant (ii) not significant (And notice the difference between these conclusions and those of 3(c), when the same data were matched.)

4 (a) Nonparametric – unless you subscribe to the view that IQ scores achieve an interval level of measurement. (b) Nonparametric, for set A scores show a bimodal distribution. (c) Nonparametric, on the grounds that attitude assessments cannot possibly give scores which are sophisticated enough to attain interval status. (d) Grams attain the ratio level of measurement; physical characteristics tend to show normal distributions, so provided the variances were similar, a parametric analysis would be fine. (e) Nonparametric, as there is too much of a discrepancy between the variances of 10 and 100 sec.

5 (a) nonsignificant (b) 0.05 (c) 0.05 (d) 0.01

Chapter 12

1 (a) simple, 2×2 (b) complex, 3×2 (c) complex, 3×3 (d) one sample, 1×2 (e) one sample, 1×6

2 $\chi^2 = 30.217$, which is significant at the 0.001 level (two-tailed test). It is concluded that there is a difference between the two groups, with the Bymor customers, indeed, buying more – or, at least, *spending* more! If it had been predicted that the Bymor customers would spend more than the Ripoff patrons, then we would have established a one-tailed hypothesis, and the results would have been significant at the 0.0005 level. However, if the opposite prediction had been made, then strictly speaking, we could not have rejected the null hypothesis.

3 $\chi^2 = 5.6516$, $df = 5$. This value does not exceed the minimum value of 11.07 (for a two-tailed hypothesis), and so we can conclude that the pattern of sickness just over a decade ago does not differ from that shown by the mediaeval monks. Did you notice that the figures given were percentages? Ideally, the statistical comparison should be based on the original numbers, not percentages, but as the samples were known to be fairly large, and the value of *chi*-square a long way off significance, this violation of the rule can be overlooked.

4 $\chi^2 = 7.840$, $df = 3$. This is significant at the 0.05 level for a two-tailed test, and so it is concluded that there is a real difference between the towns when it comes to cycle safety!

5 Using the *expected* classes of 5, 25, 40, 25 and 5, we get a χ^2 value of 26.9544. When $df = 4$, this exceeds the value of 18.47 given for the highest significance level of 0.001 for a two-tailed test. We conclude therefore that the pattern of degree classifications differs from the pattern of the normal distribution.

6 (a) p 0.025 and 0.05 (one- and two-tailed) (b) 0.05 and not significant (c) neither value significant (d) 0.0005 and 0.001 (e) 0.005 and 0.01 (f) neither probability value significant.

Chapter 13

1 IV – use of tranquillisers; DV – exam marks
2 The students and their previous exam results, IQ, sex, medical record, subject, pre-exam drug intake
3 Anxiety, fatigue, meals eaten prior to exam, body weight
4 Bias (explained in the text)
5 One-tailed
6 That there will be no difference in exam marks between students who do and those who do not take tranquillisers before exams

Answers

7 Rejected

8 Certainly a Mann–Whitney U test, but possibly an unrelated t test if the exam marks are considered to be interval data

9 There is a one in twenty chance that the difference between the two sets of results is due to the effect of chance factors.

Chapter 15

1

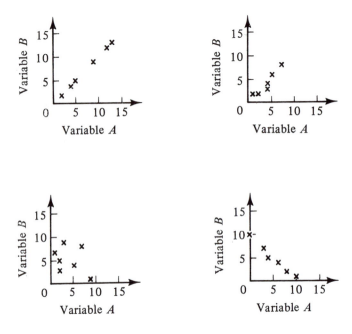

Figure 2

2 (a) +1   (b) +0.97   (c) −0.21   (d) −1

3 $r_s = 0.741$. The probability, if you decide to obtain it, for a one-tailed hypothesis, when $N = 7$, is 0.05. Note that the results would not have been significant if a one-tailed prediction had not been established.

Well, the manager of Beastly Breweries pats himself on the back here, and is so impressed by what he considers to be a correct diagnosis, that he enrols for Psychology A level! During the course he discovers that correlation need not mean direct causality; closer inspection of his staff and their working conditions reveal that the height of the counter is a crucial factor in determining the quality of staff–customer interaction. Additionally, variables other than ones directly relating to the pubs might have caused a drop in sales, e.g. stricter drinking and driving regulations, price increases, rise in unemployment.

4

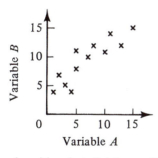

Variable *A*

(a) Good positive, but slightly curvilinear. Therefore Spearman's *rho* would be used.

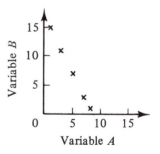

Variable *A*

(b) Perfect negative, linear. Pearson's product-moment is appropriate – and we have here a rare occasion when a line can be drawn in!

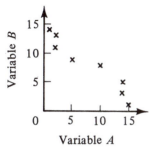

Variable *A*

(c) Spearman's *rho* can be used for this curvilinear association.

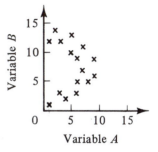

Variable *A*

(d) For this pattern, which is U-shaped, neither Pearson's nor Spearman's measures of association would be appropriate.

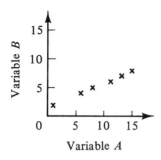

Variable *A*

(e) Almost perfect positive linear relationship. Again, Pearson's product-moment could be used, and a line could also be drawn in.

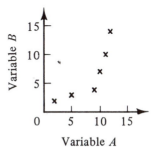

Variable *A*

(f) Almost two separate events here. As the line does not bend back on itself, we can use Spearman's *rho* here; however, the sharp bend in it precludes Pearson's *r*.

Figure 3

Answers

5 (a) $r = +1$ (b) $r = +0.937$ (c) $r = -0.358$ (d) $r = -0.987$

It is interesting to compare these values with the ones obtained using Spearman's technique. The drop from -1 to -0.99 in the final pair of scores reflects the small 'kink' evident in the scattergram.

6 (a) An indirect relationship, in that it is warm weather which makes people consume more beer. It might also be that during the summer months folk get out and about more, and visit pubs whilst on their travels.

(b) A direct link. The bus's appearance or non-appearance is a causal agent.

(c) Very difficult to tease out. It might be that events associated with being born prematurely also cause a certain amount of brain damage. However it might also be that agents which cause prematurity (rather than ones acting at the time of birth) also give rise to brain conditions which underlie later schooling difficulties.

(d) Indirect. Factors connected with standard of living come into this. The more people have cars and travel on motorways, the more likely it is that their society is one which fosters trips by plane. There may be a more direct link here, additionally. The weather conditions could affect the accident rate for cars and planes simultaneously.

(e) Not too indirect, in that surplus milk (a result of low sales) is converted into trifles.

(f) Difficult to see any connection at all between these two variables, although the more imaginative reader may be able to devise some link which explains what looks like a coincidental relationship.

7 All values are of one-tailed probabilities:

(a) $p \leqslant 0.025$ (b) $p \leqslant 0.05$ (c) $p \leqslant 0.025$ (d) $p \leqslant 0.005$ (e) $p \leqslant 0.01$ (f) nonsignificant

8 (a) ± 0.549 (b) ± 0.621 (c) ± 0.296 (d) ± 0.412 (e) ± 1.000 (f) ± 0.833 (g) ± 0.534.

Appendix

Areas under the normal curve

Standard deviations

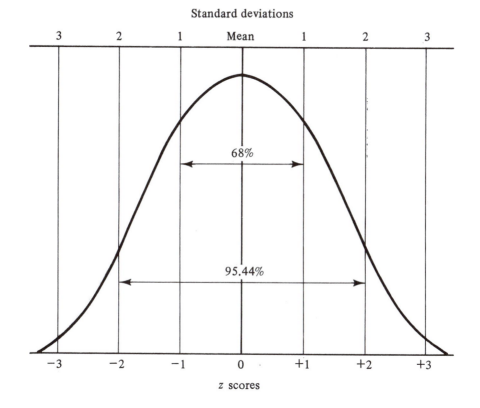

z scores

Cumulative area under the curve

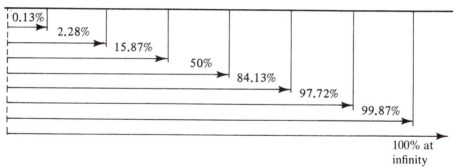

Appendix

Experimental design and statistical tests

Related (or matched) samples

Matched subjects design
Subjects are paired off, so that each score in one group can be *matched* or compared specifically with a particular score in the second group.
Pairing is in terms of relevant variables. Identical twins are often used.

Repeated measures design
Two scores are obtained from every subject, and these are then analysed. 'Before and after' types of studies are a common example of this design, which is also known as the *within subjects* design.

Unrelated (or independent) samples

Independent subjects design
All available subjects are divided into two groups which are then given different treatments. A basic assumption is that the groups are comparable at the outset on all the variables considered relevant. Because there may be a great deal of variation between all the subjects in the two groups, this design is less sensitive to slight changes which may occur as a result of the experimental treatment.
It is also known as the *between subjects* design.

Statistical tests for related samples

	Minimum data level
Nonparametric	
Sign test	Nominal
Wilcoxon	Ordinal
Parametric	
Related *t* test	Interval

Statistical tests for unrelated samples

	Minimum data level
Nonparametric	
Mann–Whitney *U* test	Ordinal
Parametric	
Unrelated *t* test	Interval

Notes

1 The division of tests is into two – related and unrelated – despite the division of designs into three. Repeated measures and matched subjects designs are given identical statistical treatment, e.g. the related *t* test if the data meet the requirements for parametric tests.

2 All the tests answer the question: 'Do the sets of scores come from one or two underlying populations?' Those listed above answer the question on the basis of the actual *values* of the scores, whilst the *chi*-square test answers on the basis of the pattern of the distribution which the scores make.

3 Don't confuse *correlation* with testing. In correlation we are simply *describing* the relationship between two sets of numbers, and sometimes using the information to make predictions.

Index

Page numbers in **bold** indicate main entries.

Index